ANIMALS, RIGHTS
AND REASON IN PLUTARCH
AND MODERN ETHICS

Plutarch is virtually unique in surviving classical authors in arguing that animals are rational and sentient and in concluding that human beings must take notice of their interests. Stephen Newmyer explores Plutarch's three animal-related treatises, as well as passages from his other ethical treatises, that argue that non-human animals are rational and therefore deserve to fall within the sphere of human moral concern.

Newmyer shows that some of the arguments Plutarch raises strikingly foreshadow those found in the works of such prominent animal rights philosophers as Peter Singer and Tom Regan in maintaining that non-human animals are the sorts of creatures that have intellectual qualities that cause them to be proper objects of man's concern, and have interests and desires that entitle them to respect from their human counterparts.

This volume is groundbreaking in treating Plutarch's views not only in the context of ancient philosophical and ethical thought but in their place, generally overlooked, in the history of speculation on human–animal relations, and in pointing out how remarkably Plutarch differs from such predominantly anti-animal thinkers as the Stoics.

Stephen T. Newmyer is Professor of Classics at Duquesne University and has published numerous articles on ethical issues relating to the treatment of animals in ancient literary and philosophical texts.

ANIMALS, RIGHTS AND REASON IN PLUTARCH AND MODERN ETHICS

Stephen T. Newmyer

Routledge
Taylor & Francis Group

NEW YORK AND LONDON

First published 2006
by Routledge
270 Madison Ave, New York, NY 10016

Simultaneously published in the UK
by Routledge
2 Park Square, Milton Park, Abingdon, Oxon OX14 4RN

Routledge is an imprint of the Taylor & Francis Group

Typeset in Garamond by
Keystroke, Jacaranda Lodge, Wolverhampton
Printed and bound in Great Britain by
The Cromwell Press, Trowbridge, Wiltshire

British Library Cataloguing in Publication Data
A catalogue record for this book is available from the British Library

Library of Congress Cataloging in Publication Data
Newmyer, Stephen Thomas.
Animals, rights, and reason in Plutarch and modern ethics /
Stephen T. Newmyer.
p. cm.
Includes bibliographical references and index.
1. Plutarch. 2. Animal rights—Moral and ethical aspects.
3. Animals (Philosophy). 4. Cognition in animals.
5. Ethics. I. Title.
HV4708.N496 2005
179′.3—dc22
2005014235

ISBN 0–415–24046–8 (hbk)
ISBN 0–415–24047–6 (pbk)

FOR CATHY

CONTENTS

PREFACE

I hope that this volume may be of interest to two groups of readers: to classicists who may be unfamiliar with one aspect of the thought of a well-loved author; and to persons involved in the struggle for better treatment for animals who may be unaware of the contribution to philosophical discourse on this topic made by a figure whose name appears only in passing historical accounts of this struggle. For the latter audience, all citations from Greek and Latin texts are at the very least summarized before they appear, and the Greek names of philosophical and ethical concepts important to this study are transliterated.

I have benefited enormously in the preparation of this volume from the guidance of the staff at Routledge. I thank Dr Richard Stoneman, Publisher in Classics and Archaeology, for encouraging me to develop ideas first presented in a conference paper into the material for a book. Matthew Gibbons, Assistant Editor in Classics, saved me from a number of embarrassing errors, and Annamarie Kino, Production Editor, answered my innumerable queries with speed and courtesy.

I would like to express my gratitude to the Administration of Duquesne University for awarding me a sabbatical leave in 2003 that enabled me to complete the composition of two chapters of the book. My special thanks go to my departmental colleague, Christine George, for her unfailing good humor and patience in guiding a technologically-challenged classicist through the mysteries of the computer.

Pittsburgh
November 2005

1

INTRODUCTION
The ancients and the moderns

Like all movements, the animal rights movement has its predecessors.
Charles R. Magel, *Keyguide to Information Sources in Animal Rights*

In his work *Animal Minds and Human Morals*, philosopher of mind Richard Sorabji analyzes a number of aspects of the ancient debate over the mental capacities of animals, a debate in which Aristotelian and Stoic notions of the nature of animalkind and humankind figure prominently.[1] As Sorabji makes clear, the issue central to this debate was that of animal rationality, a question on which virtually every school of philosophy in classical antiquity took a stand. In his investigation of the extraordinarily complex issue of animal mentation, Sorabji combines a thorough command of classical sources with a familiarity with the literature of the modern animal rights movement, using that literature, especially in the final sections of his book, to demonstrate the extent to which arguments developed by modern philosophers who grapple with the question of man's potential moral obligations toward other species have precedents in ancient formulations of these issues.[2] In the course of his work, Sorabji occasionally cites the animal-related treatises of Plutarch (*ca.* 50–120 CE), sometimes noting that Plutarch differs in opinion from other ancient writers on animal issues, in particular from the Stoics, but he seldom comments at length on Plutarch's views and rarely cites him for independent testimony on any issue.[3] In his enlightening discussion of whether the Greeks had any conception of "animal rights," for example, Sorabji cites Porphyry (*ca.* 234–305 CE) but ignores Plutarch, from whom Porphyry borrowed extensively on the questions under discussion.[4] While Sorabji is unusual, among modern scholars who discuss ancient attitudes toward animals, in acknowledging a continuity between ancient and modern philosophers, the reader does not come away from Sorabji's book with the impression that Plutarch had much to contribute to the ancient debate on animal rationality, or that his ideas on animals live on in any meaningful sense as do those of Aristotle and of the Stoics, as Sorabji so ably demonstrates.

1

Even among specialists in Plutarchan studies, his animal-related treatises remain relatively unknown. A number of general works on Plutarch and his literary legacy slight this side of their subject's oeuvre. C. J. Giankaris, for example, comments in passing on the "humanistic" side of Plutarch's personality, but ignores totally the humanity of Plutarch's pronouncements on animals.[5] D. A. Russell limits his comments on this aspect of Plutarch's work to a content summary of his treatise *De sollertia animalium* (*On the Cleverness of Animals*), which interests him primarily for the light it throws on Plutarch's teaching activities and on his circle of friends.[6] This tendency to undervalue or ignore this side of Plutarch's literary production led Francesco Becchi, an enthusiastic student of Plutarch's animal treatises, to conclude, with justification, that Plutarch's writings on animal psychology have to date attracted little critical attention.[7] In the course of Becchi's attempt to isolate the philosophical sources upon which Plutarch's writings on animals are based, he observes that Plutarch often does not seem to stand completely in the tradition of accepted notions about animals that can be traced from Aristotle down through Porphyry, and that where structural comparisons can be made among extant works, he often does not reflect structural similarities traceable among other works.[8]

The degree of neglect which Plutarch's treatises on animals have encountered, even among Plutarchan scholars, is the more remarkable when we take into account the fascination which animals held for Plutarch and the comparatively large presence which animals enjoy in his literary production. Not surprisingly, animals do not figure prominently in the *Lives*,[9] but among the extant treatises that constitute that vast collection of philosophical, religious and antiquarian essays called the *Moralia*, three deal exclusively with questions relating to animals. The most extensive of these, *De sollertia animalium*, purports to record a debate on the question of whether land animals or marine animals are more clever. No conclusion is reached, and the reader is left with the realization that Plutarch intended to show that in fact all animals possess "cleverness" and other positive intellectual attributes that cause them to be entitled to respectful treatment from human beings. While the majority of examples cited by Aristotimus and Phaedimus, Plutarch's debaters in this dialogue, are stock illustrations of animal skills familiar to readers of the Greek naturalists and of ancient catalogers of animal wonders, the thesis that underlies Plutarch's presentation is that all animals, to a greater or lesser degree, possess reason.[10] More lighthearted is the brief dialogue *Bruta animalia ratione uti* (*Whether Beasts Are Rational*), also known as *Gryllus* ("Grunter," "Oinker") from the name of one of the speakers, a comrade of Odysseus transformed into a pig by Circe. The dialogue is a parody of *Odyssey* X in which the Ithacan asks Circe to reconvert his comrades into men. In Plutarch's reworking, she suggests that he first ask them whether they in fact wish to be men again. The contented Gryllus serves as their "spokespig," rebuffing the hero's efforts and arguing that animals possess all the standard ancient virtues without any of the vices that render human life miserable.[11] Finally, in *De esu carnium* (*On the Eating of*

Flesh), the second part of which survives in a mutilated state, Plutarch offers a number of arguments, moral, hygienic and religious, in support of a vegetarian lifestyle.[12]

Animals figure prominently as well in Plutarch's work *De amore prolis* (*On the Love of Offspring*), wherein he maintains, in apparent contradiction to his position in *De esu carnium*, that the sense of justice is less well developed in animals than in humans, although he does concede there that animals love their offspring tenderly, and that animals mate only for procreation, unlike humans who are excessively devoted to bodily pleasures.[13] Animals, he argues in *De amore prolis*, are on the whole closer to Nature (*physis*) in their behavior than are humans, whose actions are at times corrupted by artifice and excess. In *De tuenda sanitate praecepta* (*On Precepts for Maintaining Health*) and in the *Quaestionum Convivalium Libri* (*Table Talk*), he raises many of the same issues touched on at greater length in *De esu carnium*. Animals appear in passing in a number of other Plutarchan treatises, frequently as examples of creatures exhibiting lifestyles superior to (or inferior to) those of their human counterparts.

In recent years, Plutarch's treatises on animals have been the subject of critical studies by a number of Italian scholars who have done much to rescue these works from the obscurity into which they had fallen.[14] These authors have made a careful attempt to isolate those concepts that contribute to what might be called Plutarch's "animal psychology." Although these scholars do not attempt to explore in any depth the topic of possible continuity between ancient thought on animal issues and the arguments of philosophers of the modern animal rights movement, a feature of Sorabji's work that renders his analysis so intriguing, their work effectively reminds us that Plutarch occupies an important position in the ancient tradition of thought on the role of animals in the sphere of man's moral concern. The thesis that underlies the present volume is that Plutarch's treatises on animals have an interest and value that has largely been overlooked in the scholarly tradition outlined above. Sorabji's contention that the ancient debate over animal rationality set the stage for many of the controversies that currently engage animal rights advocates and their opponents is certainly valid, but it can be argued that Plutarch's animal treatises shed more light on the ancient contribution to this debate than emerges from Sorabji's treatment of these works. In setting forth his case for animal rationality, Plutarch has recourse to arguments, examples and illustrations that will have a familiar ring to readers conversant with the literature of the animal rights movement.

A word of caution is in order at this point. As Sorabji argues so convincingly, it would be erroneous and anachronistic to maintain that *any* ancient philosopher held a position that could justifiably be termed "animal rightist."[15] At the same time, many of the arguments and concepts with which the modern animal rights debate is waged have ancient precedents. Plutarch's treatises on animals seem to illustrate some of these with particular clarity. He betrays a remarkably "modern" sensitivity to animals as feeling and suffering creatures that distinguishes much of the literature of the contemporary animal rights movement but which is largely absent from extant ancient works on animal issues, with the notable exception of the Neoplatonist Porphyry's treatise *De abstinentia* (*On Abstinence from Animal Food*).

It will be obvious to anyone who pays attention to the media that issues relating to the treatment of animals[16] by human beings constituted the subject of one of the central intellectual debates of the closing years of the twentieth century that shows no sign of abating in the twenty-first. One does not need to consult the sophisticated and abstractly argued treatises of ethical philosophers and ethologists, those scientists whose work entails the systematic study of animal behavioral patterns,[17] to be aware that the questions of whether animals possess "rights," what those "rights" might be, and what impact such rights possession might have upon human behavior, have far-reaching implications for the lives of all persons, and that those questions are currently the topic of lively debate. Feature stories on abuse and neglect of companion animals, poaching, endangered species, appalling conditions on factory farms, and misuse and overuse of animals in the laboratories of governments and cosmetic companies, confront readers daily. Hunters find their activities disrupted by protesters who employ more or less violent methods, and furriers find their business undermined by animal activists who bring the practices of fur production to the notice of the public. While such activities and the abuses they presently entail lay largely outside the experience of classical antiquity, the intellectual assumptions that underlie the activities of animal activists often have ancient precedents.[18] In many cases, however, the philosophers of the contemporary animal rights movement seem barely cognizant of the ancient contribution to the debate on the moral status of animals.[19]

Philosophers of the animal rights movement, and historians who chronicle its development, are virtually united in stressing its modernity. While Richard D. Ryder, whose book *Animal Revolution* traces the historical development of the concept of "speciesism," the tendency of human beings to favor human interests and to draw justification therefrom to oppress other species, may note "the gradual triumph of reason and compassion over habit, vested interest and convenience,"[20] an achievement, he observes, in which our present age can take pride, he clearly judges a philosophical concern for animals as feeling and possibly thinking creatures to be a distinctly modern phenomenon whose nineteenth-century precedents seem to him to constitute the ancient history of that idea. Ryder does devote a few pages to the classical heritage of thinking on animals, stressing the combination of reverence and cruelty that marked the curiously ambivalent ancient attitude toward animals, and he allows that Plutarch's somewhat atypical position on vegetarianism suggested belief in "a general duty of kindness to human and nonhuman alike."[21] Nevertheless, Ryder does not hesitate to proclaim the "powerful moral concern" of the animal rights movement to be a consequence of the heightened awareness of the wrongness of speciesism that accompanied the crusade for civil rights for disadvantaged classes of humans in the 1960s.[22]

A more extreme example of the historical myopia that colors Ryder's work can be seen in Peter Singer's work *Animal Liberation: A New Ethics for Our Treatment of Animals*, published in 1975 and widely regarded as the "bible of the animal liberation movement."[23] The very subtitle of Singer's work hints at the author's perception that a serious concern for animals expressed in carefully reasoned argument is a recent phenomenon. The historical sketch which opens Singer's work traces the phrase "animal rights" to the eighteenth-century Neoplatonist Thomas Taylor, whose treatise *A Vindication of the Rights of Brutes* was intended in fact as an ironic riposte to Mary Wollstonecraft's treatise *Vindication of the Rights of Woman* (1792), and while he later cites another philosopher's observation that Plutarch deserves the honor of being considered "the first to advocate strongly the kind treatment of animals on the grounds of universal benevolence," one gets the impression that for Singer, ancient thinking on animals was more quaint curiosity than valuable foundation for later debate.[24] In his Preface to the modern edition of British social activist Henry S. Salt's work *Animals' Rights Considered in Relation to Social Progress*, a treatise originally published in 1892, Singer makes the telling comment, "I marvel at how he anticipates almost every point discussed in the contemporary debate over animal rights."[25] Similarly, Ryder had asserted that the "moral basis" for the animal liberation movement was laid with the publication, in 1965, of the short essay entitled "The Rights of Animals" by British novelist and essayist Brigid Brophy.[26] Brophy herself could claim in that essay, "My views are shared by only a smallish (but probably not so small as you think) part of the citizenry – as yet."[27] The implication of Brophy's words is clear: a serious concern for animals is a distinctly modern phenomenon.

In fairness to the philosophers of the animal rights movement, the observations of their historians, including Ryder, relate, strictly speaking, to the consequences of the heightened awareness of animal suffering that arose almost as a corollary to the crusade for the betterment of oppressed classes of humans. Just as it came to be realized that denial of rights to persons on the basis of color or gender was a type of discrimination, so too could denial of rights to creatures on the basis of species be condemned as speciesism. Ryder would draw a sharp distinction between this recent drive for "animal rights" and earlier, less focused efforts which he would characterize as "animal welfare" concerns. As Ryder expresses it, "The change in phraseology from a concern for 'animal welfare' to a concern for 'animal rights' indicates the movement's increasingly ideological complexion."[28] Animal welfare efforts gained a sort of intellectual respectability when animals attracted the attention of philosophers in the mid-1960s and early 1970s. In their reasoned investigations of issues relating to animal sentience, rationality, desires and feelings, the animal rights movement was born. Recently, philosopher David DeGrazia has characterized Singer and those who immediately after supported and rejected his arguments as "the First Generation."[29]

Many of the ideas expounded by these "First Generation" philosophers, and by those who came after them in the 1980s and 1990s, have a history in ancient thought, and in some respects, Plutarch's writings on animals provide a bridge between early speculations on the nature of animalkind and the almost unbelievably sophisticated and subtle arguments evolved by contemporary ethical philosophers who contend that the mental capacities of animals entitle them to better treatment at the hands of their human counterparts than they have historically received. My intention in this volume is to examine some of those issues which are central to the contemporary debate on the moral status of animals and which have intriguing formulations in the treatises of Plutarch. I would contend that Plutarch's concomitant regard for animals as suffering creatures is in general uncharacteristic of Greco-Roman attitudes toward non-humans, while it is fundamental to the contemporary debate on the place of animals in the human moral scheme. Focusing upon Plutarch's case for animal rationality, I hope to show how some of Plutarch's insights have been developed and transformed in contemporary ethical thought and philosophical literature on animals. I do not claim that Plutarch *influenced* the thinkers whose ideas are discussed in this work, but I would maintain that Plutarch's formulations of issues relating to animal mentation at least deserve a closer look in the light of the present interest in animalkind among philosophers and laymen alike. In this respect, my approach to Plutarch's treatises on animals differs sharply from the traditional view of Plutarch's works as a repository of citations from earlier thinkers. Perhaps no Greek author has so suffered the ill-effects of *Quellenforschung* as has Plutarch, whose ideas have been consistently slighted in favor of isolation of their philosophical sources. The claim most frequently encountered in discussions of Plutarch's relation to earlier writers on animals is that much of his argumentation is directed against early Stoic doctrines.[30] R. H. Barrow has characterized Plutarch as a writer motivated by a desire to bring the achievements of the past to life in the conviction that his own age could profit from past experience. Plutarch's work reflects, in Barrow's view, the culture of the library, an approach backward-looking and pedantic, originating nothing, sincere but uninspired. At least, Barrow allows, Plutarch hated hypocrisy and false values.[31] It was such a hatred of false values that motivated Plutarch to compose his treatises on animals, as he attempted to sweep away long-standing prejudices that kept men from according animals more respectful treatment. In this, at least, Plutarch is not backward-looking, and if his treatises betray the culture of the library, his heightened sensibility toward animal issues ensures that his works are more than the sum of the sources from which he drew his material.

At the same time, however fascinating Plutarch's treatises on animals might prove to be, both for classical scholars who did not suspect the existence of this side of an otherwise much-studied author's work, and for philosophers and activists willing to countenance the notion that an ancient thinker might have something of value to say on an issue that seems so much a part of the present day and so far removed from the ancient experience, Plutarch's treatises on animals are not without formidable difficulties that hinder the formation of a satisfactory picture of Plutarch's thought on animals. Particularly troubling to the investigator is the inconsistency of some of Plutarch's pronouncements on animals. While he has left us an impassioned defense of the vegetarian lifestyle (*De esu carnium*), Plutarch elsewhere countenanced the consumption of meat, although somewhat reluctantly, on the grounds that the practice is so ingrained by custom that one may tolerate it, provided one supplements the diet with non-meat foods.[32] Moreover, the assertion made at length in *Bruta animalia ratione uti* that animal life is preferable to human life because it is more in keeping with Nature is otherwise unexampled in Plutarch's works, however much he does seem to admire animal conduct in general. Plutarch's habit of using the same piece of evidence to argue now one position and now its opposite was recently noted by Juan Francisco Martos Montiel in his study of Plutarch's use of animals as models of human behavior. As Martos Montiel observes, animal behaviors that to Plutarch suggest intemperance and irrationality show up at other places in his work as examples of the superiority of animal behavior to that of humans.[33] An apparent self-contradiction of particular importance to our investigation is Plutarch's assertion, in *De fortuna* (*On Fortune*) and in *De fraterno amore* (*On Brotherly Love*),[34] that humans are superior to animals because humans can reason, in contrast to lower species, an assertion against which Plutarch argues forcefully in *De sollertia animalium* (*On the Cleverness of Animals*). Recent scholars have downplayed such contradictions either as largely illusory or as arising from the philosophical school or literary genre which Plutarch was following in the given treatise, but they remain troubling to the investigator who seeks to gain a picture of Plutarch's animal philosophy.[35] To Plutarch's propensity for self-contradiction we may add a sometimes maddening lack of precision in terminology, a characteristic that he shares with a number of other ancient writers on animal-related topics. Adolf Dyroff, one of the earliest systematic investigators of Plutarch's animal psychology, lamented his lack of exact distinctions in psychological terminology, and charged that Plutarch interchanged terms for "soul" and "spirit" merely for artistic variation.[36] Moreover, he charged that Plutarch had at best a superficial understanding of the subtleties of the Stoic doctrines against which he frequently directed his polemic.[37]

To this catalog of pitfalls that await the student of Plutarch's animal philosophy, we may add that our author, in common with other ancient writers on animals, frequently employs a method of argumentation that relies heavily on apparent analogies between human and animal behaviors. Actions of animals that seem to parallel or imitate human actions are cited as proof that animals have mastered behaviors otherwise considered the exclusive province of human beings, an approach that lays Plutarch open to the charge of anthropomorphism. In defense of Plutarch, we may note that many modern ethologists are themselves acutely aware of the dangers of falling into this line of argumentation, and acknowledge the possibility that anecdotal evidence of apparent parallels between human and animal capacities, however convincing these may seem, may in the final analysis have no validity in proving the presence of such capacities in animals.[38]

Many of the methodological shortcomings of Plutarch's animal treatises can be explained, at least superficially, from the circumstance that he can, after all, lay little claim to being a naturalist in the manner of Aristotle or Theophrastus. One seldom gets the impression, in reading the animal treatises, that Plutarch's statements are based on close personal observation of the animal behaviors under discussion. They suggest rather a perusal of commonplace books, and his examples of animal characteristics and behaviors can often be paralleled in other ancient writers on animals who were not naturalists. Sherwood Dickerman, in his survey of ancient examples of animal intelligence, observed that Plutarch drew many of his examples from the behavior of ants, bees, spiders and swallows, precisely those animals which Galen (*ca.* 129–199 CE), Philo (*ca.* 25 BCE– 50 CE) and Cicero (106–43 BCE) cite for their comments on the mental capacities of animals, and he concluded tentatively that all of these writers, including Plutarch, had a common source, perhaps the work of Alcmaeon of Croton (fifth century BCE).[39] In this respect, however, Plutarch is no worse than other writers on animals who approached their subject as enthusiastic amateurs. Early critics of Plutarch's animal treatises were particularly harsh in their condemnation of his pronouncements. More than a century ago, Adolf Dyroff noted sourly that Plutarch's lamentable performance on animal psychology could not fairly be criticized too sharply because all he did was copy Aristotle, the Stoics and the Peripatetics, without understanding his sources completely. Dyroff felt that Plutarch simply did not possess the requisite level of care in approaching scientific questions, but rather satisfied himself by adopting a polemical tone toward those positions that he opposed. Plutarch, moreover, does not seem to distinguish between examples drawn from mythology or from fact, but contents himself with retailing foolish stories provided that they reflect well on animals.[40] In short, Dyroff concluded, Plutarch does not rise above the level of what passed for animal psychology in classical antiquity, although, in the final analysis, he cannot be faulted for this since he sought rather to offer a clever presentation of his material that is certainly superior to the dry and clipped manner of presentation seen in writers like Pliny the Elder (*ca.* 23–79 CE).[41]

Such strictures should give us pause, and caution us against the temptation to overinterpret the evidence upon which Plutarch builds his case in defense of animals and opposes the case of his philosophical opponents. Plutarch was neither a systematic philosopher nor an observational scientist, but he seems rather to have been willing to borrow ideas from a variety of schools as these suited his purposes. These limitations are starkly apparent in his pronounce- ments on animals. At the same time, however, his consistently positive attitude toward animals sets him apart from the majority of ancient thinkers who addressed the issue of animal creation and man's relation to animals. He touched upon issues not found elsewhere in extant ancient sources, and, most importantly for the present volume, he offered glimpses of arguments and solutions to ethical questions which are central to the debate on the moral status of animals as this debate is carried on today. Some of his arguments are examined in the chapters that follow, with special attention to the survival and transformation of these arguments in the work of ethical philosophers active in the modern animal rights movement. Because much of the ancient case for or against the position that human beings have moral obligations toward non-human animals rested on the answer to the question of whether reason resides in non-human species, analysis of Plutarch's case for animal rationality forms the basis for much of the discussion in the chapters that follow.

Chapter 2 explores the ancient debate on animal rationality. The chapter opens with an overview of some issues that are of central importance in the debate on the cognitive capacities of animals as these appear in the works of moral philosophers and ethologists in our time. A number of these issues will be explored in depth in subsequent chapters. At this point, the overview will serve as a backdrop against which our examination of early manifestations of arguments prominent in the current debate can be seen in higher relief. The chapter then focuses on Plutarch's case for animal rationality and on his encounter with the philosophical schools whose views he supported or refuted. The chapters that follow this preliminary discussion analyze a number of potential consequences for human behavior that arise from a positive response to the question of whether animals can reason. Chapter 3 inquires whether animals, if they are indeed rational, are therefore moral creatures entitled to a sort of relationship with human beings that could be termed "justice." Chapter 4 asks whether animals can experience pleasure, pain and other emotive states, and whether human beings should care. In Chapter 5, the possibility of altruistic behaviors in animals, exhibited both toward their own species and toward humans, is discussed in its relation to human behavior toward animals. Finally, Chapter 6 asks what bearing animal rationality should have upon human food choices. Plutarch's arguments in support of the vegetarian lifestyle are viewed in relation to the current debate on whether abstinence from meat must follow as the natural consequence of a belief in animal rationality. Plutarch devoted entire treatises, with lengthy and closely reasoned argumentation, to some of these topics, while others are touched upon in the context of his discussions of other animal-related subjects, or depend on evidence encountered only once in Plutarch's work. Our analysis of Plutarch's contribution to still other issues outlined above must rely on an assemblage of references scattered throughout his works. In any case, I hope that examination of Plutarch's treatises from a variety of perspectives that still exercise thinkers in the forefront of the debate over man's proper moral stance toward non-human species who share his world will help to elucidate Plutarch's place in the historical development of this debate, and will at the same time help to provide some answers to the questions that have long hampered an appreciation of an important side of the work of an author who, in almost all other aspects of his literary production, appears to meet only with increasing enthusiasm and respect.

2

THE NATURE OF THE BEAST
The search for animal rationality

> If it is even plausible to suggest that animals do reason, it seems to be irrational to deny them entrance into the scope of moral concern on the basis of an undecided and controversial theory of reason.
> Bernard E. Rollin, *Animal Rights and Human Morality*

Animal rationality: the current state of the debate

Since the time of Hesiod (*ca.* 700 BCE), Western thinkers have sought to determine whether an ethical relationship exists naturally between humankind and animalkind, and, if it does, what that relationship entails. The question at the core of the often acrimonious debate that has arisen around this investigation is that of whether animals are the sort of creatures that can have what philosophers term "moral status."[1] Attitudes toward the validity of investigation into the moral status of animals have varied since antiquity. Referring to the current state of the debate, philosopher Mary Midgley observes that some thinkers consider the question of man's potential moral obligations toward animals to be a central philosophical issue of our time, and that others dismiss it as perverse and sentimental.[2] Siding with this latter camp, philosopher Peter Carruthers, an outspoken critic of the notion that humans can have moral obligations toward animals, counters that "the case for attributing moral status to animals is weak, and . . . the contrary case is very powerful," and he condemns the popular concern with the rights of animals as "a reflection of moral decadence."[3] Even those who maintain that animals have some legitimate moral claims on humans cannot agree whether the interests of animals can ever matter as much as do those of humans.[4]

Throughout much of its history, speculation on the moral status of animals has been the province of philosophers, and the criteria upon which the decision to grant or deny moral consideration to animals has been based are those traditionally associated with philosophical inquiry, but with the growing acceptance of cognitive ethology as a legitimate discipline within zoology, questions of animal cognition and consciousness which occupied philosophers have been increasingly usurped by the natural sciences.[5] Lines of inquiry that since classical antiquity have relied largely on abstract speculation aided by limited use of eyewitness observation now benefit substantially from advances in neuroscience and genetics. Ironically, the growing sophistication of investigative techniques has rendered determination of the moral status of animals increasingly complex. While there is at present wider acceptance of the idea that some animals have at least limited cognitive abilities and may possess sufficient consciousness to enable them to experience such affective states as pain and pleasure, scientists now struggle with the question of how far down the ladder of animal creation such consciousness extends. Some of the most vocal advocates of the position that animals deserve moral standing seem willing to include only conscious, or "sentient" beings in the scope of human moral concern.[6] At the other end of this scale, research into the impressive intraspecies communication skills of such mammals as dolphins and gorillas has led some philosophers to conclude that these creatures qualify for personhood, a prospect which has enormous moral and legal ramifications.[7]

As our discussion suggests, determination of the moral standing of animals has, since antiquity, tended to center upon speculation on the nature of animal mentation. Cognitive ethologists ask whether animals have on the one hand consciousness, or awareness of their surroundings to the extent that their interactions with those surroundings involve purposeful thought of some sort, and on the other whether they possess cognitive abilities, including problem-solving skills and the ability to process information, that humans can detect and measure. As animal rights philosophers prefer to phrase the question, do animals in fact "reason"? The quest to isolate and analyze the mental capacities of animals stands at the forefront of the current debate on the nature of animals, and it has proven a minefield both for those who maintain that animals have moral claims on humans and those who deny this assertion. A great deal is at stake, both for humankind and for animalkind. Determination that the mental processes of at least some animals are akin to those of human beings would necessitate a radical reassessment of much of human behavior toward other species in such areas as animal experimentation, food choices, farming techniques, confinement of animals in zoos, and a myriad other aspects of human life that involve interaction with animals, since our attitudes toward consciousness in animals seem to condition much of our treatment of them. It is no wonder, then, that some contemporary philosophers have been eager to prove that the gulf between the mental capacities of humans and those of even the most intelligent animals is unbridgeable, and that animals consequently cannot fall within the purview of human moral concern.

Some philosophers maintain, however, that there is no necessary connection between mental capacities and moral worth. This position in itself is not new, but can be seen in embryonic form in the work of the nineteenth-century Utilitarian philosopher Jeremy Bentham, who substituted the capacity to feel pain for the ability to think as the central issue determining the moral status of animals. "The question is not, Can they *reason?*," Bentham argued in an often-quoted dictum, "nor, Can they *talk*? but, Can they *suffer*?"[8] Ethicist Bernard E. Rollin expanded Bentham's position by arguing that neither the ability to reason nor the capacity to experience pleasure or pain seems adequate to make a creature worthy of moral consideration. For Rollin, a moral being is one who possesses needs, desires, goals, aims, wants and interests.[9] Similarly, animal rights philosopher Steve F. Sapontzis rejected the emphasis on reason as the sole criterion for determining a being's moral worth, and advanced instead a pluralistic ethic that combines a consideration of animal interests and of what Sapontzis terms "animal virtues," like kindness and courage, with a goal of minimizing animal suffering in determining the proper relationship between humans and other species.[10]

In recent decades, the quest to isolate the cognitive capacities of animals has advanced impressively through the research of cognitive ethologists who remain, however, extremely cautious in their assertions because of fear of charges of sentimentality and of anthropomorphism that is eager to take every animal behavior and reaction resembling a human behavior or reaction as evidence of mental kinship. An excellent example of this cautious approach is the work of biologist Marian Stamp Dawkins, who modestly describes her book *Through Our Eyes Only? The Search for Animal Consciousness* as "an attempt to account for what we now understand of the experiences of other species."[11] Her goal is to ascertain whether we can comprehend what goes on inside non-human minds, with a view toward measuring the conscious experiences of animals. Beginning with the premise that being conscious would seem to be advantageous to an animal, at least in keeping it out of trouble, she reminds us that complexity of behavior is not in itself proof of consciousness since computers can perform complex functions. Arguing that adaptability of behavior to changing circumstances might better suggest conscious experience, Dawkins cites examples of animals that clearly adapt their behaviors to the needs of the moment. Vervet monkeys, for example, employ different grunts in response to different circumstances in their environment, as when they greet social inferiors, superiors, or strangers, behavioral patterns that suggest that each form of greeting has a distinct meaning that their peers can interpret.[12] Baboons can even learn to practice deception by pretending to look for predators when none are present in order to frighten rival baboons away from a food source that the deceivers covet.[13] Although Dawkins remains tentative in her conclusions, she is willing to assert that such cognitive capacities as ordering, numbering, and deceiving do not seem to be restricted to human beings, and that it is therefore unscientific not to consider that we are in the presence of outward and visible signs of conscious awareness when these capacities appear in animal behaviors.[14]

Biologist Rosemary Rodd goes a step further than Dawkins in arguing that even such evidences of consciousness as self-awareness and self-consciousness, which philosophers frequently demand as prerequisites for humanity, can no longer be considered the exclusive province of human beings, since chimpanzees have been shown to have the ability to recognize themselves in mirror images.

For Rodd, this argues for a "sophisticated ability to think about the self from 'outside.'"[15] If animals are to this degree self-aware, they must be capable of learning about themselves through some exercise of cognitive skills and, in Rodd's view, they are consequently sophisticated enough actively to experience their own lives.

Cognitive ethologists place considerable weight on the fact that the structure and function of neurons and synapses are similar in all creatures endowed with a developed central nervous system, while at the same time there is no evidence from neuroanatomy to suggest that the human brain has any special features unique to it.[16] Although the thoughts of even the most advanced non-humans may be limited in type and number, they should not therefore be considered inconsequential. Cognitive ethologist Donald R. Griffin argues that, while the thoughts of animals are probably limited to their immediate survival needs, such as attainment of food and avoidance of enemies, scientists should not on that ground avoid employing such terms as thoughts, intentions, beliefs and feelings to refer to the mental processes involved.[17] Rats learn to move to another part of a cage to avoid an electric shock after a warning signal has been given, and will seek that safe spot even if no shock follows the signal, suggesting to Griffin that animals expect a particular outcome to ensue from a given set of circumstances. This may indicate, in his view, that animals have a primitive understanding of conditionality, or "if . . . then" thought patterns.[18] Griffin concludes that so many species of animals display evidence of adaptability to changing circumstances that some conscious thought must accompany their actions, and he does not rule out the possibility that even those behaviors that scientists like to call "instinctual" may be accompanied by awareness on the part of animals that they are engaged in these behaviors.[19] Moreover, the fact that the behavior of rats described above can be duplicated in laboratories or, as in the case of vervet monkeys and baboons, can be observed to occur regularly in nature under similar circumstances, suggests that this is not likely to be the result of coincidence or the type of evidence that could justly be labeled anecdotal.

Perhaps the most controversial area of ethological research is that which seeks to explore the emotive states of animals. While some philosophers and ethologists may be willing to countenance the notion that at least some species may feel fear, pain or pleasure, the assertion that some may also experience such emotions normally considered to be uniquely human as grief, compassion and joy remains for many scientists the stuff of children's tales defensible only by recourse to anecdotes and anthropomorphizing analogies. Scientists are often so hesitant to ascribe emotions to animals that when they encounter in them what they reasonably conclude to be emotions in human beings, like love or hate, they have recourse to designations like "attachment" or "aggression" to conceal the apparent similarity to human emotions that they may in fact believe to be at work.[20] The explanation for this hesitation is not far to seek. Not only does the ascription of emotions to animals imply that humans may not be the only creatures capable of behaving "humanely," but exercise of emotions seems to contradict evolutionary theory that teaches that traits should benefit their possessors while emotions may entail self-sacrifice and a concern for collective interests.[21] At the same time, however, emotions have clear survival value. Fear, for example, may lead to flight and escape from a predator. Mapping the emotional lives of animals has implications for human morality that are as compelling as those that follow the documentation of other aspects of animal cognition. If an animal can feel pain or can mourn the loss of its peers, humans might need to take its feelings into consideration in their interactions with it.[22]

Emotion is an aspect of cognitive behavior since emotions help creatures to relate to their external environments. Despite the claim of some who oppose attributing emotions to non-human animals, the expression of emotions does not require the capacity for language to prove their presence. Animals share with humans such non-verbal communication modes as gesture, facial expression and movement, although ethologists caution us here against facile analogies, since, for example, a chimpanzee grins when angered or frightened. Yet ethologists have documented innumerable instances of behaviors which would without hesitation be declared expressions of emotions if observed in humans. It is well known, for example, that elephants will slow their march if a member of their troop is injured, and that animals will adopt orphans of other species, as dogs and cats will sometimes adopt orphaned piglets or skunks.[23] Elephants have been observed to kneel down and pull baby rhinos from mud holes in which they had become mired.[24] Dolphins may swim underneath injured dolphins and carry them safely to shore.[25] If these actions were seen in humans, they would be praised as instances of altruism or at least kindness, but scientists hesitate to attach such labels to animal behavior. While it might be an exaggeration to claim that these actions are motivated by a "code of ethics" by which the animals involved live, it is worth noting that ethologist Frans deWaal reminds us that it is scientifically demonstrable that concepts like guilt, honesty and the weighing of moral dilemmas are traceable to certain areas in the human brain, and that since the nervous systems of animals are similar to those of humans, there is no cause for surprise in finding parallel behaviors in animals.[26]

A conclusion frequently encountered in ethological literature, and in the treatises of animal rights philosophers who take account of ethological evidence, is that the mental capacities of animals and those of humans stand in a relationship which might justly be called an evolutionary continuum, and that that continuum might include the emotions as well, so that differences between humans and animals should properly be considered ones of degree.[27] A number of animal rights philosophers have asked whether any of these differences are morally relevant after all. If they are not, man has no justification in excluding animals from the scope of his moral concern.[28] This position stands in sharp contrast to that prevalent since classical antiquity and bolstered by the interpretation which has rather consistently been placed on the biblical concession of "dominion" over animals,[29] which posits an uncrossable gulf separating mankind from the rest of animal creation that allows man to claim for himself a unique place above the rest of creation granted to him largely on the strength of his supposedly superior mental endowments.[30] This position has been jealously guarded and ingeniously defended by philosophers through the ages who have sought to isolate skills which are uniquely human, most of which have involved some aspect of man's capacity for reason. As one after another of the ostensible proofs of man's uniqueness has fallen to evidence from ethological research, opponents of granting moral status to animals have raised the bar and placed ever higher demands on animals before they can be admitted into the scope of human moral concern. The case of tool usage by animals provides an instructive example.

The purposeful use of tools had long been believed to be a skill that humans shared at most with their ape and monkey relatives, until ethologists beginning in the 1950s challenged this assumption. Elephants, they noted, use sticks to scratch parts of their bodies that they cannot easily reach, while herons drop berries and even inedible objects into water to attract fishes which they spear when the fishes come to inspect the objects.[31] In light of such evidence, behavioral scientists who rejected the idea that animals think or plan were forced to alter their position to maintain instead that, while animals may after all use tools, they cannot *make* tools. This claim too has been challenged. Capuchin monkeys, for example, have been observed to strike stones against hard surfaces and to use the stone flakes that result to scrape flesh from bones and to cut through objects.[32]

The intellectual faculty which philosophers have most jealously guarded as the exclusive province of human beings, indeed as the embodiment of what it means to be human, separating man irrevocably from the rest of animal creation, is the ability to learn and use language. In his study of animal thought, psychologist Joseph Mortenson eloquently expresses the importance of this faculty to man's view of himself as the pinnacle of creation, "Language is the most highly regarded human trait. Man is the speaker, the listener, the reader, the symbol-user."[33] Entire ethical systems have been constructed on the proposition that man has the ability to invent and use language because he is rational, while animals do not possess language because they are irrational. Influential philosopher R. G. Frey is most closely associated with the stance that the ability to engage in symbolic communication constitutes the essence of morality. As the author of the first systematic treatise in recent decades that attacks the concept of animal rights on moral grounds, Frey maintains that animals cannot have rights because they cannot have interests, and they cannot have interests because they cannot have desires. This is in turn the case because animals cannot reflect on what their desires might be, and this is so because they do not have language. Since animals have no interests, they cannot be harmed.[34]

More recent thinkers have challenged Frey's position on a number of grounds. It has not been obvious to other philosophers why having desires requires language.[35] In addition, it has been objected that, in Frey's system, human babies, because they are not yet in possession of language, cannot have rights, a position which few ethicists would be eager to embrace. When Frey's argument is followed to its conclusion, in fact, it emerges that in his ethical system, not even adult human beings have rights because there is no such thing as a moral right![36]

A contemporary ethical stance of more immediate interest to us because of its debt to classical ethical theory is that which is called Contractualism or Contractarianism. Contractualism argues that individuals must be sufficiently "like" human beings in their mental capacities to be able to enter into contracts with humans to have their interests respected and in turn to respect the interests of humans. Only what contractualists term "rational agents" can enter into such contracts and can respect the interests of others. Even if it could be proven that animals possess such mental constructs as beliefs and desires, they could not, in contractualist theory, act on the basis of these to the extent that they could agree on the rules needed to govern their interactions with humans, which would qualify them for moral consideration. The doctrine that individuals must be "like" enough to human beings to be morally considerable is the cornerstone of the Stoic position on animals, and the debt of Contractualism to its Greek model is evident as well in the corollaries that arise from the initial requirement of "likeness." In the contractualist stance, language possession is obviously presupposed, since contract formers must be able to voice their interests to other contract formers, and contractualists deny that animals possess the faculty of language. The case against according moral status to animals that is advanced by Carruthers, to which we have made reference above, is grounded in contractualist theory.[37] Contractualists admit that human beings may have what philosophers term "indirect duties" to animals which make it morally wrong to harm them gratuitously because such behavior may harm the interests of humans. This notion takes a page from the ethical philosophy of Kant, who held that those who harm animals unnecessarily are likely to harm humans as well. In Kant's view, animals "matter" only insofar as human interactions with them have an impact on the interests of humans.[38]

The positions of Frey and Carruthers betray a tendency to beg the question of what language is by assuming that, whatever it is, it is possessed only by humans, and they and other philosophers who oppose according moral status to animals have found corroboration for their stance in the theories of such linguists as Noam Chomsky. Chomsky maintained that the ability to learn languages is unique to humans because an understanding of grammar and other linguistic concepts is "hard wired," so to speak, in the human brain, but is absent from the brains of non-human animals. Hence, language is "natural" to humans, but not to other animals.[39] Already in the 1960s, however, primatologists challenged the claim of linguists that only humans could use symbolic, artificial language through a series of now-famous experiments to teach chimpanzees and gorillas such forms of communication as American Sign Language (AMESLAN). Although it is now known that some early successes were aided by "cueing," a process of intentional or unintentional prompting on the part of researchers that enabled them to elicit desired responses,[40] later results have been impressive. The chimpanzee Washoe and the gorilla Koko not only mastered and correctly used hundreds of signs in AMESLAN, but taught some to their peers and used correct signs to identify pictures in magazines while sitting alone. Koko seemed to be able to formulate answers to such abstract questions as what death meant to gorillas, and she created social scenes when alone with her toys, signing to her dolls to "kiss" her or scolding them as "bad."[41] In such situations, cueing is clearly not at work.

Opponents of according moral status to animals, including Frey and Carruthers, brand such results as mere anecdote, and charge that, however clever this behavior may be, it does not suggest that animals use language to plan or express beliefs or demonstrate evidence of rational agency.[42] Philosophers now demand that animals be able to manipulate languages more syntactically sophisticated and more highly inflected than the English used in AMESLAN before humans can judge animals to be worthy of inclusion in man's moral concern. As each goal is met, a new demand is made, thus guaranteeing man his place at the pinnacle of creation.

Plutarch in the ancient debate on animal rationality

I have prefaced our examination of some of the more important arguments and assumptions concerning the intellectual capacities and moral status of animals that were developed before Plutarch undertook the composition of his animal treatises, with an overview of the state of the debate over animal mentation as it has developed since the reawakening of interest in animal issues that activists date to the 1960s, in order to underscore the fact that, as the debate has taken shape in our time, mind and morals have become inextricably connected. In no extant ancient writer on animals is this connection so fully explored as in Plutarch. The arguments advanced by both sides in the modern controversy over animal minds and their implications for human morality, the examples cited in support of both positions, and even the latent preoccupations and presumptions that inform the controversy, are mirrored in Plutarch's presentation of his case for animal rationality and in his representation of the stances of philosophers whose ideas he adopts or refutes. While Plutarch's arguments are not always original with him, he does bring to the ancient debate a strong belief that animals are proper objects of man's moral concern.

A number of scholars have detected in Plutarch a quality of mind that served to predispose him to a sympathetic attitude toward animals. While some detractors charge that his observations on animals smell more of the library than of the stable, other scholars have noted that Plutarch obviously admired animal creation to a degree not common in classical antiquity. Vittorio d'Agostino, in his early study of Plutarch's animal psychology, praised Plutarch's generous sense of humanity, and he asserted (unfortunately without elaborating) that Plutarch's ideas on animals conformed to "modern" sensibilities on man's duties toward other species.[43] In his survey work on Plutarch, R. H. Barrow observed, with perhaps a trace of bemused apology, "That Plutarch takes more sympathetic note of the animal creation than any other Greek writer, except the naturalists, would be a thesis no doubt impossible to prove. Yet, for what it is worth, the impression remains."[44] This aspect of Plutarch's psyche has been commented upon as well in works of classical scholarship not specifically devoted to Plutarch. Jacqueline de Romilly, in her study of the concept of *douceur* in Greek thought, judged Plutarch to be a prime example of the operation of πραότης, "gentleness," as a guiding principle in a Greek's life, for she finds that he possessed great tenderness that manifested itself in his relations with his wife, his children, and, not least, the denizens of the animal world.[45]

Some recent writers who stress the unusual depth of Plutarch's humanity have seen this trait as a potent influence on his mode of argumentation on animal issues. Damianos Tsekourakis, in the course of his argument against the commonly held belief that Plutarch enjoined abstinence from meat out of a sympathy for the Pythagorean doctrine of metempsychosis, counters that he was motivated rather by a sentiment of fellow-feeling toward animals than by adherence to any philosophical school. "Being himself a man of charitable character," Tsekourakis argues, "he felt very sympathetic toward animals and also felt pity when they were mistreated."[46]

Plutarch's obvious affection for animal creation has been a source of admiration as well to ethicists and to animal rights philosophers with a sense of history. In his study of the development of European moral thinking, nineteenth-century ethicist William Lecky claimed of Plutarch, "He was the first writer who advocated very strongly humanity to animals on the broad ground of universal benevolence, as distinguished from the Pythagorean doctrine of transmigration."[47] Animal rights philosopher Stephen Clark admired Plutarch's argument that humans can have no claim on animals if animals have none on humans.[48] Recently, Matt Cartmill, in his fascinating historical study of attitudes toward hunting, judged Plutarch to be "probably the only important ancient authority actually to denounce hunting as morally wrong," and he cites him for the idea that hunting is a source of man's inhumanity to man.[49] In his treatise *De virtute morali* (*On Moral Virtue*), Plutarch had argued that humans possess an emotive side that cannot justifiably be suppressed. Virtue, he held there, arises in humans from the correct regulation of the emotions, not from the denial of their operation (*De virtute morali* 443C–D). In Plutarch's view, questions relating to man's proper treatment of animals should be decided by a style of argument that allows room for both logic and emotion, a position which Plutarch seems about to articulate in the mutilated final sentence of *De esu carnium*. Humans, he maintains there, must decide moral issues by focusing on their emotions and weighing evidence with these in mind (τοῖς πάθεσιν ἐμβλέψαντες τοῖς ἑαυτῶν καὶ πρὸς ἑαυτοὺς ἀνθρωπικῶς λαλήσαντες καὶ ἀνακρίναντες, 999B).[50] In Plutarch's animal philosophy, logic and emotion are not mutually exclusive avenues of inquiry.

While animal advocates employing a style of argumentation that combined rigorous logic with an appeal to the emotions, in the manner of Plutarch's approach, did much to improve the lot of animals in many nations through the past several decades, the arguments of sympathetic Greek and Roman thinkers, in contrast, had little practical effect upon ancient policies on the treatment of animals, nor did they inspire a more charitable attitude toward animal suffering on the part of the common man. The reasons for this are obvious. Societies that rely heavily on slaves are not likely to spare much thought for what are considered an even lowlier class of beings. At the same time, pagan religions required a steady supply of animals for ritual sacrifice. Moreover, the brutality of arena sports was never lessened by attention to the arguments of philosophers sympathetic to animals, and only occasionally did spectators feel moved to express themselves in support of animals mistreated in the arena. The most famous instance of a public outcry against cruelty to arena animals occurred during the ceremonies that marked the opening of Pompey's theater on the Campus Martius in 55 BCE. On that occasion, the elephants, sensing that they could not escape, seemed to beg for mercy, which, as Pliny the Elder tells us, moved the spectators to rise in anger against Pompey.[51] More often, however, criticisms of arena sports focused on the brutalizing effects such sports had on the spectators, not to mention on the human participants, but they seldom evinced sympathy for the animals involved. Seneca's famous condemnation of arena sports (*Epistulae* 7. 4), for example, spares no thought for the sufferings of the lions and bears who were forced to confront human combatants.[52] On rare occasions, we do find mention of legal action taken on an *ad hoc* basis against persons guilty of unusual acts of animal cruelty. Plutarch himself notes (*De esu carnium* 996A) that the Athenians punished a man who flayed a living ram. Still, we do not find instances of what we would now call animal protection legislation in the case of either domesticated or wild animals. Historian of ancient ecology J. Donald Hughes laments that even the powerful example of Plutarch did little to better the lot of animals, "Plutarch exhibited admiration and sympathy for the myriad forms of living things and was an early defender of animal rights. Unfortunately, neither in his case nor in any other known from ancient times does it seem that such ideas resulted in practical programs to help wildlife."[53]

In seeking to inject an element of humane feeling into contemporary attitudes toward the treatment of animals, Plutarch stood outside the mainstream of thought in the first century CE, but, while Dierauer feels confident enough to assert that he is unique among ancient thinkers in taking account of the sufferings of animals and in claiming that humans have no right to cause them pain,[54] Plutarch may in fact have found inspiration for this attitude in earlier Greek thinkers. Pythagoras (sixth century BCE) in particular is often cited for his sympathetic views toward animals, most especially in connection with his doctrine of metempsychosis, but it is far from easy to ascertain the reasons for his adherence to this doctrine. It is not certain that concern for animals as suffering creatures motivated his stance to any significant degree. Diogenes Laertius (VIII. 36) tells us that the Presocratic Xenophanes of Colophon (sixth century BCE) recounted the tale that Pythagoras, on seeing a dog being beaten, interceded for it, warning that the beast might be the reincarnation of a friend or relative. Likewise, Pythagoras' notion of justice toward animals may suggest more concern for human moral excellence than for the feelings of animals. The philosopher seems to have held that while both humans and animals are besouled, the sacrifice of an animal forces a human to act unjustly in eradicating a creature that bears a kinship to humans, a line of argument mentioned as Pythagorean both by Diogenes Laertius (VIII. 13) and by Porphyry (*De abstinentia* [*On Abstinence from Animal Flesh*] III. 26). Diogenes is also our source for the Pythagorean belief that consumption of meat tends to dull the human soul and injure the human body (VIII. 13), although Pythagorean vegetarianism is often taken as the surest evidence of Pythagoras' enlightened attitude toward animals. In fact, only Ovid (*Metamorphoses* XV. 75–142) seems to argue that concern for the sufferings of animals was the motivating force in Pythagoras' doctrine of abstention from meat.[55] Porphyry also mentions (I. 26) that some persons maintained that Pythagoras sanctioned the eating of meat by athletes to improve their performance.[56] It is worth noting as well that Plutarch, in the opening sentence of *De esu carnium*, brushes aside the question of what led Pythagoras to abstain, and states that he would rather ask what first led humans to taste meat (993A), while he also mentions (*De sollertia animalium* 959F) that the Pythagoreans, with a view toward instilling humane feeling and compassion in humans (πρὸς τὸ φιλάνθρωπον καὶ φιλοίκτιρμον), enjoined gentleness toward animals (τὴν πρὸς τὰ θήρια πραότητα μελέτην ἐποίησαντο), an "indirect duty" view of man's obligation toward non-humans that recalls Kant's position.

Pythagoras' notion of man's "kinship" with animals, which seems to be a corollary to his doctrine of metempsychosis, manifested itself in a form more overtly sympathetic toward animals as suffering creatures in the lost treatise *De pietate* (*On Piety*) of the Peripatetic Theophrastus (*ca.* 372–288 BCE), excerpts of which are preserved in Porphyry's discussion of animal sacrifice in his *De abstinentia*, a treatise which dates from the latter decades of the third century CE. Porphyry relates there (II. 12) that the arguments against animal sacrifice which he offers are derived from Theophrastus' sensible discussion (εἰκότως ὁ Θεόφραστος ἀπαγορεύει μὴ θύειν τὰ ἔμψυχα τοὺς τῷ ὄντι εὐσεβεῖν ἐθέλοντας, χρώμενος καὶ τοιαύταις ἄλλαις αἰτίαις). Later (III. 25), in the course of his own argument that humans owe a debt of justice to animals, Porphyry mentions that Theophrastus had argued that, just as humans recognize that they have a kinship (οἰκείους εἶναι) to each other, so do they recognize that animals are akin to humans in having flesh, passions, and soul, even if they differ from humans in their manner of life. If one admits these principles, Theophrastus held, it becomes clear that humans have a kinship to animals too (Θεόφραστος δὲ καὶ τοιούτῳ κέχρηται λόγῳ . . . εἰ δὲ ἀληθές ἐστι τὸ λεγόμενον, ὡς καὶ ἡ τῶν ἠθῶν γένεσίς ἐστι τοιαύτη, φρονοῦσι μὲν ἄπαντα φῦλα, διαφέρουσι δὲ ταῖς τῶν πρώτων κράσεσι, παντάπασιν ἂν οἰκεῖον εἴη καὶ συγγενὲς ἡμῖν τὸ τῶν λοιπῶν ζῴων γένος, Porphyry, *De abstinentia* III. 25). Theophrastus believed that this kinship forbade the eating of flesh, as Porphyry reports (*De abstinentia* II. 28).

As we observed above, the issue of man's natural "kinship" with animals has become a cornerstone of the modern ethical stance called Contractualism or Contractarianism, which is distinctly hostile to the idea of according moral standing to animals on the grounds that they do not possess the requisite mental capacities to enter into rational contracts with human beings to respect the interests of humans and to have their interests respected in turn. If we may trust the testimony of Porphyry, Theophrastus used the idea of kinship to argue that man owed a debt of justice toward animals because of their kindredness to humans that required humans to refrain from sacrificing them and eating them, not least, as Porphyry reports of Theophrastus' position, because such actions deprive animals of their lives and thereby cause them unjustifiable injury (ὅτι γε ἐπιθυομένων τῶν ζῴων φέρει τινὰ βλάβην αὐτοῖς, ἅτε τῆς ψυχῆς νοσφιζομένων, *De abstinentia* II. 12). Theophrastus' argumentation entails a remarkable anticipation of the so-called "harm as deprivation argument" that has been used by prominent animal rights philosopher Tom Regan to argue that causing the death of an animal is morally wrong because it necessarily deprives it of the opportunity to experience any future choices. In Regan's view, death is the ultimate harm because it entails the ultimate loss.[57]

The ancient doctrine at issue in Theophrastus' discussion is the complex concept of οἰκειότης (*oikeiotês*), which combined the ideas of belonging, kinship and relationship. While it has frequently been considered to be Stoic in origin, and while, as we shall see below, it was central to the Stoic denial of moral standing to animals, some scholars have seen it as Theophrastean in origin, and it is clear from Porphyry's presentation of Theophrastus' case that Theophrastus believed, against the Stoics, in human kinship with animals that necessitated a sympathetic treatment of animals by human beings.[58]

This same sympathy for animals as suffering creatures that seems to have inspired Theophrastus to develop his conception of *oikeiotês* is in evidence elsewhere in Porphyry's remarkable treatise *De abstinentia*, which displays a close familiarity with all previous Greek speculation on animals and which serves, as we have observed, as the principal source of extracts from the lost *De pietate* of Theophrastus. Constituting, with Plutarch's earlier *De esu carnium*, one of the two extant ancient defenses of the vegetarian lifestyle, the Neoplatonist Porphyry's *De abstinentia* offers a carefully argued defense of the position that humans owe a debt of justice to animals because they share with animals a kinship (*oikeiotês*), as Theophrastus had argued, and shares Theophrastus' position that so long as early man acknowledged that kinship, he properly refrained from sacrificing animals (οὐδεὶς οὐθὲν ἐφόνευσεν, οἰκεῖα εἶναι νομίζων τὰ λοιπὰ τῶν ζῴων, *De abstinentia* II. 22). In Porphyry's view, humans are akin to animals not only with respect to the constitution of their souls, passions, drives and senses, but in their faculty of reason as well (πολὺ δὲ μᾶλλον

21

τῷ τὰς ἐν αὐτοῖς ψυχὰς ἀδιαφόρους πεφυκέναι, λέγω δὴ ταῖς ἐπιθυμίαις καὶ ταῖς ὀργαῖς, ἔτι δὲ τοῖς λογοσμοῖς, καὶ μάλιστα πάντων ταῖς αἰσθήσεσιν, *De abstinentia* III. 25).[59]

However enlightened Porphyry's conception of animal rationality, with its consequences for human behavior, may seem to us, his position, like that of Pythagoras, seems to have been motivated to some extent by a concern for the welfare of the human soul, although he does seem to have been more genuinely sympathetic to animals as sentient beings than was Pythagoras, to the extent we may judge this from extant testimonia relating to the Presocratic. The Neoplatonist Porphyry enjoined vegetarianism on the grounds that animal food arouses passions and mental disturbances that must be avoided by the philosopher, because these pull the human soul down and hamper its ascent to true Being (ἐκ δὲ τούτων ἐγειρόμενα τὰ πάθη καὶ πᾶσα ἡ ἀλογία παχυνομένη κατάγει τὴν ψυχὴν καὶ τοῦ οἰκείου περὶ τὸ ὂν ἀποστρέφει ἔρωτος, *De abstinentia* I. 33). Porphyry does not altogether avoid an appeal to the self-interest of human beings.

As it was construed by both Theophrastus and Porphyry, the doctrine of *oikeiotês* accorded moral status to animals and placed them firmly within the sphere of man's moral concern. The relationship which animals have with human beings is, in their view, juridical in nature, for humans *owe* just treatment to creatures that are somewhat akin to them in their intellectual capacities.[60] Yet it would not be the animal-friendly conception of kinship espoused perhaps by Pythagoras and certainly by Theophrastus and Porphyry, who borrowed from Theophrastus on this issue, that would prove influential in later centuries, for, as Sorabji's analysis makes abundantly clear, a philosophical "crisis" in discussion of man's relationship with animals had already been engendered when Aristotle denied rationality to animals, a denial which was subsequently accorded a distinct moral dimension by the Stoics.[61] It is against the background of this crisis that the animal philosophy of Plutarch must be understood.

Although he appears to have vacillated somewhat in his estimation of the overall intellectual capacities of animals, allowing them more developed capacities in his zoological treatises while portraying them as more distinctly inferior to humans in his anthropocentric treatises,[62] it is undeniable that no figure has exercised a more profound influence, for better or worse, on subsequent speculation on the animal estate than has Aristotle (384–322 BCE). Moreover, his interest in animals differed substantially from that of other members of his school, not least from that of his more radical follower Theophrastus, whose arguments for man's fundamental kinship with animals we outlined above, for, as Sorabji has argued, Aristotle's case against animal rationality was grounded in scientific considerations with little concern for the moral consequences of his arguments.[63] Only in succeeding generations would Aristotle's scientific observations be used to build a case for the moral inferiority of animals to humans, especially by the Stoics and Epicureans, who saw in Aristotle's ideas of continuous gradations in nature, the so-called *scala natura*, or Great Chain of Being, as it was styled in later ages, and in the philosopher's frequent reliance on a "man alone of animals" argument, sufficient cause to allow them to conclude that animals stood so far below humans in the scheme of creation that humans could have no moral obligations toward them. In its moralized Stoic guise, Aristotle's denial of reason to animals would form the basis for much of the Western Christian attitude toward animals as creatures to whom humans could not owe justice but whom they could use as they pleased for their own purposes, while the more sympathetic doctrines of Pythagoras, Theophrastus, Plutarch and Porphyry were thrown into the shade.[64]

In the seventh chapter of *De motu animalium* (*On the Movement of Animals*), Aristotle came closest to crediting animals with rationality, a circumstance that has contributed to doubts as to the genuineness of the work, since the philosopher's stance there seems at odds with his position elsewhere. In the course of a discussion of syllogistic thinking, he cites a number of instances of the operation of such thinking in humans. For example, when a human sees water, he thinks, "I need water; I see water; therefore, I drink." Aristotle elaborates this example by noting that animals are impelled to movement and action by a similar desire, which comes about through sensation or imagination and thought (οὕτως μὲν οὖν ἐπὶ τὸ κινεῖσθαι καὶ πράττειν τὰ ζῷα ὁρμῶσι... ταύτης δὲ γινομένης ἢ δι' αἰσθήσεως ἢ διὰ φαντασίας καὶ νοήσεως, 701a33–36). Aristotle *may* mean here that, if an animal can draw conclusions from observing its surroundings, and act upon this observation, it can engage in a form of reasoning, although one must keep in mind the possibility that Aristotle believed that an animal could act on its observation without intervening rational action. Nevertheless, he seems to come close in this passage to granting some degree of rationality to animals.[65]

A passage of considerable importance to understanding Aristotle's concept of animal mentation is the often-cited opening chapter of the eighth book of *Historia animalium* (*History of Animals*), wherein the philosopher maintains that, while animals may have *traces* (ἴχνη, 588a20) of some human characteristics, they possess only *resemblances* of intelligence (τῆς περὶ τὴν διάνοιαν συνέσεως ὁμοιότητες, 588a23–24). Throughout this passage, Aristotle develops his doctrine of biological gradation or continuity (συνέχεια, 588b5; also *De partibus animalium* [*On Parts of Animals*] 681a12–15), whereby nature advances by degrees to humankind, and according to which such human attainments as skill, wisdom and intelligence (ἐν ἀνθρώπῳ τέχνη καὶ σοφία καὶ σύνεσις, 588a29–30) are present in animals only by a kind of *similar* natural capacity (ἐστί τις ἑτέρα τοιαύτη φυσικὴ δύναμις, 588a30–31). Scattered throughout the zoological treatises are assertions that, although other animals may possess intellectual and behavioral characteristics *analogous* to those of humans, only humans can reason. Earlier in *Historia animalium*, Aristotle had acknowledged that other animals may be lively or shy or affectionate or proud, but only the human being is a deliberative animal (βουλευτικὸν δὲ μόνον ἄνθρωπός ἐστι τῶν ζῴων, 488b24–25). Similarly, in *De partibus animalium*, the philosopher maintained that while other animals may possess locomotion, only humans possess intellect (ὑπάρχει ἡ φορὰ καὶ ἐν ἑτέροις τῶν ζῴων, διάνοια δ' οὐδενί, 641b8–9).[66]

Some of Aristotle's examples of human uniqueness seem to betray the beginnings of an ethical dimension, and suggest that the philosopher was occasionally willing to abandon the scientific objectivity which Sorabji claims was the hallmark of his zoology. Perhaps no example that Aristotle cites has had more far-reaching consequences in the history of man's relationship with animals than his assertion that, while some animals can use their voices to give information or to communicate sensations of pleasure and pain, only man has a language that allows him to communicate knowledge and ethical values (λόγον δὲ μόνον ἄνθρωπος ἔχει τῶν ζῴων . . . τοῦτο γὰρ πρὸς τἄλλα ζῷα τοῖς ἀνθρώποις ἴδιον, τὸ μόνον ἀγαθοῦ καὶ κακοῦ καὶ δικαίου καὶ ἀδίκου καὶ τῶν ἄλλων αἴσθησιν ἔχειν, Politica [Politics] 1253a10–19). We have seen above that the denial of language possession to animals would come to form the cornerstone of the Stoic case against including animals in the sphere of human moral concern on the grounds that animals cannot assert their right to just treatment from humans and cannot respect in turn a human's claim to justice, the principle upon which the contractualist stance is based. Even some of Aristotle's claims of human uniqueness which are apt to strike the reader as rather far-fetched, as, for example, his assertions (Ethica Eudemia [Eudemian Ethics] 1236b1–6) that only humans are capable of real friendship based on exchange of affection; that only humans can experience hope and expectation of the future (De partibus animalium 669a20–22); and that only humans can experience true happiness that comes through contemplation of the divine (Ethica Nicomachea [Nicomachean Ethics] 1178b21–28), were not without influence upon post-Aristotelian animal philosophy, when the Stoics came to moralize Aristotle's animal science.[67]

From its foundation, the Stoic school relied on Aristotelian zoology to bolster its own system in which rationality was regarded as a prerequisite for moral consideration. The Stoics saw Aristotle's doctrine of the continuous gradation of species and his quest to isolate the uniqueness of human beings as justification for a moral system in which man occupied a position forever out of reach of other species. While Aristotle asked what animals are and how they differ anatomically and physiologically from human beings, questions fundamentally zoological in inspiration, the Stoics asked a question still alive in the debate on the rights of animals: do animals differ from humans in any *morally* significant sense? Their answer, like that of modern thinkers who oppose according moral status to animals, was affirmative, and they based that answer upon a vision of animals as beings so unlike humans that we can have no fellow feeling for them. This process of welcoming kindred individuals into the moral compact, the *oikeiôsis* discussed above,[68] was for the Stoics as well as for the Epicureans the foundation of justice. This bond of kindredness did not subsist with animals in Stoic thinking, because of the imperfection of their souls.

Although the Stoics, in common with most ancient philosophical schools,[69] did not deny a soul to animals, they did deny that the animal soul contained a rational element and the absence of this element kept the animal soul from ever attaining to the perfection of the human soul.[70] We learn from Aetius that Chrysippus (*ca.* 280–207 BCE), the influential Stoic who was particularly vehement in his denial of reason to animals, held that the soul is constituted of eight parts, the first seven of which make up the irrational elements of the soul: the five senses, the capacity for utterance, and the reproductive capacity. A mysterious eighth element, called the ἡγεμονικόν (*hêgemonikon*), functions as a sort of "governing principle" over the whole.[71] This ἡγεμονικόν, which in human beings eventually develops into the faculty of reason or λόγος (*logos*), remains irrational in animals. Hence, while animals and humans are born with souls of similar constitution, the human soul in time outstrips that of the animal, whose subsequent behaviors are of the sort which the Stoics called impulse, or ὁρμή (*hormê*), as, for example, the tendency of animals to move toward sources of food. The Stoics contrasted this with the rational desire or movement termed ὄρεξις which governed human action, while the irrational impulse of animals was mere self-interestedness that led animals to approach what is useful and avoid what is harmful.[72]

In Stoic doctrine, the imperfection of the animal soul had grave consequences, for it precluded any possibility of affinity between humans and animals that could cement a moral relationship between the species. This affinity existed between animals and their offspring and their own kind, and between humans and their offspring and their own kind, but not between animals and humans because the imperfection of the animal soul, which forced animals to remain forever irrational, denied them the capacity for language and therefore made moral discourse between the species impossible. The Stoic connection between reason, language and interspecies affinity is made strikingly clear by Cicero, who argued that we are nowhere further removed from animals than in our possession of reason and speech, in consequence of which we may speak of strength in them, but never of justice (*De officiis* I. 50):

> Sed, quae naturae principia communitatis et societatis humanae repetendum videtur altius; est primum, quod cernitur in universi generis humani societate. Eius autem vinculum est ratio et oratio, quae docendo, discendo, communicando, disceptando, iudicando conciliat inter se homines coniungitque naturali quadam societate; neque ulla re longius absumus a natura ferarum, in quibus inesse fortitudinem saepe dicimus, ut in equis, in leonibus, iustitiam, aequitatem, bonitatem non dicimus; sunt enim rationis et orationis expertes.

Cicero's point, and that of his Stoic sources here, is that humans can owe nothing to creatures that are so alien to themselves that they cannot understand and verbalize a conception of morality: that is, animals cannot express their intention to respect the rights of humans and their desire to have their rights respected in turn by humans. In this connection between language and moral considerability, we glimpse the Stoic contribution to the modern ethical stance called Contractualism that we outlined above.[73]

In practical terms, the assertion of an unbridgeable gulf between animalkind and humankind gave humans permission to use animals as they saw fit. Cicero again elucidates the Stoic position as it appeared in Chrysippus, who held that no covenant of justice exists between humans and animals (*De finibus* III. 67):

> Sed quomodo hominum inter homines iuris esse vincula putant, sic homini nihil iuris cum bestiis. Praeclare Chrysippus cetera nata esse hominum causa et deorum, eos autem communitatis et societatis suae, ut bestiis homines uti ad utilitatem suam possint sine iniuria.

At the same time, in his presentation of the Stoic position here, Cicero hints, certainly unintentionally, at the peculiar ambiguity that the Stoic view of animals entailed which forced them to regard them as a necessary evil, a class of beings to which humans can owe nothing but which is at the same time absolutely essential to their lifestyle. The Stoics themselves acknowledged this debt with a kind of perverse humor, maintaining that animals would have no value at all if they did not serve the needs of humans. Porphyry records that Chrysippus held that the pig has a soul in place of salt to preserve it until humans can eat it,[74] and Plutarch (*De stoicorum repugnantiis* [*On the Self-Contradictions of the Stoics*] 1044D) adds that the Stoics argued that bugs were intended to prevent humans from oversleeping, while mice forced them to stay neat and tidy. Porphyry saw that the Stoics attached momentous importance to the need to regard animals as subservient to humans for, he tells us (*De abstinentia* I. 4), they held that human life would be impossible if humans refrained altogether from using animals in support of their lifestyle, a situation which would turn the world upside-down, if justice were accorded to irrational beings by rational ones, and would eventually force humans to live a life no better than that of brute beasts.

The connection in Stoic thinking between reason and meaningful language is accentuated by the fact that the same word, *logos*, is employed in Greek to encompass both concepts, a circumstance which allowed the Stoics to imply that absence of the one entailed absence of the other. Reason, as it manifested itself in language, was bipartite in Stoic doctrine, its two parts sharply differentiated in operation: one type of reason, λόγος ἐνδιάθετος (*logos endiathetos*), "inner reason, thought," exercises control over and gives meaningful vocal expression to λόγος προφορικός, "uttered reason, meaningful speech." Since the capacity for meaningful expression arises in the *hêgemonikon* and this remains irrational in animals, λόγος ἐνδιάθετος would lie outside the realm of possibility for them, and their utterances would remain meaningless. Porphyry (*De abstinentia* III. 2) notes that the doctrine of the twofold *logos* was central to the Stoic case against animals, while Philo (*De animalibus* 98–99), defending the Stoic position, argues that animal utterances have no more meaning than do the notes of a flute, lyre or trumpet.[75]

In addition to their denial of meaningful language to animals, which foreshadows the intellectual assumptions of Contractualism, certain other corollaries that follow from the Stoic denial of reason to animals will have an equally familiar ring to readers conversant with the modern debate on the mental capacities of animals. Sorabji notes that the Stoics were the first ancient philosophers to make moral responsibility dependent upon reason.[76] In the case of human beings, actions are "up to us" (ἐφ' ἡμῖν, in Stoic phraseology), despite the operation of fate or necessity in the universe. Aulus Gellius explains the position of Chrysippus on the relationship between fate and human will by noting that the Greek had argued that, although fate may set things in motion in human life, it is human will and mind that determine the course of fate (*sic ordo et ratio et necessitas fati genera ipsa et principia causarum movet, impetus vero consiliorum mentiumque nostrarum actionesque ipsas voluntas cuiusque propria et animorum ingenia moderantur*, Noctes Atticae [*Attic Nights*] VII. 2.11). Human beings, that is, have, as rational beings, the capacity to withhold assent from action. As Cicero explains the Chrysippean position (*De fato* [*On Fate*] 43), assent rests with us humans (*assensio nostra erit in potestate*). In contrast, animals, as non-rational beings, cannot withhold assent from action. Their actions, therefore, are not "up to them," and they cannot in consequence be praised or blamed for their actions. In Stoic ethics, moral agency is associated with rational assent. In modern parlance, animals, in Stoic doctrine, cannot be "moral agents," beings who effect moral actions, but only "moral patients," those beings who are the objects of moral actions.[77] In the thinking of the Stoics and of their modern philosophical descendants, only moral agents fall within the scope of human moral consideration.

The question of moral agency has taken on considerable importance in the thought of some prominent animal rights philosophers. Tom Regan agrees with the Stoics that animals are not moral agents and cannot therefore do right or wrong, but the conclusion he draws from this position differs radically from that implicit in Stoic doctrine. Because animals cannot act morally, the Stoics conclude, human beings have the right to use them as they see fit since, after all, moral discourse with them is precluded by their irrationality. Regan concludes, in contrast, that moral patients are of necessity innocents because they cannot perform an action which is anything but innocent, and Regan maintains that absolute prohibitions exist against harming innocents.[78]

Since the publication of Regan's influential and controversial treatise, what has been termed the "argument from moral agency" has been subjected to searching criticism. David DeGrazia, who coined this term, observes that an implicit belief in its validity conditions how many persons think about animals, and he critiques two commonly advanced arguments for its validity: that only moral agents have inherent value and dignity which entitle them to equal consideration of their interests; and (a Stoic-inspired argument) that only moral agents can have duties toward other moral agents, so that humans can have no duties to animals, a position that DeGrazia calls the "principle of reciprocity" which is a linear descendant of the Stoic doctrine of *oikeiotês* and of the contractualist stance.[79] DeGrazia counters that a number of objections might be raised against the argument from agency. One cannot be sure, to begin with, that moral agents might not after all have some duties toward individuals who have no duties toward them in return (as, for example, in the case of babies). Moreover, the concept of inherent dignity of moral agents seems to have no philosophical grounding, but seems rather to reflect a species bias. Yet DeGrazia's most telling argument, which he terms the "gradualist thesis," falls outside the scope of Stoic morality in maintaining that moral agency is a matter of *degree*, so that not all humans have all attributes of agency while not all animals have none. "The capacities to project into the future," DeGrazia argues, "to learn from experience, to keep multiple considerations in mind, to feel for others, to make decisions, and so on are found, to some degree at least, in many mammals. . . . Dolphins and Great Apes quite arguably demonstrate as much moral agency as, say, the moderately retarded."[80] DeGrazia concludes his discussion by stating that the argument from moral agency is itself a product of species bias.

The question of the fundamental moral relevance of rational agency was subjected to yet further criticism by biologist and bioethicist Bernard E. Rollin, the author of the epigraph which opens this chapter, who traces speculation on the significance of rational agency to the Greek Sophists.[81] Rollin objects to the contractualist stance, which he classifies as a social contract theory, arguing that just because moral agents set up the rules, it does not follow that moral patients cannot be allowed to benefit from them and be protected by them if it can be demonstrated that such patients as animals do not differ clearly from those whose interests moral agents wish to protect. Nor is it easy to see how animals differ in morally relevant ways, in Rollin's view, from certain classes of humans whose interests moral agents would wish to protect but who cannot enter into contracts as, for example, future generations of humans, babies, the retarded, the comatose, and so on. The conclusion which Rollin reaches from this line of reasoning is compelling:

> If the contractualist wishes to include these humans as entities to whom we have obligations, then he must admit that entities become moral objects in virtue of characteristics other than the rational ability to enter into contracts – characteristics like the ability to suffer, or to have needs. But if that is the case, then animals must be covered by moral rules, since they, too have these characteristics.[82]

From the foundation of the school, the Stoics would have rejected Rollin's argument that the capacity for emotion is a valid substitute for reason as the basis for a claim to moral consideration, since the Stoics regarded emotions as dependent upon the function of certain rational actions of which they considered animals to be incapable. The Stoic theory of emotions is complex. In his life of Zeno, Diogenes Laertius informs us that the founder of the school defined emotion, or πάθος (*pathos*) as an irrational movement of the soul, or as an excessive impulse (ἔστι δὲ αὐτὸ τὸ πάθος κατὰ Ζήνωνα ἡ ἄλογος καὶ παρὰ φύσιν ψυχῆς κίνησις καὶ ὁρμὴ πλεονάζουσα, VII. 110). He elaborates the Stoic position by observing that the school further regarded emotion as entailing a kind of judgment, or κρίσις (*krisis*) (δοκεῖ δ' αὐτοῖς τὰ πάθη κρίσις εἶναι, VII. 111). The emotion of avarice, for example, is a judgment that money is a good thing. Now, while the Stoics held that animals are capable of impulse, or ὁρμή (*hormē*), as we observed above,[83] they denied that they are capable of judgment, which is a function of rationality, and declared that they can therefore not have emotions.[84] Later Stoics seem to have felt a certain vulnerability on their doctrine of animal emotions because of arguments from opponents who reasoned that since animals certainly do show at least some evidences of emotions, they must therefore possess some traces of rationality. The Stoics responded, as they so often did, by "raising the bar," and making further demands on animals before they could be acknowledged to be rational. Seneca, for example, saw how the doctrine of rationality as a necessary consequence of emotion could be used against the school, and he responded by redefining the concept of emotion to involve a four-stage progression to full-blown emotion. The third step in this progression, which he defined as a kind of rational assent of the mind (*adsensus animi*), was impossible for irrational animals, who remained at stage two, experiencing only a sort of involuntary mental agitation (*agitatio animi*).[85]

What emerges from our examination of the Stoic case against animals, influential through the ages in various guises and constantly "updated" and elaborated to meet the objections of its opponents, is a picture of an ethic of exclusion designed both to justify any human action taken against animals and to assure humans that they are an order of beings favored by their creator. Yet the Stoic heritage has never been without its detractors. However it has been articulated, Stoicism and its modern descendants like Contractualism assume that animals have no claims on us because of their supposed irrationality. Some modern animal rightists, however, counter that even if animals can make no moral claims upon us on the basis of their own attainments, we cannot necessarily be certain that we do not owe them our protection on other grounds than the possession of reason. Perhaps we owe them that protection simply because they are our fellow-creatures and, with us, part of the community of life. We may after all owe something to those who cannot owe us anything in return. Philosopher Stephen R. L. Clark eloquently expresses his doubts concerning the assumptions of the Stoics and their contractualist offspring:

> Contractual theorists from Protagoras onward have imagined society as a sort of corporation. Stoics employed this analogy to give men a sense of companionship in the whole kin-group of humanity. My

suggestion is that society is much more like a household, including different age-groups, ranks and species, and that a similar analogical process reveals the wider Household which is the community of living creatures.[86]

Clark, who demonstrates a deeper appreciation for the ancient contribution to philosophical speculation on the intellectual and moral status of animals vis-à-vis their human counterparts than is in general encountered in contemporary animal rights literature, advocates what might be termed an ethic of inclusion that focuses on what he perceives to be similarities between human beings and animals as the starting point for ethical discourse on man's proper stance toward non-human species, in contrast to the ethic of exclusion observable in the Stoics and their intellectual descendants. Animals, like humans, act correctly, in Clark's view, when they carry out the activities proper to their lives, and when humans do not allow animals to carry out their proper actions, both animals and humans are deprived thereby and their lives diminished.[87] Thinkers in the Stoic tradition fail to see that animals may after all be more than mere tools for man's use, but may be what Clark calls "ends-in-themselves."[88] Even supposing it is true, as some philosophers have asserted, that there is a "hierarchy of ability" in nature, Clark insists that this should not be allowed to end up a tyranny.[89] It would be difficult to imagine that Clark, who cites Aristotle, Theophrastus, the Stoics and Porphyry, has not taken a page from Plutarch's animal ethics in formulating his own doctrine of ethical inclusiveness.

Plutarch's case for animal rationality

In some cases, the Latin titles by which the treatises contained in his *Moralia* are conventionally known do a disservice to Plutarch by imperfectly representing their contents.[90] This is strikingly true of our author's animal-related treatises. The longest and most carefully reasoned of these, *De sollertia animalium* (*On the Cleverness of Animals*), in which Plutarch's case for animal rationality is laid out in detail, is not so much a random investigation of the "cleverness" or "ingenuity" (*sollertia*) of animals, as the somewhat colorless Latin noun of the title suggests, as it is a comparative analysis of the intellectual endowments of land-dwelling and sea-dwelling creatures, a fact which is more accurately reflected in the Greek title of the work, Πότερα τῶν ζῴων φρονιμώτερα τὰ χερσαῖα ἢ τὰ ἔνυδρα (*Whether Land or Sea Animals Are Wiser*). Similarly, the humorous dialogue *Bruta animalia ratione uti* (*Whether Beasts Are Rational*) touches on the question of animal rationality only briefly (991F–992C), despite the work's title, although in this case, the Latin title is a close translation of the common Greek title of this work whose principal thesis is that animals are superior to humans in their greater natural propensity toward the virtues. In this final section of our chapter, we will examine the case for animal rationality that Plutarch develops in *De sollertia animalium* and supplements with arguments advanced elsewhere in the treatises included in the *Moralia*, as we turn our attention to Plutarch's contribution to the debate, ancient and modern, on the moral ramifications of reason possession in animals.

Plutarch scholars have long maintained that among his most cherished activities was the teaching of philosophy in his native town of Chaeronea. Almost a century ago, Max Schuster analyzed *De sollertia animalium* expressly for the light it throws on Plutarch's activities as a teacher of Platonic bent, and he argued that Plutarch maintained a kind of "mini-Academy" in his home, the significance of which to local intellectual life remains unclear because of Plutarch's native modesty in referring to it.[91] Some of the treatises included in the *Moralia* appear to reproduce the deliberations of this informal school, as Plutarch at times lectures his pupils and at other times records the discussions led by them. In *De sollertia animalium*, Soclarus, a family friend of Plutarch who appears elsewhere as an interlocutor in Plutarch's dialogues, reflects the position of the Stoics in the course of the discussion, while Autobulus, Plutarch's own father, advances throughout a position more sympathetic toward animals. In the course of the comparative analysis itself, which follows preliminary comments by Soclarus and Autobulus, one Aristotimus advances the case of land-dwelling animals, while one Phaedimus takes the side of sea-dwellers. Neither of these individuals is otherwise known.

In the opening paragraphs of *De sollertia animalium*, Plutarch invites his readers to overhear this discussion which, we are given to understand, is already in its second day, and the tantalizing references to conclusions reached in the previous day's deliberations make readers interested in ancient attitudes toward animals sorry to have missed the earlier debate. Plutarch's interlocutors had already the day before discussed the moral issues involved in hunting when a treatise on the subject was read before the group,[92] and, more importantly for our purposes, the thesis had been advanced, apparently by Autobulus, that all animals possess some degree of understanding and reason (ἀποφηνάμενοι γὰρ ἐχθές, ὡς οἶσθα, μετέχειν ἀμωσγέπως πάντα τὰ ζῷα διανοίας καὶ λογισμοῦ, 960A). This thesis will be tested on the second day of discussions by means of a comparative examination of the intellect (περὶ συνέσεως, 960A) demonstrated by land and sea creatures. Although it is impossible for us to gauge the overall importance of the discussion of hunting to the previous day's deliberations because of the allusive references to the subject (959A), the motif of the hunt has an important structural function in the subsequent debate. Soclarus makes the argument, still favored by hunters today, that hunting affords a pure spectacle (καθαρὰν θέαν, 959C) of human intellect pitted against the mindless strength (ἀνόητον ἰσχύν, 959C) of animals. Autobulus reminds him, however, that the possibility of intellect in animals had been raised in the previous day's deliberations (960A), so that the question of the justification of hunting must be reformulated to ask whether land-dwelling or sea-dwelling creatures will constitute the worthiest adversaries of human beings (960B). Soclarus' position on hunting is precisely what might be expected from an individual sympathetic to Stoic ideals, for underlying his attitude is the Chrysippean doctrine that animals have value only insofar as they contribute to the betterment of the lifestyle of humans.[93] Indeed, we can hardly read Soclarus' statement here without recalling Porphyry's observation (*De abstinentia* I. 4) that the Stoics held that all human life would collapse if we refrained from using animals to support it.

Soclarus' estimation of hunting, with its Stoic-colored assertion that humans are by nature intellectually superior to animals and that the lives of animals are expendable, is consistent with the Greek belief that hunting is in a sense a matter of self-defense on the part of humans since animals wrong humans by injuring them. According to some Greek thinkers, humans wage a war against animals which is both natural and just. Porphyry, for example, succinctly presents this notion when articulating the position of those who would defend meat eating against his arguments (ἀλλὰ μὴν πρός γε θήρια πόλεμος ἡμῖν ἔμφυτος ἅμα καὶ δίκαιος, *De abstinentia* I. 14). Hunting is the noble and controlled pursuit of this goal, Greek supporters of hunting maintained, in which humans can succeed only by virtue of their intellect. Through Autobulus' reply to Soclarus' assertion, however, Plutarch introduces a note of sympathy and "fellow-feeling" for animals as suffering creatures that is by no means common in ancient discussions of man's relations with other species, whether in the context of hunting or elsewhere, but which sets the tone for Plutarch's subsequent argumentation in *De sollertia animalium*, and lends a distinctly "modern" tone to his animal psychology. Autobulus is willing to concede that hunting may have been justified at a point in human history when man limited such activity to the destruction of noxious animals like bears and wolves, but he laments that men have moved on almost exclusively to the slaughter of innocuous beasts like rabbits, deer and sheep (959E). Man has descended from a potentially defensible activity to a blameworthy desire to inflict pain.

The argument that hunting may be ethically unjustifiable because it causes pain and injury to sentient beings was not likely to carry much weight with philosophers who taught that humans can owe nothing to creatures that are utterly unlike us in their nature (the *oikeiotês* doctrine). Yet this is precisely the argument that Autobulus makes in reply to Soclarus as he charges that humans have, through their love of hunting, become inured to animal suffering and have even come to delight in the slaughter and death involved (αἷμα καὶ τραύματα ζῴων μὴ δυσχεραίνειν ἀλλὰ χαίρειν σφαττομένοις καὶ ἀποθνῄσκουσιν, *De sollertia animalium* 959D). It is highly significant, and completely in keeping with Plutarch's technique of using Stoic technical terms to refute Stoic doctrines, that Autobulus calls this callous attitude toward animals a case of ἀπάθεια (*apatheia*), apparently in the meaning of "insensibility" (959D), although the Stoics had used the term to characterize the goal of their ethical system, that freedom from the passions for which their devotees strove.[94] Sorabji makes the interesting comment that Plutarch believed that humans may owe a debt of benevolence to animals even if they cannot be said to owe them a debt of justice.

On this attitude, Sorabji remarks, "I have not found this argument anywhere else."[95] Autobulus argues against hunting precisely because it deadens any human inclination toward this benevolence. Man thinks nothing of killing for pleasure, which renders him immune to pity (πρὸς οἶκτον ἀκαμπές, 959E). This Plutarchan sensitivity, while seldom encountered in ancient sources, has become increasingly prominent in modern discussions of the ethics of hunting, and it is nowhere more eloquently expressed than in the words that close Cartmill's history of the practice, "Throughout Western history, the hunt has been defined as a confrontation between the human world and the wild. Giving up the distinction between those two worlds means discarding the whole system of symbolic meanings that have distinguished hunting from mere butchery and given it a special importance in the history of Western thought. If the edge of nature is a hallucination, then hunting is only animal-killing."[96] Autobulus' tone of indignation at the suffering of other species, found so strongly in Cartmill's indictment of hunting, weaves through De sollertia animalium like an emotional counterpoint to the logical argumentation in defense of the position that animals are rational offered by Plutarch in his treatise, and, when it is seen beside the equally strongly held views of Soclarus, it places in high relief the peculiarly ambivalent attitudes toward animals that both ancients and moderns evince.

The dialogue De sollertia animalium is bipartite in its overall structure. In the first seven chapters (959A–965D), Plutarch defends his thesis that all animals partake in reason to some degree and refutes the case of those thinkers, in particular the Stoics, who denied this. The remaining thirty chapters (965E–985C) constitute the comparison of the mental endowments of land and sea creatures. In the final analysis, neither is judged superior. The treatise ends inconclusively and rather abruptly, leaving the reader with the impression that Plutarch was more interested in convincing him that all creatures have a share of reason than that creatures pursuing one mode of life are superior to those pursuing the other. In the course of Plutarch's defense of animal rationality, scarcely any argument employed in ancient discussions for or against its existence fails to appear, and a number that are prominent in modern animal rights literature are encountered in remarkable anticipations. In De sollertia animalium and its sister-treatises Bruta animalia ratione uti and De esu carnium, and here and there in such works as De amore prolis (On Love for Offspring), the reader will discover that Plutarch has taken a stance on such issues of central importance in ancient speculation on animal psychology as the nature and extent of the "gulf" that separates humans from animals, the nature of the emotional life of animals, the linguistic capacities of animals, and the ability of animals to enter into contracts with humans based on their linguistic capacities.[97]

When Plutarch has Autobulus remind his companions that on the previous day, the idea had been advanced that all animals *partake in* or *have a share of* (μετέχειν) reason (λογισμοῦ), he not only states what will be the thesis of

De sollertia animalium, which Plutarch will prove to his satisfaction in the subsequent argumentation of the treatise, but he both hints at the course that his argument will take and explicitly takes a stance in opposition to Stoics like Chrysippus. For Plutarch, who focuses on what he views as similarities between animals and humans and not, in the manner of the Stoics, on their differences, animal rationality is rather an issue of "more or less" than of "either–or," as the Stoics, in their eagerness to protect man's privileged position in creation, would view it. At the same time, by choosing the verb μετέχειν, "share in," Plutarch allows the reader to see that part of the task he sets himself in *De sollertia animalium* will be to determine the dimensions and limits of animal rationality. While acknowledging that animals do not possess the level and range of rationality that humans do, Plutarch insists that they cannot therefore be denied reason altogether. Autobulus argues that it would be absurd to maintain that creatures not designed to exhibit perfect reason do not therefore possess any reason (τὸ μὴ πεφυκὸς ὀρθότητα λόγου δέχεσθαι <μηδὲ λόγον δέχεσθαι>, 962C).[98] After all, Autobulus continues (962C), if philosophers demand perfection of wisdom, they will not find it even in humans (ἣν δὲ ζητοῦσιν ὀρθότητα καὶ σοφίαν οὐδ' ἄνθρωπον εἰπεῖν κεκτημένον ἔχουσιν), although humans have access to those advantages that would raise reason implanted by nature in all creatures to a state of perfection, namely attentive care and education (λόγος μὲν γὰρ ἐγγίνεται φύσει, σπουδαῖος δὲ λόγος καὶ τέλειος ἐξ ἐπιμελείας καὶ διδασκαλίας, 962C). Consequently, the rational faculty implanted by nature in humans is potentially infinitely perfectible, while that of animals is of a lower and more limited grade, and is not so perfectible. Even in the case of animals themselves, the difference between one animal and another lies in the degree of intellectual development that nature has accorded to each (ἄλλοις δ' ἄλλως κατὰ τὸ μᾶλλον καὶ τὸ ἧττον παροῦσα τὰς ὁρωμένας διαφορὰς πεποίηκεν, 963A). The reasoning ability of animals may prove to be less highly developed than that of humans, but to deny animals a share of intellect and understanding because they do not possess them in the degree that humans do is, Plutarch insists, as absurd as to deny that humans can see, hear or run because they cannot do these things as efficiently as can some animal species (963A). Therefore, he allows Autobulus to proclaim (963B), we should more correctly state that animals possess less acute intellect than do humans rather than that they possess none (οὐκοῦν ὁμοίως μηδὲ τὰ θηρία λέγωμεν, εἰ νωθρότερον φρονεῖ καὶ κάκιον διανοεῖται, μὴ διανοεῖσθαι μηδὲ φρονεῖν ὅλως μηδὲ κεκτῆσθαι λόγον). Their intellect is weak (ἀσθενῆ) and "muddy" (θολερόν), but it is not absent (963B). Francesco Becchi has recently observed, quite aptly, that Plutarch sees animal rationality as a question of quantity rather than of quality.[99]

In Plutarch's view, common sense itself suggests that animals are rational, for to assume the opposite leads one into logical absurdities, as happens to the Stoics when their assumptions on animal rationality are followed to their conclusions. The Stoics held that the rational must be counterbalanced in the universe by the irrational, just as all would agree that the mortal must be counterbalanced by the immortal and the destructible by the indestructible (960B). This Stoic "theory of opposites" was developed by Chrysippus in his treatise Περὶ ἐναντίων (*On Opposites*).[100] Autobulus counters Soclarus' reliance on the theory of opposites by admitting that no one would deny that there are irrational creatures in nature, but these are such entities as are not endowed with soul, while every besouled creature possesses at birth the intellectual faculties of sensation and imagination (πᾶν τὸ ἔμψυχον αἰσθητικὸν εὐθὺς εἶναι καὶ φανταστικὸν πέφυκεν, 960D). Not even the Stoics had denied that animals possess souls.[101] Autobulus counts himself among those who hold not only that sentient beings possess intelligence, but that they naturally (κατὰ φύσιν, 960D) likewise possess opinion (δόξα) and reason (λογισμός). Autobulus then cites as collaboration the Peripatetic philosopher Strato's assertion that it is impossible for a creature to possess sensation without also possessing intellect (καίτοι Στράτωνός γε τοῦ φυσικοῦ λόγος ἐστὶν ἀποδεικνύων ὡς οὐδ' αἰσθάνεσθαι τὸ παράπαν ἄνευ τοῦ νοεῖν ὑπάρχει, 961A).

Plutarch allows that philosophers, including Aristotle, are at least correct in asserting that nature does everything toward some purpose or end, so that it would be counterintuitive to maintain that nature could create any sentient being for the sole purpose of its being sentient, without intending that sentience to be exercised toward some useful end (960E). In fact, Plutarch argues, nature has provided creatures with the capacity to distinguish between that which they should avoid and that which they should pursue. This capacity cannot reside in creatures that do not have some ability to reason (λογίζεσθαι, 960F), to judge (κρίνειν), to remember (μνημονεύειν), and to attend (παρέχειν). This ability in animals to recognize things that are akin to themselves or foreign to them (πρὸς τὸ οἰκεῖον καὶ τὸ ἀλλότριον ἡ αἴσθησις, 961B) is of course the origin of that *oikeiotês* which underlies a creature's affection for its offspring and forms the basis for its sense of self-preservation. Moreover, an animal could not be expected to keep things in mind once the immediate perception of them is past, if the animal did not possess that function of intellect called memory (961B). Otherwise, an animal could never recall what prey is proper to it. The fact that animals obviously do recall their prey likewise argues, in Autobulus' estimation, that animal perceptions possess as well that ingredient which the Stoics dubbed "conceptions" (ἔννοίας, 961D), which become, when activated, as in the recollection of absent prey, what the Stoics termed "thoughts" (διανοήσεις). The Stoics denied that animals were capable of concepts and they held that an animal's recognition of its prey did not involve any mental representation that might require verbalization inside the brain of the animal. As Chrysippus held, an animal can recognize without being rational, a position which Autobulus would have rejected.[102] Subsequently in *De sollertia animalium*, Plutarch expands this assertion by citing some unnamed philosophers who agree with him that animals have a share of reason and who base their case on the principle that irrational creatures could not demonstrate instances of a sense of purpose (προθέσεις, 966B), preparation (παρασκευαί), memory (μνήμη), emotions (πάθη) and care for their offspring (τέκνων ἐπιμέλειαι) if they did not possess that share of reason. It is precisely the possession of these faculties, Plutarch argues, that allows these philosophers to declare that animals have a share of reason (δι᾽ ὧν οἱ φιλόσοφοι δείκνυουσι τὸ μετέχειν τοῦ λόγου τὰ ζῷα, 966B).

Plutarch once again takes on the Stoics in his defense of emotions in animals that follows the above discussion, developing a line of argument clever in its strategy of turning Stoic notions against them but at the same time open to a charge of that anthropomorphism that has dogged advocates for animals through the ages. Plutarch allows Autobulus to complain that, while the Stoics spend their time defining emotions abstractly as functions of logical analysis, calling them judgments (κρίσεις) and opinions (δόξαι), they ignore the evidence of their senses that tell them that animals do many things that indicate the presence of anger, fear, jealousy and envy.[103] If they deny emotions in animals, the Stoics catch themselves up in a self-contradiction when they punish their horses in hopes, through the application of pain, of instilling in them that sense of grief which is called repentance (μετάνοια, 961D), which would be pointless if the animals could not reflect upon the purpose of their chastisement. Autobulus here ignores the knotty problems that trouble modern ethologists who ask whether a behavior that would in humans be acknowledged to be a particular emotion is in fact that emotion when similar behavior is witnessed in animals, and he chastises the Stoics for allowing only that a deer "as it were" (ὡσανεί, 961F) feels fear, or a lion "as it were" shows anger. By the same token, he charges, one would have to conclude that an animal only "as it were" sees or even lives at all. Such assertions on the part of the Stoics, Autobulus concludes, are contrary to the clear evidence of the senses (παρὰ τὴν ἐνάργειαν, 961F).

While Soclarus confesses to being convinced by Autobulus' exposition of the content of animal perception and emotion to this point, he maintains that animals nevertheless exhibit many other evidences of shortcomings (φλαυρότητα, 962A) vis-à-vis human beings, most importantly in their failure to demonstrate any evidence of aiming toward virtue or of progress toward it (προκοπήν) or yearning for it (ὄρεξιν, 962A). Since this virtue is the end toward which reason was established by nature, Soclarus declares himself unable to see how nature could have given animals the beginnings of reason if they cannot attain its perfection. Soclarus' word choice here again betrays the Stoic inspiration of his argument. The concept of ὄρεξις, "yearning, desire," was viewed by the Stoics as a function of reason, and since they denied reason to animals, they judged them consequently incapable of desires as well.[104]

Autobulus replies that he does not wonder that the Stoics cannot see that the apparent lack of striving toward virtue in animals is not to be ascribed to a lack of reason in them rather than to an imperfection of reason since they are equally blind to the fact that, although they assert that love of offspring (φιλοστοργία, 962A) is the origin of justice and fellowship among living creatures, and they do not deny that animals love their offspring dearly, they refuse nevertheless to acknowledge that animals partake of justice.[105] It stands to reason, he observes, that since some animals fly and see better than do some others, some animals possessed of the capacity to reason more closely approach the perfection of that faculty than do some others (962D).

Here, at the endpoint of the exposition of his case for rationality in animals, just as he takes up the issue of the potential juridical relationship between humans and reason-possessing animals (963F–965B), and shortly before he undertakes the comparative examination of land and sea animals, in the course of which his thesis of animal rationality is supported by practical examples, Plutarch brings his argument full-circle by harkening back to his original thesis, stated at the beginning of the debate (960A), that animals *share in* (μετέχειν, 962C) the faculty of reason, the idea which had formed the cornerstone of Plutarch's argument. While Plutarch had at no time in the development of his case claimed that reason ever manifests itself in so developed a form as it does in human beings, he had advanced the belief that no sharp intellectual distinction exists between humans and animals. For Plutarch, biological gradualism, the συνέχεια of Aristotle,[106] does not require us to draw the line at the point where rationality enters the picture. Animals, in Plutarch's view, share the conscious world of humans, however dim their consciousness may be, and do not, in his view, have to be equal to humans to matter to them.

In the first seven chapters of De sollertia animalium (959A–965D), wherein the bulk of his case for rationality in animals is set forth, Plutarch employs forms of the word φύσις (*physis*) seventeen times, as he grapples with the questions of what constitutes the "nature" of animalkind and whether the nature of animals differs in any morally significant aspect from that of humankind. Plutarch's numerous appeals to the concept of *physis* in the chapters that develop his case for animal rationality suggest that, for him, rationality is a constituent of the nature of animalkind. Similarly, in his treatise Bruta animalia ratione uti, Plutarch's philosophical pig Gryllus explains that sexual passion in animals is strictly seasonal and always restrained, for in animals, *physis* is the supreme motivating factor in their behavior (τὸ δ' ὅλον ἡ φύσις, 990D). Slightly later in that treatise, the pig claims that *physis* is the teacher of skills in animals (τούτων διδάσκαλον εἶναι τὴν φύσιν, 991F), and that if humans believe that this *physis* is not equivalent to reason and intellect, they had better look for a more appropriate term for it (ἢν εἰ μὴ λόγον οἴεσθε δεῖν μηδὲ φρόνησιν καλεῖν, ὥρα σκοπεῖν ὄνομα κάλλιον αὐτῇ καὶ τιμιώτερον). While we might justly hesitate to accept the word of a pig, even of one so clever as Gryllus, we should note that here, as in De sollertia animalium, Plutarch is suggesting that *physis* and reason, or λόγος (*logos*), are not incompatible, but are rather to be seen as equally responsible for guiding the actions of animals.

One might be tempted to conclude that, in his use of the term *physis*, Plutarch is speaking of a kind of unalloyed "instinct," that sort of hard-wired, pre-programmed behavior of animals that some psychologists and ethologists with behaviorist sympathies like to posit to account for all animal actions that seem to be purposeful and guided by some intellectual activity, yet Plutarch is careful to suggest that *physis* and *logos* work in tandem in motivating animal behaviors, and that what we might be tempted to term "instinct" may in fact be infused with some rational activity. Plutarch understands the "nature" of animals to include a kind of innate rationality that guides behaviors that are instinctual to the extent that they are natural to a given species. In his recent work *Dominion: The Power of Man, the Suffering of Animals, and the Call to Mercy*, Matthew Scully adopts a view strikingly similar to that of Plutarch when he questions the tendency of some psychologists to explain all animal behaviors as predetermined, instinctual responses unaided by any feelings or intentionality, observing, "*Something* has to choose, to mediate, to organize, which is why identical animals will often react differently to identical circumstances. And whatever that something is, it cannot itself be instinct. It must logically stand above instinct, presiding and selecting as it does in us. In our case we call it consciousness. What could it be in their case but a humbler version of the same thing?"[107] Like Plutarch, Scully sees the *physis* of animals as informed by some intellectual activity.

That the *physis* of animals consists not of "mere" instinct but entails a decision-making component that argues for the presence of some degree of rationality was obvious to Plutarch from the tendency of an animal to seek that which is akin to it and to avoid that which is foreign to it, an intellectual capacity which animals receive from nature, as he states in his defense of the vegetarian lifestyle, in a passage in which he argues that animals possess perception, hearing, sight, imagination and, in particular, intelligence that enables them to distinguish between the two (ἀλλ' αἰσθήσεώς γε μετέχουσιν, ὄψεως ἀκοῆς, φαντασίας συνέσεως, ἣν ἐπὶ κτήσει τοῦ οἰκείου καὶ φυγῇ τοῦ ἀλλοτρίου παρὰ τῆς φύσεως ἕκαστον εἴληκε, *De esu carnium* 997E). This element of rationality natural to animals that allows them to recognize that which is akin to them (τὸ οἰκεῖον) is the cornerstone of that sense of belonging and of relationship, that *oikeiotês*, which the Stoics declared to be impossible between humans and animals precisely because they held that animals lack reason, and which they considered to be the basis of justice between humans but which they maintained was impossible between humans and irrational creatures. While Plutarch's phraseology here is quite close to his formulation of the concept of kinship in *De sollertia animalium* 961B, he now specifically states that it arises from the nature of animals and is derived from that rationality which is natural to them.[108]

The rational instinct that constitutes the *physis* of animals may, as Plutarch acknowledges, operate at a level forever below that at which the reasoning powers of humans function, affording them mental capacities that he variously terms inferior, dim and muddy, but Plutarch singles out one notable area in which the *physis* of animals is superior to that of humans: animals live lives that are more in tune with their nature than do humans who tend over time to be corrupted by vices which do not infect animals. Plutarch had remarked (*De sollertia animalium* 962C) that while humans have access to those advantages that could grant them genuine and perfect reason (σπουδαῖος λόγος καὶ τέλειος) in the form of education and practice at virtue, we do not in actuality find that perfection of reason in humans. We are told why this is so by Plutarch's philosophical pig Gryllus in *Bruta animalia ratione uti* (989C). Animals, unlike humans, live lives free from false opinion (κενὴ δόξα) and alien passions (ἐπείσακτα πάθη), so that they do not fall victim to unnatural desires. Since in this treatise, and nowhere else in the *Moralia*, Plutarch advances the position that animals are superior to human beings, we must conclude that this assertion is yet another example of that superiority. Plutarch had developed a somewhat similar argument in his treatise *De amore prolis*, wherein he maintained that nature preserves in an unadulterated form the traits peculiar to animals (ἄκρατον γὰρ ἐν ἐκείνοις ἡ φύσις καὶ ἀμιγὲς καὶ ἁπλοῦν φυλάττει τὸ ἴδιον, 493C) while humans are led by the very force of their reason and character (ὑπὸ τοῦ λόγου καὶ τῆς συνηθείας, 493C) into more sorts of judgments and opinions than lie open to the mental powers of animals. Indeed, in beasts, such versatility and freedom of expression by the intellect is not so abundantly available (τοῖς δὲ θηρίοις τὸ μὲν πολύτροπον τοῦ λόγου καὶ περιττὸν καὶ φιλελεύθερον ἄγαν οὐκ ἔστιν, 493D). In humans, reason is master (αὐτοκρατὴς λόγος, 493D), while animals are less led astray from their humbler nature by the weaker force of their intellect. Animals live in a sense closer to nature, and are, ironically, in this respect at least superior to humans in whom autocratic reason, when allowed free rein to indulge in passions and desires, leaves no trace of nature (αὐτοκρατὴς λόγος . . . οὐδὲν ἴχνος ἐμφανὲς οὐδ' ἐναργὲς ἀπολέλοιπε τῆς φύσεως, 493E). In other words, when animals obey the dictates of their dimmer powers of reasoning, they are acting according to nature (κατὰ φύσιν), while humans are liable to act contrary to nature (παρὰ φύσιν) when they indulge their stronger but sometimes wayward powers of reasoning. This enables animals to live lives that are more naturally virtuous than are those of humans.[109]

The idea that animals are naturally inclined to aim at virtuous behavior surfaces as well in Gryllus' exposition of the excellences of the animal estate, when the pig forces Odysseus to acknowledge that the animal soul is by its very nature so constituted (ὁμολογεῖς τὴν τῶν θηρίων ψυχὴν εὐφυεστέραν εἶναι πρὸς γενεσιν ἀρετῆς καὶ τελειοτέραν, *Bruta animalia ratione uti* 987B). Slightly later in that treatise, the pig makes the same point developed at length in both *De sollertia animalium* and *De amore prolis*, that the intellect of animals allows them no room for useless pursuits (ἡ τῶν θηρίων φρόνησις τῶν μὲν ἀχρήστων καὶ ματαίων τέχνων οὐδημιᾷ χώραν δίδωσι, 991D). Unfortunately, this observation immediately follows a lacuna in which we might well have expected to encounter once again some variation of Plutarch's idea that animals live closer to their *physis* than do humans and are therefore more naturally virtuous. Gryllus seems at least to hint at this in 991E, where he claims that animal intellect (θηρίων φρόνησις) engenders by itself and unaided those skills that animals require for life, and demands that Odysseus acknowledge that this must constitute an instance of the workings of animals' reason (λόγος), unless Odysseus can think of another name for it (991F). He finally declares himself at a loss to explain, now that he has experienced the animal estate, how he could ever have been led to believe that only humans are rational (καταδὺς εἰς τουτὶ τὸ σῶμα θαυμάζω τοὺς λόγους ἐκείνους, οὓς ἀνεπειθόμην ὑπὸ τῶν σοφιστῶν ἄλογα καὶ ἀνόητα πάντα πλὴν ἀνθρώπου νομίζειν, 992C). Despite its light and jocular tone, and the relatively few references to the topic in the brief compass of the treatise, *Bruta animalia ratione uti* agrees with Plutarch's thesis in *De sollertia animalium* that animals are rational, that their reason differs from that of man quantitatively rather than qualitatively, and that animals live closer to their nature and are therefore less corrupted by potential misuse of their rational faculties.

The concluding reflections of Autobulus and Soclarus (962B–965D) that immediately precede the comparative analysis of the lifestyles of land and sea animals, and incorporate as well the discussion of the possibility of justice toward animals, serve to recapitulate a number of salient points in Plutarch's case for rationality in animals, in particular his fundamental thesis that the reasoning faculty in animals differs from that in humans quantitatively rather than qualitatively. Foreshadowing the manner of argumentation employed in the comparative chapters, Plutarch now relies more heavily on specific examples of animal behaviors to support his observations. To illustrate the topic just discussed at length, namely that some species naturally aim more toward virtue than do some others, Autobulus observes (962F) that hippopotamuses will eat their parents while storks care for theirs, just as some species of birds are more solicitous in caring for their nestlings than are others. To make such observations, Autobulus argues (963A), strikes us as perfectly sensible, while to assert that one tree is less intelligent than another strikes us as absurd, and this is so precisely because all animal species have some share of the rational faculty while we tacitly recognize that mute creations like trees do not. Again, it is a question of quantity rather than quality of this capacity to think (ἡ φρονεῖν δύναμις, 963A) that leads to observable differences since some species possess this capacity more or less than do others (ἄλλοις δ' ἄλλως κατὰ τὸ μᾶλλον καὶ ἧττον παροῦσα τὰς ὁρωμένας διαφορὰς πεποίηκεν, 963A).

Continuing along similar lines, Autobulus notes (963D) that we do not fault the imperfection of a sensation in an organ that is not created to possess that sensation in the first place. That is, we do not fault an organ for blindness if that organ was not created to see. Similarly, we do not call a creature mentally deranged if it was not created to possess reasoning power in the first place (ᾧ μὴ τὸ φρονεῖν καὶ διανοεῖσθαι καὶ λογίζεσθαι κατὰ φύσιν ὑπῆρχεν, 963D). Now, when an animal becomes rabid, it suffers a type of disturbance exactly parallel to that suffered by insane humans: they do not experience any damage to their sight or hearing but only to their judgment and memory. Even the Stoics admit that dogs become rabid, which these animals could not do if they did not possess mental capacities that were liable to become disturbed in the first place (963F). At this allusion to the Stoics, Soclarus admits himself won over by at least this part of Autobulus' argument against the school.

The chapters of *De sollertia animalium* in which Plutarch's case for rationality in animals is developed have received at least a modicum of respect from scholars, if for no other reason than that they serve as testimonies to the beliefs of those schools whose positions Plutarch attacks, in particular those of the Stoics. The remaining chapters of the treatise, entailing the comparison of the lifestyles of land-dwelling and sea-dwelling creatures, have, in contrast, been condemned as mere borrowings from commonplace books of which a number of other ancient writers who fancied themselves naturalists availed themselves, and have been dismissed as worthless zoology.[110] Such strictures abound already in the earliest analyses of Plutarch's animal psychology. Dyroff brands the land–sea dichotomy as primitive, even if Pliny the Elder likewise employed it.[111] Schuster judges the direct comparison to be a technique influenced by Plutarch's activity as a schoolmaster trained in rhetoric, since the style of argument that combines comparison, or σύγκρισις (*synkrisis*), with use of abundant examples suggests the teaching style of the rhetorical school. Indeed, Schuster finds Plutarch at times constrained by this rhetorical antithesis which occasionally comes off as artificial and far-fetched.[112] He concludes that no real decision is reached on the question of whether land or sea creatures are more clever because the entire comparative investigation was nothing more than a rhetorical exercise to begin with, having no deeper purpose than mere display of rhetorical dexterity.[113]

If Plutarch's zoological observations are judged solely by their scientific acumen, it becomes difficult to disagree with Dyroff and Schuster. Almost a century ago, Sherwood Dickerman showed that Cicero, Philo, Pliny the Elder, Plutarch, Galen and Aelian cite identical instances of animals' behaviors as evidence for the presence of such traits as prudence, wisdom, courage and justice in animals. Ants, for example, are universally cited as creatures remarkable for their strong sense of social responsibility and foresight, while swallows are seen as prudent and tender parents.[114] Virtually no anecdote on animal behavior that Plutarch retails is found uniquely in his work. Yet Plutarch's interest in such lore is less in its scientific validity than in the moral lessons that he can extract from it, for the *synkrisis* allows him to provide specific examples of rational behavior in animals and, more importantly to his purposes, to suggest from these examples that animal excellences may have consequences for human behavior toward other species.

In the manner of a true debate, the interlocutors in the comparative analysis are allowed an "opening statement." Aristotimus, defender of the superiority of land-dwellers, reintroduces the motif of the hunt at the opening of the *synkrisis*, asserting that the comparison of the two lifestyles should properly be viewed as a debate on the question of which sort of animals more successfully sharpen the wits of the hunter by pitting a human being against the craftiness and bravery of animals, qualities which no one would reasonably claim for sea-dwelling animals (966A). He declares it downright dishonorable and mean-spirited to hunt some fishes because they are utterly lacking in cleverness and guile (ἀμήχανον ὅλως καὶ ἀπάνουργον, 966B). A subtle difference is detectable in this second discussion of hunting. Whereas earlier, Soclarus had maintained that the pleasure afforded by hunting arises from the pitting of human wit against mindless animal strength (ἀνόητον ἰσχύν, 959C), now Aristotimus modifies this significantly to declare that hunting is a battle of wits between adversaries who differ in strength and wit. While some fishes may lack wit, some animals, namely land-dwellers, decidedly do not. Aristotimus' change of perspective on the issue of hunting is unquestionably prompted by the extended argument for animal rationality that has intervened between the earlier discussion of hunting and its reintroduction here. This becomes immediately clear from his next comments, for he declares that land-dwellers, in contrast to denizens of the sea, exhibit all of those properties by which philosophers are wont to recognize that creatures have a share of reason (μετέχειν λόγου τὰ ζῷα, 966B): purposefulness (προθέσεις), memory (μνῆμαι), emotions (πάθη), and care for their offspring (τέχνων ἐπιμέλειαι), precisely those properties which Plutarch had earlier claimed for animals (961C). Aristotimus' presentation is in large measure a demonstration of those traits in land animals.

Although Phaedimus, the defender of sea creatures, acknowledges himself at a distinct disadvantage since the lives of sea creatures are not so readily observable to humans as are those of land-dwelling creatures, he promises nevertheless not to rely on unsubstantiated anecdotes and imported tall tales, but to build his case exclusively on eyewitness accounts (τῇ ὄψει πίστιν, 975D). In fact, he almost immediately invokes the sort of anecdotal material that he decries, but his point is well taken. He recognizes that, because land animals are right before our eyes in a manner that sea creatures seldom are, they are more appealing to humans who perceive them as more "like" them than are the remote and often unseen creatures of the sea. Human contact has therefore tended to imbue land creatures with human traits (ἀνθρωπίνοις ἤθεσιν, 975E). Phaedimus perceives the tendency of humans to anthropomorphize land animals, to the disadvantage of sea creatures. The excellences of these animals, he counters, lie open to us in a pure and unadulterated state, untainted by human contact (975F). In cases where such contact has been possible, sea creatures show themselves to be less alien to human experience than Aristotimus claims. Crocodiles and even eels kept as pets will respond to the voices of their masters, and allow themselves to be handled (976A–B). Phaedimus also takes up the motif of hunting to counter Aristotimus' assertion that sea creatures are not worthy adversaries for the hunter, declaring it common knowledge that fishes are difficult to catch because they are by nature suspicious of every human effort to ensnare them, a circumstance that arises from their unadulterated native intelligence (τῆς δ' ἀκράτου καὶ φυσικῆς συνέσεως μέγα δήλωμα τὸ κοινόν ἐστιν, 976C). Slightly later, he supplements this observation by recounting that some fishermen employ dragnets rather than hooks to catch fish in the belief that their prey could not evade capture in this manner even with the use of reason and cleverness (σαγηνεύοντες, ὡς τοῖς ἐνσχεθεῖσιν οὐδεμίαν ἐκ λογισμοῦ καὶ σοφίας διάφευξιν οὖσαν, 977E). Whatever his differences with his opponent, it is clear that Phaedimus has accepted Autobulus' case for animal rationality and argues from the position that sea creatures provide evidence of such rationality as abundant and convincing as that afforded by land-dwellers.

After Phaedimus has concluded his defense of sea-dwellers, Aristotimus invites the audience to vote for the side whose arguments they find more convincing (985C), but the treatise ends with no vote taken. Early critics of *De sollertia animalium*, including Schuster, confessed their frustration at this abrupt and inconclusive outcome, a circumstance which led Schuster to dismiss the latter half of the treatise as nothing more than rhetorical performance.[115] In his recent study of Plutarch's *Lives*, however, Tim Duff makes a valuable comment concerning Plutarch's use of the σύγκρισις in the treatises of the *Moralia*, "He often uses *synkrisis* not to demonstrate the superiority of one side of the equation over the other, but rather to explore the issues raised as a whole."[116] He then cites the comparative chapters of *De sollertia animalium* as a case in point, observing that they function as "a tool of discussion rather than as a means of grading."[117] Plutarch himself hints that this is the proper reading of the σύγκρισις when, in the closing sentence of the treatise, he has Soclarus remark that if the observations of the two opponents are considered together, they provide a strong case against those who would deny reason and intellect to animals (συνθέντες εἰς ταὐτὸν ἀμφότεροι καλῶς ἀγωνεῖσθε κοινῇ πρὸς τοὺς τὰ ζῷα λόγου καὶ συνέσεως ἀποστεροῦντας, 985C).

On several occasions in the course of the *synkrisis*, Plutarch abandons the technique of bald enumeration of anecdotal *mirabilia* that characterizes the latter chapters of *De sollertia animalium*, and dilates on topics of particular importance to his thesis of animal rationality. On these occasions, he seems to be engaged in a kind of dialogue with philosophical schools whose doctrines he seeks to refute. In these extended discussions, Plutarch anticipates ideas that continue to resonate in the modern debate over the rights of animals. He touches upon the issues of logical thinking in animals (969A), of tool usage in animals (967A), of language capabilities in animals (972B–973E), of altruism and cooperative behaviors in animals (972B, 977C and 984B–F), and, perhaps most importantly, of man's potential debt of justice toward animals (970B). Since the questions of animal altruism and of justice toward animals form the subjects of subsequent chapters in our study, we will examine here Plutarch's discussion of logical thinking and of language and tool usage in animals.

Our examination of Plutarch's case for rationality in animals set forth in the first seven chapters of *De sollertia animalium*, and our analysis of the vocabulary in which he couches his case, have suggested that his argumentation is intended to a significant degree as a refutation of the Stoic case against reason possession in animals, in particular as it was developed by earlier Stoics including Zeno (*ca.* 335–263 BCE) and Chrysippus. We have noted as well his fondness for employing technical terms used in Stoic philosophy to turn Stoic doctrines upside-down. Similarly, in the course of the *synkrisis*, Plutarch examines at some length a peculiarity of animal behavior that had caught the attention of no less a figure than Chrysippus himself and that might be taken as evidence of rational activity in animals. What renders his discussion so intriguing is that the behavior under discussion has been cited again in modern ethological literature as potential evidence of traces of a rational capacity in some animals. The question at issue is that of whether some animals are capable of logical deduction. The old Stoic, Plutarch tells us (969A), claimed that when a hunting dog stops at a crossroads and, after sniffing two of three paths and detecting no scent at the two, follows the third path which he has not sniffed at all, the dog performs an operation which *resembles* a kind of syllogistic reasoning that proceeds along these lines: "the prey did not go this way or this way; it must therefore have gone this third way." According to Plutarch, the Stoics designated this kind of syllogistic thinking as "multiple disjunctive" (τῷ διὰ πλειόνων διεζευγμένῳ, 969B). In his life of Zeno, Diogenes Laertius (VII. 81) terms it the fifth indemonstrable syllogism, so called because it is self-evident and requires no demonstration. What troubled the Stoics in the behavior of the dog was its apparent employment of reason, which of course they denied to animals. They were forced to account for the action by some other explanation and to declare the action merely *analogous* to reason. Yet what mental processes were after all involved in what clearly required a choice on the part of the animal made after some intellectual activity? Chrysippus went only so far as to state that the dog shares in dialectic, not that it reasons. In our passage in *De sollertia animalium*, Plutarch rejects all talk of logic and analogy with human reason, and asserts that the dog's actions were the products of perception and reason alone (διανοίᾳ καὶ λόγῳ μόνον, 969C), as will be obvious to anyone who observes countless other actions performed regularly by dogs. The fault of the Stoics, as Plutarch sees it here and elsewhere, is their tendency to reject the evidence of their senses when they stand in the presence of clear truth. The example of Chrysippus' dog continued to fascinate ancient thinkers, not least because it seemed to contradict the Stoic denial of reason to animals, and they wrestled with the question of what sort of mental activity might be involved in the dog's behavior. Sorabji concludes that the Stoics must have allowed what he calls "propositional content" to animals that is apprehended solely through the senses and does not involve any intervening rational action.[118] In any case, the Stoics were clearly troubled by the example of the dog.[119]

The possibility of logical deduction in animals, which might take the form of syllogistic reasoning, has been hypothesized by some ethologists who have observed the remarkable adaptability of some animals to the circumstances of their environment, especially in cases of avoidance of danger and pursuit of food. Donald R. Griffin, a vocal proponent of the position that animals have conscious mental experiences, cites experiments in which rats that have learned to run complex mazes at the end of which food awards awaited them, appeared confused when the expected reward was absent and set about searching for it. His conclusion on this sort of behavior is illuminating, "Naturalists and ethologists have gathered abundant evidence that such needs do arise very commonly in the natural lives of animals, and the resulting behavior strongly suggests that they understand in an elementary fashion what the problems are and how their behavior is likely to solve them. Animals appear to think in 'if, then' terms. 'If I dig here, I will find food.'"[120] Whereas Chrysippus satisfied himself with calling attention to an intriguing instance of animal behavior that appeared to him analogous to syllogistic thought in humans, Griffin's interpretation of the behavior of the rats combines the belief that animals are indeed capable of such syllogistic thought, if only in a limited degree, with Plutarch's contention that some rational activity must accompany this kind of behavior.

In the opening section of this chapter, we noted the prominent place that the issue of tool use and production by animals has assumed in the modern debate over the intellectual endowments of animals.[121] This aspect of the debate well illustrates the propensity of philosophers and scientists who oppose the inclusion of animals in the moral scope of humans to "raise the bar" against animals each time it is proven that animals are capable of an action formerly thought impossible for them, in this case demanding tool production by animals after tool usage by them has been demonstrated. Plutarch includes examples of tool usage by animals in the course of the *synkrisis* which, although not unique to him, gain in significance because he relates them as evidence of rational action in animals. Phaedimus tells us, for example, that crows (κόρακες) are known to fill vessels with stones to cause the water in the vessels to rise to a level at which they can drink it (967A). Ethologists have noted numerous instances of such purposeful use of tools on the part of a number of bird species that enable them to secure food that would otherwise be unattainable to them, and among bird species, crows are consistently singled out for their purposeful tool usage. Rogers, noting that "crows are particularly prone to using tools,"[122] recounts a sophisticated operation on the part of a crow that learned to insert a stick into a hole in order to push a key to secure a food reward. Hauser, always cautious in his assertions about the mental capacities of animals, reminds us that most tools used by animals are "gifts of nature,"[123] rather than "artifacts" produced by the animals themselves, but he does note that crows in New Caledonia create two distinct types of tools from twigs to extract insects from trees, one tool curved and thin and the other wider and barbed, each to be used as the particular problems of extraction dictate.[124]

Modern scientific and philosophical literature has devoted much more attention to the issue of language possession in animals than to their ability to make and use tools since the capacity for meaningful symbolic language is widely viewed as man's last best claim to a singularly favored position in creation. Only humans, it is argued, possess this capacity, and only they can articulate a claim to have their interests respected by other language possessors. We have shown above that this position, which has its origins already in the Stoic doctrine of the imperfect soul of animals, has in recent decades been called into question by ethologists.[125] In the *synkrisis* of *De sollertia animalium*, Plutarch offers an ingenious argument for language possession in birds that once again, as its use of Stoic technical vocabulary makes clear, is aimed against the school of Chrysippus.

For the Stoics, the lack of language capacity in animals was the result of the imperfect nature of the animal soul.[126] While Chrysippus acknowledged that the soul of animals possesses all eight parts that the human soul possesses, that is, the five senses, the capacities for utterance and for reproduction, and the highest element, the so-called *hêgemonikon* or "governing principle," the *hêgemonikon* in humans goes on to develop into reason but remains forever irrational in animals. Since meaningful language, as opposed to the sort of squeaks and chirps that all animals can produce in some form, was a product of reason in Stoic teaching, and animals remain irrational, it was clear to the Stoics that such language was closed to animals. Plutarch sets out in the *synkrisis* to refute the Stoic contention that only humans, with their developed rational *hêgemonikon*, are capable of meaningful, indeed purposeful utterance, employing one of only a handful of examples in *De sollertia animalium* drawn from a Roman context. A Roman barber kept a fantastically talented jaybird (θαυμαστόν τι χρῆμα . . . κίττης, 973C) that was capable of reproducing a wide range of human and animal sounds. On one occasion, a funeral procession passed the barber's shop, accompanied by loud brass instruments. The jay thereupon fell silent and could not be encouraged to vocalize, leading some to believe that it had been poisoned while others concluded that it had been rendered deaf by the musical instruments. Plutarch's reading of the case is different. The jay, he maintains (973D), had withdrawn into itself, and when it eventually used its voice again, it henceforth reproduced only the sounds of the musical instruments. For Plutarch, the explanation for this phenomenon is obvious: during its period of self-imposed silence, the bird was meditating on what it had heard, and consciously chose to utter only certain sounds, which, Plutarch concludes, shows that self-instruction involves a greater level of reason than does mere mimicry of others (ὥστε, ὅπερ ἔφην, τῆς εὐμαθείας λογικωτέραν εἶναι τὴν αὐτομάθειαν ἐν αὐτοῖς, 973E). Other talking birds, Plutarch argues, provide equally compelling evidence that they possess not only the capacity for this "uttered reason" (λόγος προφορικός) but for articulate speech as well (ψᾶρες δὲ καὶ κόρακες καὶ ψιττακοί . . . ἐμοὶ δοκοῦσι προδικεῖν καὶ συνηγορεῖν τοῖς ἄλλοις ζῴοις ἐν τῷ μανθάνειν, τρόπον τινὰ διδάσκοντες ἡμᾶς, ὅτι καὶ προφορικοῦ λόγου καὶ φωνῆς ἐνάρθρου μέτεστιν αὐτοῖς, 972F–973A). It was the period of silence and inner meditation on the part of the jay that proved, for Plutarch, that the "uttered reason" of birds is prompted by "inner reason" (λόγος ἐνδιάθετος) that inspires and guides the utterance. Once again, Plutarch's word choice here makes it clear that he is taking aim at the Stoics, and may in fact have some specific Stoic text in mind in his attack. In his discussion of the Stoic theory of voice (φωνή), Diogenes Laertius informs us that Diogenes the Babylonian held that while the utterance of an animal is merely the percussion of air caused by impulse, the voice of a human being is "articulate" (ἔναρθρος) and the product of reason (ζῴου μέν ἐστι φωνὴ ἀὴρ ὑπὸ ὁρμῆς πεπληγμένος, ἀνθρώπου δ' ἔστιν ἔναρθρος καὶ ἀπὸ διανοίας ἐκπεμπομένη, VII. 55).

Twice in the course of *De sollertia animalium*, once briefly in the *synkrisis* (970B) and once at length in the final chapters of his argument for rationality in animals (963F–975B), Plutarch formulates his answer to that question which, since antiquity, has motivated much of the inquiry into the intellectual capacities of animals: if animals are indeed the sort of creatures that are akin to humans to the extent that they possess some degree of reason, as Plutarch has been at pains to show in *De sollertia animalium*, and that behave toward each other and toward humans in ways that humans would consider to be virtuous if observed in human interactions, how then should humans conduct themselves toward animals? Plutarch grapples here with the issue of man's potential debt of justice toward animals, an ancient concern that remains one of the most contentious issues in the animal rights debate of the present century. Plutarch's contribution to that debate forms the subject of our next chapter.

3

JUST BEASTS

Animal morality and human justice

You know, my Brethren, we, in our turn, have no duties toward the
brute creation; there is no relation of justice between them and us. . . .
They can claim nothing at our hands; into our hands they are absolutely
delivered.

John Henry Cardinal Newman, *Sermons Preached on Various Occasions*

It is no exaggeration to state that the determination of acceptable criteria for
deciding what constitutes man's obligations toward animals has been the central
preoccupation both of ancient philosophers who speculated on animal issues
and of animal rights advocates in our own age. Simply put, much of the
argumentation on the nature of animalkind has since antiquity been directed
to the question of whether humans owe what is generally termed "justice" to
other animals. If it is determined that they do, what then constitutes that
justice, and which animal species are entitled to share in it? As the epigraph to
this chapter makes abundantly clear, some thinkers of recent date harbor no
doubts that the position espoused already by the Stoics was after all correct. Yet
if we look more closely into the issue that Cardinal Newman decides here with
such finality, we find that the question of man's potential debt of "justice"
toward animals is as complex as is the issue of animal rationality itself.

The position of many recent philosophers and ethicists opposed to the idea
that animals are entitled to "justice" at the hands of humans, including
contractualists like Frey and Carruthers whose arguments we examined above,
has been, like that of Newman, developed under the influence of Stoicism, and
relies on the criterion of reason possession as the deciding factor in assigning
moral considerability.[1] In contrast, philosophers and ethologists who seek to
accord justice to animals have evolved ethical systems that are considerably
more varied and less uniform in approach, some of which reject rationality
altogether as a valid criterion for moral inclusion. In his work *Taking Animals
Seriously: Mental Life and Moral Status*, philosopher David DeGrazia offers a
valuable overview and critique of a number of influential recent contributions
to the debate on the moral status of animals.[2] He asks preliminarily a series of

questions that bear on the issue of justice and that have been central to recent investigations of the moral status of animals: are animals after all due any moral consideration from humans and, if not, why not? If they are, is it simply because their welfare affects humans, or do they deserve consideration in their own right? Can they have what philosophers term "interests," and what might the interests of animals be? Can the interests of animals matter as much as do those of humans? Is it reasonable to advance a principle of "equal consideration of interests" for animals, as some philosophers have done, even if they have failed, in DeGrazia's view, to specify what they mean by that concept? Equal consideration of interests, DeGrazia maintains, does not mean that animals might have interests identical to those of humans, but he does hold that avoidance of suffering is an interest of humans that animals would seem to have as well. He notes that Peter Singer, in his work *Animal Liberation: A New Ethics for Our Treatment of Animals*, had early on called attention to the prominence of the concept of equal consideration of interests in philosophic debate on animals, although Singer himself recognized how vague previous discussion of animal interests had been.[3] DeGrazia observes too that Contractualism also presupposes the concept of equal consideration of interests, but applies it solely to human interests. In light of the complexity involved in defining equal consideration, DeGrazia concludes his survey by offering his understanding of the concept, "Equal consideration for animals entails giving equal moral weight to their relevantly similar interests. It forbids generally devaluing their interests relative to ours just because the interest-bearers are animals."[4]

Informing DeGrazia's position is the belief that there is something intrinsic to animals that makes them worthy objects of human moral consideration, and he agrees with those who maintain that animals have sufficient mental experiences to allow them this consideration. He cites scientific evidence that animals have feelings and desires, beliefs, and, in the case of some species, self-awareness. For Singer, whose part in the discussion of equal consideration of interests DeGrazia had noted, it is sentience, the capacity to feel pain, that entitles a creature to moral considerability. While humans may have superior memories and more detailed knowledge of what is happening to them, Singer feels that there is no reason to conclude that animals experience pain to a lesser degree than do humans. Indeed, he maintains that their suffering may be the more intense because they understand it less.[5] The suffering of animals has for Singer the same moral weight as does that of humans. Singer has been attacked on a number of grounds, including his neglect of the possibility that the life of a human being may be intrinsically more valuable than that of an animal.[6] Although he avoids the use of the word in *Animal Liberation*, Singer argues from the point of view of Utilitarianism, so that maximizing pleasure and minimizing pain is paramount in his approach to the question of the moral status of animals. Since both humans and animals are capable of experiencing pain, their lives must be valued equally. Critics have seen a sinister side to Singer's Utilitarianism, charging that, if carried to its natural end, it countenances all sorts of euthanasia.

Parents can dispose of their retarded offspring if so doing adds to the sum total of the parents' pleasure.[7] It would in his system always be possible to value the pleasure of a pack of healthy dogs over that of a sick or retarded human being. Sorabji offers a graphic example of where Singer's Utilitarianism can lead, "If it is really true that we are obliged to conduct medical or scientific experiments on living beings, we should be ready to do so on an orphaned imbecile with few preferences rather than on a vivacious animal with many."[8]

Philosopher Tom Regan, whose treatise *The Case for Animal Rights* remains the most elaborately argued case for according "rights" to non-human species, faults Singer's utilitarian stance for failing to take account of individuals in its appeal to the greatest good without regard for how that good is to be shared. In formulating a case for what he terms "formal justice," Regan posits the equality of individuals who possess what he terms "inherent value."[9] Individuals having lives that are less happy or that involve fewer cultural advantages do not have lives that are less valuable than those whose lives are richer and more varied, since the value of their lives does not depend on other individuals' estimation of the value of those lives. What matters is that an individual's life has such features as desires, beliefs, goals, feelings of pain and pleasure, and preferences. Individuals who possess these fulfill what Regan calls the "subject-of-a-life criterion."[10] Such individuals can suffer harm if they are deprived of those experiences that are natural to them. To deprive an animal of light or movement, for example, is, in his view, intrinsically wrong because it deprives the animal of experiences that are naturally desirable to it. Nor does it matter that the natural desires of an animal, such as the desire of a chicken to scratch the ground, strike humans as trivial. The moral wrong involved in so depriving an animal of its natural desires constitutes what Regan calls the "harm as deprivation" principle.[11] In contrast to Singer, Regan argues from an animal rights stance, as the title of his treatise makes clear, and he concludes that those creatures that are subjects of a life have a right not to be harmed, for this would be a violation of justice. At the same time, Regan and Singer are agreed in holding that animals must be accorded equal consideration of their interests, whatever those may in fact be, and that animals do indeed have interests in the first place, a position that would seem, in view of the treatment traditionally accorded to animals since antiquity, hardly obvious to the vast majority of mankind.

Since the publication of Regan's treatise, ethical systems have been evolved which question the earlier assumption that moral status for animals is dependent upon their mental capacities. Stephen R. L. Clark, for example, suggests that even if animals cannot lay claim to "rights" because of any intellectual endowments, they may still have at least the "negative right" not to be harmed.[12] He rejects reason out of hand as a criterion for according justice to animals, remarking, "I have attempted to put, and rebut, the thesis that only those creatures with whom we share a 'community of reason' should be counted as worthy of our concern."[13] He rejects likewise the Stoic demand for a human–animal contract as a prerequisite for according justice to animals, preferring to see life as a household of differing species. Similarly, Clark discounts the long-standing emphasis on language as a prerequisite for moral considerability, arguing, "Common sympathies and purposes, mutual attractions and puzzlements are quite enough to provide a mutual sense of fair dealing at least with our most immediate, mammalian kin."[14] He would agree with Regan that animals may be harmed by being deprived of the pleasures natural to them, and he demands for them "happiness according to their kind," although humans cannot always determine what constitutes the happiness of animals.[15]

Ethicist Bernard E. Rollin agrees with Clark that rationality is at best a questionable criterion for moral considerability. What connection is there, he asks, between reason and moral status, and how can we be sure that only humans are after all capable of reason? How can we be certain that the vaunted human capacity for language is itself evidence of rationality?[16] He dismisses the Stoic-inspired argument of the contractualists that only those beings can be accorded justice who can agree to behave toward others as they would wish others to behave toward them, by arguing that animals are in fact "contractors," for any person who has observed animals at a watering hole is aware that animals agree on the procedure for taking turns at drinking.[17] Rollin evolves a theory of moral considerability that is somewhat Aristotelian in inspiration, according to which an animal is held to have a *telos*, which is, as Rollin defines it, a nature or function that the animal strives to carry out. A creature has a number of desires and needs which the successful realization of its *telos* demands, although a given creature may not be totally aware of its own needs and desires.[18] For Rollin, the possibility that a human may thwart another being's *telos* is an intensely moral issue, not least because Rollin believes that neuroscience tells us that most animals have at least minimal nervous systems and pain receptors. Being alive and having interests, like avoiding pain, places a creature in the moral arena, and the right to life is inalienable for animals, in Rollin's view.[19] To deprive an animal of life is morally wrong, and humans must prove that their right to life is morally superior to that of any creature whose life they take.

The results of experimentation in neuroscience have been cited by some biologists in support of the claims of philosophers that animals may be moral creatures. In her work *Biology, Ethics and Animals*, biologist Rosemary Rodd concludes that since study of the nervous systems of animals suggests that many species are capable of feeling pain, determination of the extent to which a given animal feels pain becomes central to answering the question of how we are to treat it. Even to claim that we can end an animal's life painlessly carries no moral weight, both because we would not necessarily wish our lives to be ended even if it could be done painlessly and we have no right to assume an animal would either, and, perhaps more importantly, because, in her view, it may after all be impossible to end an animal's life painlessly. She notes that since rats will jump away from a place where they have received an electric shock when a light comes on, even if the light comes on and no shock follows, it is reasonable to conclude that animals do anticipate frightening events and that they have "at least a hazy idea of a future self to which the frightening events will happen."[20] This might, in Rodd's view, indicate that animals have a preference for life and a fear of death. Rodd accepts Regan's "harm as deprivation" principle on the grounds that killing an animal removes from it all possibility of future enjoyment. As a biologist, Rodd offers an intriguing argument against the influential Aristotelian and Stoic claim of a vast gulf separating animals and humans by arguing that for millennia, human achievement was not markedly superior to that of other primates, and that great strides are in fact quite recent in the overall timeline of human history. It is only fair, therefore, to acknowledge that animals, which have helped us in farming and building, are in fact partners in human achievement.[21]

Some biologists have advanced considerably beyond the relatively cautious assertions of Rodd and, relying on the results of recent studies in neurobiology, have asked a provocative and highly controversial question that has enormous implications for human morality: could it be that some animal species have themselves at least an elemental understanding of a concept of "justice," and live their lives in accord with it? Although the idea might strike some investigators of animal behavior as far-fetched, it has been seriously proposed in some scientific literature. Already in the 1970s, psychologist Herbert Terrace reported that a chimpanzee that he had studied named Nim Chimsky, whose name is a parody of that of linguist Noam Chomsky who denied the capacity of language to non-humans,[22] would expect praise from his trainers for good deeds and punishment for bad deeds. He was observed to sulk if not praised by one trainer for deeds which his other trainers had praised, or if he received punishment for deeds that other trainers allowed. Terrace took this as evidence that Nim was developing a sense of justice.[23] Terrace's position has received support from the researches of ethologist Frans de Waal at the Yerkees Regional Primate Research Center in Atlanta. de Waal has collected numerous examples of primate behavior that he considers to be possible instances of a sense of justice in animals. On one occasion, a chimpanzee named Puist aided her friend Luit in chasing off a rival named Nikkie. Nikkie thereupon turned on Puist and threatened her, leading Puist to extend her hand to Luit for help. Luit ignored her, and after Nikkie left the scene, Puist proceeded to shout at Luit. de Waal's conclusion on this behavior is thought-provoking, "If Puist's fury was in fact the result of Luit's failure to help her after she had helped him, the incident suggests that reciprocity in chimpanzees may be governed by obligations and expectations similar to those in humans."[24] For de Waal, the behavior of the chimpanzee illustrates what ethologists call reciprocity, that is, the tendency of animals to give, trade or exact revenge for acts performed on them. In this instance de Waal illustrates "reciprocal justice" in animals. If his reading of the behavior of the chimpanzees is correct, it would appear that some species can "contract," at least with their conspecifics, and it affords ammunition against the contractualist assertion that only humans can form contracts. de Waal points out further that since the nervous systems of other mammalian species are fundamentally similar to those of humans, and since, as he puts it, "honesty, guilt and the weighing of ethical dilemmas are traceable to specific areas of the brain,"[25] we should not be surprised if animals display some behaviors that appear to parallel what humans call "justice." If animals behave toward each other in a manner that suggests that they abide by moral principles, including what resembles a sense of justice, it is obvious that humans must rethink any denial of justice to them. Opponents of this radical reading of animal behavior would argue that only if an animal *intends* to be "just" can we take its behaviors into account in formulating our own moral positions. The issue of intentionality is seen by some as fundamental to any evaluation of apparent instances of moral behaviors in animals, and of course the thorny issue of anthropomorphism once again enters the picture.

What could rightly be considered the logical final stage in the argument for according justice to animals is reached in the work of Steven M. Wise. An attorney who specializes in animal rights law, Wise has argued, in his book *Drawing the Line: Science and the Case for Animal Rights*, that creatures possessing what he terms "practical autonomy" are entitled to "liberty rights." Creatures with practical autonomy are those that can desire, try to fulfill their desires, and demonstrate self-sufficiency to the extent that they can understand, if only dimly, that they want something and are trying to secure it.[26] Wise numbers chimpanzees, bonobos and dolphins among such creatures. These are creatures with highly developed consciousness, which allows them the "liberty rights" of immunity to any form of enslavement or torture. It is clear that Wise's position has been influenced by the thought of such figures as Singer and Regan among philosophers, and Griffin among ethologists, but he ventures beyond their conclusions to argue that highly conscious animals qualify for legal personhood, an assertion that even the boldest ethologists are hesitant to countenance. Wise's conclusion is highly controversial, "Judges must recognize that even using a human yardstick, at least some nonhuman animals are entitled to recognition as legal persons."[27] With this assertion, Wise has reached the outside edge of any debate on justice toward animals, far beyond the tentative explorations of animal rights philosophers who hesitate to assert what the interests of animals might be.

In the final chapter of his work *Animal Minds and Human Morals*, Sorabji offers a valuable critique of some of the ethical theories discussed above, in particular those of Singer and Regan, both of whose approaches he faults as "one-dimensional," although together their work constitutes the two main streams of thought on animals in recent years.[28] In neither case, Sorabji notes, is rationality a paramount consideration. For Sorabji, the mere satisfaction of preferences, as Singer expounds the principle, is inadequate as the foundation of a moral system governing human treatment of animals, and he rejects as well Regan's absolute reliance on a doctrine of inherent value that allows for no degrees.[29] Sorabji envisions an ethic in which what he terms "multiple considerations"[30] figure, including kindness and gratitude, along with a regard for relationships, a requirement that recalls the Stoic doctrine of *oikeiotês* that worked so strongly against animal interests through the ages. Our examination of ethical theories developed in the post-Regan era and bolstered by the findings of neuroscience suggests that philosophers are in fact moving in the direction that Sorabji envisions, as they abandon the monolithic approach of earlier decades that relied heavily on the criterion of rationality in animals, and they answer in the affirmative DeGrazia's question of whether animals matter in their own right and have interests that humans must respect. Benevolence and kindness now enter into ethical discussion of justice toward animals.

Sorabji notes likewise that the ancient quest for a definition of "justice" toward animals was as complex and subtly nuanced as anything observable in modern ethics, but he laments that it was at times as limited and one-dimensional in application as anything observable in modern ethical philosophy. He remarks of the Stoic understanding of the concept, for example, "The Stoic idea of animals as occupying a circle beyond the outermost limit of concern overlooked the variety of connexions we may have with them. The idea that all just dealing depended on contract and expediency overlooked the many other springs of justice. Moral theories may seek to make things manageable by reducing all considerations to one. Insofar as they do, this is so much the worse for them."[31] Sorabji reminds us that, in ancient parlance, "justice" (δίϰη, διϰαιοσύνη) encompassed more than considerations of wronging others, and involved all aspects of conduct toward others.[32] Aristotle had called justice the perfect or complete virtue (τελεία μάλιστα ἀϱετή . . . ἐστιν, *Ethica Nicomachea* 1129b31). In this understanding of the concept, it is obvious that one could wrong another individual without committing an injustice toward that individual. Hence, as Sorabji points out, to kill an animal for food or for medical research might be a wrong, but it would not necessarily be an injustice. It is significant that at this juncture, Sorabji cites Plutarch's famous discussion of Cato's treatment of animals (*Cato* 339A), wherein Plutarch states that although one might not owe animals justice, one might nevertheless owe them at least benevolence, and he correctly notes that elsewhere, Plutarch maintains that humans do indeed owe animals a debt of justice.[33] The case for justice toward animals that Plutarch develops comes close to the ideal of a multi-dimensional ethic that Sorabji demands. Not totally dependent upon an appeal to rationality in animals as the overriding consideration in according justice to animals, Plutarch maintains as well that animals can be injured and not merely damaged. In his presentation of the case, animals are entitled to compassionate treatment and, no less importantly, to a general acknowledgment of their varied and considerable intellectual endowments, as he has attempted to present these in the comparative chapters of *De sollertia animalium*. Plutarch argues for the kindness and benevolence that Sorabji finds conspicuously lacking in both ancient and modern ethical theory relating to animals, and at the same time his works contain striking anticipations of a number of the arguments advanced by the ethical philosophers discussed in the opening pages of this chapter. We find in the text of Plutarch a clear instance of the "harm as deprivation" principle that has come to be associated closely with Regan, and he offers a number of examples of the "reciprocal justice" that deWaal and other ethologists now cite as evidence that some animals have an elemental concept of justice that they apply in their lives. Most importantly, Plutarch maintains that animals do indeed possess that kinship with humans that the Stoics demand for moral considerability because they demonstrate that rationality that the Stoics make the cornerstone of that kinship.

Although the development in antiquity of a systematic and thoroughgoing case against according justice to animals is most closely identified with the Stoics, they were by no means the first Greeks to articulate a position on the ethical relationship between humans and animals. In what constitutes the earliest extant passage in Greek literature in which men are specifically contrasted with animals, rather than, as in Homer, with the gods,[34] Hesiod remarks (*Opera et Dies* [*Works and Days*] 276–279) that Zeus accorded justice to humans but not to animals. For Hesiod, this is proven by the fact that animals eat each other because they lack this conception of justice (ἐπεὶ οὐ δίκη ἐστὶ μετ᾽ αὐτοῖς, *Opera et Dies* 278). To humans, in contrast, Zeus gave the excellent gift of justice (ἀνθρώποισι δ᾽ ἔδωκε δίκην, ἣ πόλλον ἀρίστη / γίνεται, *Opera et Dies* 279–280). Hesiod is concerned here with his legal problems with his brother and does not demonstrate any abiding interest in relations between the species, but it is interesting to observe that Hesiod seems to believe that the sense of justice does not reside in animals (οὐ δίκη ἐστὶ μετ᾽ αὐτοῖς). The notion that animals have no innate understanding of the concept of justice experienced a modest afterlife in Greek thought, if we may trust Plutarch, who allows his Stoic mouthpiece Soclarus to assert (*De sollertia animalium* 964B) that creatures that do not understand how to treat humans justly (δικαιοπραγεῖν πρὸς ἡμᾶς) cannot be treated unjustly by us. Significantly, Soclarus had just cited these Hesiodic verses in which a sense of justice is denied to animals. Similarly, Epicurus (341–270 BCE) (*Kuriai Doxai* [*Principal Doctrines*] 32) claimed that justice does not exist among beasts that cannot make agreements with one another to avoid mutual harm.[35] Aelian (*ca.* 170–235 CE), the tireless cataloguer of animal wonders, offers a particularly charming refutation of Hesiod's contention that animals have no sense of justice. After citing the Hesiodic verses (*De natura animalium* VI. 50), Aelian counters that the Stoic Cleanthes (331–232 BCE), himself an opponent of the concept that animals can reason, observed some ants carrying from their nest the body of an ant that had been a member of some other nest. Before the other ants accepted their dead comrade, they went into their own nest and brought up a worm, as if for a ransom (οἱονεὶ λύτρα). What could Hesiod say to that, Aelian asks, when he says that animals do not understand justice? Sorabji, following a brief discussion of the notion of a sense of justice in animals, points out that the relative paucity of ancient sources makes it difficult to draw many conclusions on the degree to which it was accepted in antiquity, and he denies that the concept has any necessary connection in ancient thought with the question of man's potential debt of justice toward animals.[36] It would seem, however, that the ancients were sensitive to the possibility of what deWaal and others call reciprocal justice.

A second, seemingly related, question bearing on the issue of justice toward animals appears already in the Presocratics: are animals responsible for and accountable for their own actions? If they are, humans can justly punish them on the grounds that they can purposely harm humans. The Presocratic Democritus (*ca.* 460–357 BCE) had argued, for example, that animals might indeed be willing to harm humans, and that he who kills such animals does so without penalty (τὰ ἀδικέοντα καὶ θέλοντα ἀδικεῖν ἀθῷος ὁ κτείνων, Democritus fr. 257 DK). Animals that seek to kill humans act in a manner contrary to justice (παρὰ δίκην, Democritus fr. 258 DK). In their willingness to commit injustice (θέλοντα ἀδικεῖν), they bear responsibility for their actions. Animals can be, as modern animal rights philosophers put it, moral agents in Democritus' view. Although Aristotle had claimed that animals do act voluntarily (ἑκουσίως, *Ethica Nicomachea* 1111a27), and would therefore seem to be capable of blame, he held elsewhere that justice toward a horse or an ox is not possible (οὐκ ἔστι δίκαιον πρὸς ἵππον ἢ βοῦν, *Ethica Nicomachea* 1161b2–3), precisely because humans have nothing in common with them (οὐδὲν γὰρ κοινόν ἐστιν, *Ethica Nicomachea* 1161b4). We might be tempted to see in this line of argument the origin of the ancient concept of the "just war" (δίκαιος πόλεμος) against animals, especially since Aristotle also held that the warfare against animals which we call hunting is a just war by its nature (φύσει δίκαιον τοῦτον ὄντα τὸν πόλεμον, *Politica* 1256b26–27), but, as Sorabji correctly reminds us, this war was just not because we are justly retaliating against animals who harm us but because nature intends animals for human use.[37] Slightly earlier in the *Politics*, Aristotle had stated that since only man has language, which is intended for the articulation of what is good and bad, only man has the perception of good, bad, the just and the unjust (τοῦτο γὰρ πρὸς τἆλλα ζῷα τοῖς ἀνθρώποις ἴδιον, τὸ μόνον ἀγαθοῦ καὶ κακοῦ καὶ δικαίου καὶ ἀδίκου καὶ τῶν ἄλλων αἴσθησιν ἔχειν, *Politica* 1253a11–14). It is obvious, from these examples, that the ancients failed to reach a consensus on the question of whether animals can act justly and unjustly toward humans, since Democritus taught that humans could kill animals that acted unjustly toward us while Aristotle made the killing of animals a function of human justice alone.

It is noteworthy that Aristotle's case here against according justice to animals is developed in his political and ethical treatises rather than in his zoological works, for he is eager to show here that humans are an order of beings different from other animals, with which humans have nothing "in common" (*Ethica Nicomachea* 1161b4). We have seen, in our discussion of Porphyry's exposition of the contents of Theophrastus' system of animal psychology,[38] that Aristotle's successor expressly contradicted his great master and, in emphasizing such characteristics that humans have in common with animals as passions (ἐπιθυμίαι), drives (ὀργίαι) and reason (λογισμοί), he argued that animals are indeed akin (οἰκεῖοι) to humans (Porphyry, *De abstinentia* III. 25). It is regrettable that we must approach Theophrastus through the medium of Porphyry's exposition of his views, for he seems to have aimed at a comprehensive theory of justice toward animals, but it is clear that the Stoics, whose theory of animal psychology and its relation to human morals would dominate in later ages, reached back to Theophrastus' master to develop their theory of man's juridical relationship toward animals in which the criterion of reason would become the paramount consideration.[39]

We have already touched upon a number of the most prominent elements in the Stoic case against according justice to animals in our discussion, in Chapter 2, of ancient theories of animal rationality, not only because, in the case of the Stoics, considerations of animal rationality and human justice cannot be separated but are viewed as two sides of the same issue, and because the question of kinship between humans and animals takes center stage in Stoic discussion of man's relationship with other animals, but no less importantly because Stoic theory has exercised a particularly potent influence upon subsequent thought on man's relationship with other species, as is observable, for example, in the case of modern Contractualism. For the Stoics, man's ultimate unlikeness to animals erected an insurmountable barrier between the species and made any thought of human justice toward animals impossible. In his life of Zeno, Diogenes Laertius reports that already Chrysippus, in the first book of his treatise *On Justice*, had declared that the impossibility of a relationship of justice between humans and animals because of this unlikeness was an accepted position in Stoic philosophy (ἔτι ἀρέσκει αὐτοῖς μηδέν εἶναι ἡμῖν δίκαιον πρὸς τὰ ἄλλα ζῷα, διὰ τὴν ἀνομοιότητα, VII. 129). The origin of this unlikeness is, as we have seen, the absence of reason in animals, which excludes them forever from that fellowship that exists only between rational creatures. Arius Didymus tells us that this was Chrysippus' view on the subject (κοινωνίαν δ' ὑπάρχειν πρὸς ἀλλήλους διὰ τὸ λόγου μετέχειν, *Stoicorum Veterum Fragmenta* II. 528). This fellowship is, of course, the οἰκειότης upon which the Stoic theory of justice rested. Cicero offers a particularly eloquent account of how this fellowship serves as the origin of justice in Stoic thinking (*De finibus* V. 65):

> In omni autem honesto de quo loquimur nihil est tam illustre nec quod latius pateat quam coniunctio inter homines hominum et quaedam societas et communicatio utilitatum et ipsa caritas generis humani, quae nata a primo satu, quod a procreatoribus nati diliguntur.

Here Cicero makes clear that this fellowship (*quaedam societas et communicatio*, the Stoic οἰκειότης) arises from the love that humans naturally have for their offspring (*quod a procreatoribus nati diliguntur*), and he goes on to state that this in time reaches out from us as individuals to embrace our fellow-citizens and friends and eventually the entire human race. This recognition of our kinship with others is the origin of justice (*quam dico societatem coniunctionis humanae munifice et aeque iustitia dicitur*, V. 65). Animals are notably absent from Cicero's account here. Moreover, Cicero's rosy picture of Stoic *oikeiotês* does not reveal the sinister consequences that strict adherence to the doctrine entailed. Under this doctrine, humans were freed from any requirement to help animals in need. Even if we are not intellectually akin to another creature, it seems obvious that we might still feel moved to help that creature if it was injured. The Stoics admitted no such obligation to act on the creature's behalf. Early on in the course of his treatise *De abstinentia*, Porphyry, relying to some extent on material he draws from Plutarch's own case for justice toward animals, outlines the Stoic view on some of the negative consequences that arise if humans overlook their fundamental lack of kinship with animals and admit them into the company of justice-sharers. To treat animals justly, according to the Stoics, ruins the entire concept of justice by forcing it to bear a burden it cannot bear (προσάπτων τῇ δικαιοσύνῃ ὃ μὴ δύναται φέρειν, I. 4) and destroyed that which is akin by mingling it with that which is alien (διαφθείρει τῷ ἀλλοτρίῳ τὸ οἰκεῖον, I. 4). The logical conclusion to this line of argument was obvious to the Stoics: animals have no right *not* to be harmed by humans. Unfortunately for animals, the natural alienation that separated humans from animals at birth only became exaggerated with the passage of time as the *hêgemonikon*, or guiding principle of the soul, went on in the case of humans to attain full rationality while it remained irrational in animals.[40]

Since the publication a century ago of the first critical studies of Plutarch's animal psychology, scholars have charged that much of Plutarch's anti-Stoic polemic is directed against the "older Stoics," especially against Zeno, Chrysippus and Cleanthes, a position voiced already in Schuster's 1917 study of *De sollertia animalium*,[41] while Plutarch ignores the milder "later Stoics" for whom the topics that he debated so passionately were no longer burning issues, so that his animal treatises betray the quaint anachronism of an author tilting at windmills. Similarly, Barrow charged that Plutarch's understanding of Stoicism was simply too weak to allow him to recognize that the Stoics of his own time held many of the same views that he held.[42] Recently, Jackson Hershbell reiterated these long-standing charges, observing that Plutarch may have been unfair in presenting Stoic ideas, particularly because he may not have adequately distinguished ideas prevalent in the various periods of the history of the school.[43] It is certainly true that, in the presentation of his case for rationality in animals and in his plea for justice toward them that arises from his proof for that rationality, he mentions by name and alludes to the theories of these "older Stoics." Unfortunately, even when he appears to be citing a passage from a Stoic treatise, he seldom refers by name to its author. Chrysippus, whose ideas Plutarch especially opposes in the animal-related treatises, is himself mentioned by name only once (*De sollertia animalium* 980A), in a disparaging reference to the Stoic's marine biology. In his study of Plutarch's relationship to Stoicism, Hershbell notes that, in the treatises included in the *Moralia*, Plutarch refers to Zeno largely for anecdotal and proverbial material, and that he seldom refers specifically to the works of Cleanthes, the successor of Chrysippus as head of the school, but he feels that, in contrast, Plutarch probably studied Chrysippus' text with some diligence.[44] Plutarch obviously considered Chrysippus to be that Stoic whose ideas were particularly to be confronted in his case for a moral relationship between humans and animals.

It is likely that Plutarch's own position on animal mentation and its consequences for human morality relies so heavily upon a refutation of the theories of these "older Stoics" precisely because Plutarch recognized that the Stoic stance on animals and their relation to humans had crystallized already in the earlier period of the school's history, as seems in fact to be the case to the extent that we can judge this from the extant fragments and testimonia of both the earlier and the later Stoics on the topic of animals. We can form some judgment of the contribution of the "later Stoics" from the fragments of Posidonius and from the works of Rome's greatest representative of Stoicism, Seneca. The polymath Posidonius (*ca.* 135–51 BCE), the most eminent and influential of the later Stoics and a man often credited with instituting substantive changes in long-standing teachings of the school, opposed Chrysippus' theory that animals are devoid of emotions because these arise from reason and animals are irrational. Galen tells us that Posidonius maintained that Chrysippus' theory flies in the face of observable fact (μάχεσθαι τοῖς ἐναργῶς φαινομένοις, fr. 159),[45] and that he held as well that animals obviously feel desire and anger (τῶν ἀλόγων ζῴων ἀφαιρεῖται τὰ πάθη φανερῶς, fr. 33). Further, Posidonius taught that the souls of animals, like those of humans, contain certain forces that stir them to pleasure, power and victory (fr. 158). Posidonius got around the problem posed by Chrysippus' theory of emotion by positing the existence of two non-rational parts of the soul, from which emotions could arise in animals even if they are otherwise irrational (fr. 33). Dierauer considers Posidonius' rethinking of the school's position on animal emotions to be a significant change in Stoic thinking in its rejection of the earlier Stoic separation of human and psychic life, a shift instituted by Posidonius in recognition of the overly intellectualized conception of Chrysippus.[46]

Further post-Chrysippean refinement of the Stoic position is traceable in Seneca (*ca.* 4 BCE–65 CE), a figure who, like Posidonius, is often credited with introducing a more humane face to Stoic ethics and whose life for a time overlapped that of Plutarch. We have noted already that Seneca attempted to defend the Stoic denial of emotions to animals by positing a four-stage progression to full emotion, only two stages of which animals can attain.[47] In so doing, he seems to have been addressing the same Chrysippean problem that Posidonius recognized in his predecessor. Seneca elaborated his ideas on animals at length in the 121st of his *Epistulae Morales*, a document which, according to Daniel Dombrowski in his study of ancient philosophical vegetarianism, Seneca uses to "criticize the anthropocentric heart of Stoicism."[48] In fact, however,

Seneca seems to adhere to the Chrysippean position in the letter. He agrees with his predecessor that animals have some awareness of their own constitution (*omnibus constitutionis suae sensus est, Epistulae* 121. 9), and when he goes on to explain the nature of the constitution of the human child, we observe the same distinction made between the *potentially* rational human and the irrational animal. Humans and animals may start out at the same place in having some conception of themselves, but humans move on to become reasoning creatures because the human is adapted at each age in its growth to the constitution appropriate to it at that stage (*omnes ei constitutioni conciliantur in qua sunt, Epistulae* 121. 15). Diogenes Laertius, in his life of Chrysippus, tells us that the Stoic had taught that that which is dearest to an animal is its own constitution and its awareness of it (ὁ Χρύσιππος . . . πρῶτον οἰκεῖον λέγων εἶναι παντὶ ζῴῳ τὴν αὐτοῦ σύστασιν καὶ τὴν ταύτης συνείδησιν, VII. 85). Seneca makes precisely this point, and, as Diogenes' account of Chrysippus' position makes clear, the Roman philosopher was hinting at the old Stoic doctrine of *oikeiotês*, suggesting that the fundamental distinction between rational humans and non-rational, if clever, animals makes this kinship impossible. It is difficult to agree with Dombrowski's assessment of this letter as an attack on older Stoic anthropocentrism since it seems rather to reinforce the Chrysippean position.

Judging from the examples of Posidonius and Seneca, to whom we might well add the case of Cicero, in view of his frequent appeals to Chrysippean doctrines in his account of Stoic attitudes toward animals interspersed throughout his philosophical dialogues, it might be justifiable to conclude that, however much Stoicism was "softened" by its post-Chrysippean practitioners, philosophers still understood the Stoic stance toward animal mentation and consequently toward man's obligation of justice toward animals to be to a substantial degree dominated by Chrysippus' ideas, to which later additions were more often refinements than rejections of his ideas. Perhaps Plutarch was not after all so antiquarian and out of step as his critics have charged in his refutation of so-called "older Stoics" and in his defense of the idea that animals are after all moral creatures to whom we may have an obligation of justice.

Situated immediately following Plutarch's case for rationality in animals, in which he had been at pains to refute the Stoic position which we have outlined above, Plutarch's longest continuous discussion of man's juridical relationship with other species (*De sollertia animalium* 963F–965B) stands as the culmination of the polemic portion of the dialogue, as if constituting the natural corollary to a demonstration of rationality in animals. Plutarch seems to ask, by so placing his case for justice toward animals, how we can be justified in treating them as Stoic philosophy condones if they indeed possess traces of that rationality which that school demands. In these chapters, Plutarch sets down what he considers to be the limits of human justice toward animals, and he answers the question of how humans may without violating the demands of justice make use of animals. As with his much more far-reaching and elaborately developed case for rationality in animals, Plutarch's reflections on justice in *De sollertia animalium* are supplemented by material in *De esu carnium*,[49] as he examines the possibility that the need for just treatment toward animals may place restrictions on human diet, and he raises the possibility that animals live themselves by a code of justice. Also as in the case of his arguments for rationality in animals, Plutarch on occasion seems to contradict himself in his pronouncements on justice that appear in certain treatises of the *Moralia*, where he seems to deny that animals have an understanding of the concept.

Although they have not attracted the critical attention that Plutarch's apparent denials of reason to animals have aroused, his contradictions on the question of justice require some examination because they seem to stand in stark contrast to his call for justice toward animals. In the dialogue *Adversus Colotem* (*Reply to Colotes*), Plutarch refutes the assertion of the Epicurean Colotes of Lampsacus, contained in a now-lost treatise by that author, that conformity to the teachings of certain philosophers renders life impossible. While defending Democritus, Parmenides, Empedocles, Socrates, Melissus of Samos, Plato and Stilpon of Megara against Colotes' charges, Plutarch, never an admirer of Epicureanism, attacks what he considers to be the base morality espoused by the school's founder and by his most distinguished disciple Metrodorus of Lampsacus (*ca.* 331–278 BCE).[50] At one point, Plutarch states that animals live the lowly life they do because they have no knowledge of anything finer than pleasure, and do not understand the justice of the gods, caring nothing for the beauty of virtue (ὁ τῶν θηρίων βιὸς τοιοῦτός ἐστιν ὅτι τῆς ἡδονῆς οὐδὲν ἐπίσταται κάλλιον οὐδὲ δίκην θεῶν οἶδεν οὐδὲ σέβεται τῆς ἀρετῆς τὸ κάλλος, *Adversus Colotem* 1125A). It is obvious that Plutarch, in expressing an opinion that agrees so closely with Hesiod's pronouncements on justice in animals and indeed with Epicurus' own denial of a debt of justice toward animals (*Kuriai Doxai* 32), is not disparaging animals, but intends rather to liken the "beastly" life he describes to that envisioned for humans in the Epicurean system, for he immediately after observes that this life of lawless pleasure is precisely what Metrodorus recommends for human beings (καθάπερ οἴεται δεῖν ὁ σοφὸς Μητρόδωρος, *Adversus Colotem* 1125A).

A similar motivation seems to stand behind Plutarch's apparent denigration of the sense of justice in animals that appears in *De amore prolis*. As we have noted above,[51] scholars have been troubled by statements in that treatise which downplay the moral qualities of animals in a manner that contrasts with views expressed in the animal-related treatises. In *De amore prolis*, Plutarch declares that nature has implanted the principle of love of offspring even in irrational animals, although that sense remains incomplete and inadequate in animals in the matter of justice (ἡ γὰρ φύσις ... τοῖς ἀλόγοις τὸ πρὸς τὰ ἔγγονα φιλοστοργίαν ἀτελὲς καὶ οὐ διαρκὲς πρὸς δικαιοσύνην, *De amore prolis* 495B–C). Although this treatise has long been considered to reflect a stage in Plutarch's thought in which he was more well-disposed to Stoic ideas, recent scholars have suggested that *De amore prolis* is intended more as an indictment of human moral failings than as a reflection on the imperfections of animals.[52] In this work, Plutarch argues that humans, who have the advantage over animals in the keenness of their reasoning powers, still contaminate their reason with acquired beliefs and judgments, while animals follow their nature more closely and cannot rebel against their inferior intellectual capacities to the extent that they are led into vice (493B–D). It is important to note of the passage cited above (495B–C) that Plutarch allows that animals, however dim their moral sensibilities may be, love their offspring. In *De Stoicorum repugnantiis* (*On the Contradictions of the Stoics*), Plutarch had noted that Chrysippus himself had attributed love of offspring even to animals in the first book of his treatise on justice (ἐν τῷ πρώτῳ περὶ Δικαιοσύνης καὶ τὰ θηρία φησὶ συμμέτρως τῇ χρείᾳ τῶν ἐκγόνων ᾠκειῶσθαι πρὸς αὐτά, *De Stoicorum repugnantiis* 1038B). Once again, we encounter the Stoic doctrine of *oikeiotês*, as ᾠκειῶσθαι (*ôkeiôsthai*) makes clear. The Stoics had themselves placed the origin of justice in this principle, as Porphyry reminds us (τὴν δὲ οἰκείωσιν ἀρχὴν τίθενται δικαιοσύνης οἱ ἀπὸ Ζήνωνος, *De abstinentia* III. 19). Since love of offspring is the origin of this sense of kinship, and since this kinship is the origin of justice, animals, who love their offspring, cannot be devoid of a sense of justice. Plutarch's meaning in *De amore prolis* is that animals may have an inferior sense of justice in keeping with their lowlier mental capacities, but they are no more devoid of it than they are of reasoning ability itself.

The preponderance of evidence in his animal treatises suggests that Plutarch, in contrast to Hesiod and Epicurus and in agreement with Aelian, believed that animals have a lively sense of justice which they exercise even in their relations with human beings. In his defense of vegetarianism, in one of the most affecting passages to be found in Plutarch's writings on animals, he envisions an animal at the point of slaughter pleading with his slayer to spare him if he seeks by his death only a more elaborate meal and not relief from hunger (994E). We humans mistakenly think that the animal's cries on this occasion are merely inarticulate sounds (φωνὰς ἀνάρθρους εἶναι δοκοῦμεν, 994E) and do not recognize that they are cries for justice (δικαιολογίας, 994E).[53] Significantly, Plutarch hints here at the issue of language in animals, as he suggests that animals themselves have a sense of justice which they try unsuccessfully to make humans understand in their utterances (δικαιολογίας). The true horror of the scene emerges only when we realize that, in this case, the animal has a sense of justice superior to that of the humans who exploit it. We should not fail to note that Plutarch injects here an appeal to human emotion in his plea of the wretched beast at slaughter, indicating that he does not consider such an appeal out of place in serious philosophical discourse. Indeed, in the final incomplete sentence of the mutilated second part of his defense of vegetarianism, where he is once again about to take up the question of whether a relation of justice subsists between humans and animals (σκεψώμεθα, τὸ μηδὲν εἶναι πρὸς τὰ ζῷα δίκαιον ἡμῖν, *De esu carnium* 999B), he pointedly articulates his belief that such an inquiry can legitimately include an appeal both to reason and to emotion (τοῖς πάθεσιν ἐμβλέψαντες τοῖς ἑαυτῶν καὶ πρὸς ἑαυτοὺς ἀνθρωπικῶς λαλήσαντες καὶ ἀνακρίναντες . . . , *De esu carnium* 999B). His direct appeal to emotion here renders the loss of the remainder of the treatise particularly lamentable.

Plutarch also furnishes multiple examples of the "reciprocal justice" in animals which deWaal analyzes.[54] He tells us, for example, that a captive elephant at Rome that had been tormented by children who pricked his trunk with their styluses, picked one of the children up and appeared about to hurl him to the ground. Instead, the elephant put him down gently and walked away, thinking that he had exacted a sufficient justice by causing fear in the child (ἀρκοῦσαν ἡγούμενος δίκην τῷ τηλικούτῳ φοβηθῆναι, *De sollertia animalium* 968E). The elephant reciprocated hurt with hurt, but proved superior to the child in freeing his victim from that hurt. Similarly, Plutarch recounts a tale of a dolphin who enjoyed swimming with a boy, who once during a storm fell off the dolphin's back as he tried to carry him to safety. The animal took the lifeless body to shore and lay beside it until he too had died, judging himself responsible for the boy's death and feeling obliged therefore to share in that death (δικαιώσας μετασχεῖν ἧς συναίτιος ἔδοξε γεγονέναι τελευτῆς, *De sollertia animalium* 984F).[55] The topic of reciprocal justice resurfaces in the σύγκρισις of *De sollertia animalium* when Aristotimus, defender of the primacy of land animals, states that we must agree with those who say there is no debt of justice owed to sea creatures because they are devoid of pleasantness of demeanor and friendliness (970B). Land animals, on the other hand, display these attractive qualities in their dealings with humans. His opponent cannot rightly deny, Aristotimus asserts, that justice was involved when the corpse of Alexander the Great's friend Lysimachus was guarded by his dog, who jumped into the funeral flames of his master. Similarly, the eagle kept by King Pyrrhus sat down on his master's pyre and allowed himself to be consumed with the king's body. The elephant belonging to King Porus pulled the spears from his master's body, though wounded himself, and gently lowered the king to the ground when he feared the king would fall from his back in his debilitated state. Aristotimus seems to take these as examples of animals repaying their masters for their care in earlier days.

In the course of his discussion of Greek views on whether animals have a sense of justice by which they live, Sorabji had observed that the Greeks did not articulate the Kantian position that humans are not obligated to accord justice to animals who lack the sense of justice. He makes the intriguing observation, "The only case I have noticed of such an argument is one attributed to the Stoics and Peripatetics (i.e. Aristotelians), that there can be no such thing as wronging those who do not exercise justice (*dikaiopragein*) towards us."[56] The passage he cites as uniquely representing this position is *De sollertia animalium* 964B–C. Although Sorabji does not develop his observation here, our discussion above of Plutarch's justice-observing animals suggests that he contributed to the ancient debate more substantially than Sorabji allows.

Plutarch's argument for justice toward animals (*De sollertia animalium* 963F–965B) had opened on a surprising note of agreement on the part of

Plutarch's interlocutors Soclarus and Autobulus, as Soclarus acknowledges the correctness of his opponent's last statement (ὀρθῶς μοι δοκεῖς ὑπονοεῖν, 963F). Although Autobulus had once again just raised the possibility that animals possess reason because we recognize departures from their normal behavior as examples of irrationality, it is not in fact the evident participation of all animals in some form of intellectual activity that inspires Soclarus' agreement but his acknowledgment that what separates his view from that of Autobulus are the consequences for human morality that must follow from the assertion that animals possess this activity. Specifically, both speakers are in agreement that rationality in animals has profound moral and juridical implications for human conduct. Soclarus here acknowledges the dilemma that the possibility of rationality in animals posed for his Stoic forebears: how can one reconcile the claims of justice with the desirability of making use of animals in human life? The Stoics had contended that, if we extend justice to animals and refrain from making use of them, we force ourselves to live lives like those of the beasts themselves (τρόπον τινὰ θηρίων βίον βιωσόμεθα τὰς ἀπὸ τῶν θηρίων προέμενοι χρείας, 964A). Soclarus' portrayal here of the miserable lives left to mortals if they take regard of animals marshals, in short compass, all the prerequisites for according justice to other individuals which the Stoic case demanded: if we live alongside without harming them (ἀβλαβῶς, 964A) and with circumspection and discretion (μετ' εὐλαβίας, 964B), *as one should with those who are rational and are akin to us* (ὡς προσήκει λογικοῖς καὶ ὁμοφύλοις πᾶσι τοῖς ζῷοις οὖσιν . . . προφέρεσθαι, 964B), what will be left of our civilized life? The Stoic linkage of kinship (*oikeiotês*) with rationality appears once again, as often in Plutarch's case against the school. Plutarch's overriding mission, throughout the animal treatises, has been to show that animals do in fact share this kinship because they share the rationality upon which it depends and even have traces of a language with which they seek, however ineffectually, to impart to humans their desire to be included in the sphere of human moral concern, as is clear from his sacrificial animal's fruitless attempt to communicate with humans.

Autobulus agrees with Soclarus that human life is by its nature fraught with injustice. Human beings cannot even come into the world without committing injustice as they are, in a manner that seems contrary to nature itself, nourished off the limbs of their parent (τρέφεσθαι τὸ γεννώμενον παρὰ φύσιν μέλεσι τοῦ γεννήσαντος ἀποσπωμένοις, 964E). Ironically, nature herself is the source of injustice, but humans, according to Autobulus, can work around this necessity to be unjust in a manner that neither denies rationality to animals nor requires humans to forgo totally the use of animals, as the Stoics had feared. As Pythagoras, whom Plutarch cites comparatively rarely in support of his ideas, had long ago argued, there is nothing intrinsically unjust in *using* animals, provided we do not *misuse* them (964F). Enlisting tame animals to assist us in farming is not unjust by nature, whereas actions that force animals to defend themselves or allow them no exit, like blood sports and arena entertainments, are unjust, while sports in which animals play alongside humans as their partners are to be encouraged. Plutarch's mouthpiece employs here an argument that would resonate with animal rights philosophers who argue that animals have interests to which humans must be sensitive in their actions. Autobulus ends this plea with a sobering anecdote intended to illustrate his belief that humans must have regard for the interests of animals when they contemplate actions that may seem inconsequential to them but which have lethal consequences for animals. The philosopher Bion, Autobulus reminds his audience, observed that when children throw rocks at frogs to have fun, the frogs die not for fun but in earnest (βατράχους μηκέτι παίζοντας ἀλλ' ἀληθῶς ἀποθνήσκειν, 965B).

The dilemma posed by Soclarus is shown up as being, in the final analysis, illusory. It is not impossible for humans to live without mistreating animals, and humans cannot take refuge in the arguments of the Stoics that we cannot act unjustly toward creatures that do not understand justice (οἷς δ' οὐκ ἔστι τὸ δικαιοπραγεῖν πρὸς ἡμᾶς, οὐδ' ἡμῖν πρὸς ἐκεῖνα γίγνεται τὸ ἀδικεῖν, De sollertia animalium 964B), as Hesiod had contended was true of animals. Plutarch has provided ample examples of reciprocal justice in animals, proving that they understand the concept of justice after all and have been known to act justly toward humans. We cannot therefore, in Plutarch's estimation, do less toward them.

Having reached the end of our examination of Plutarch's argument for according "justice" to animals, we return to the question with which our inquiry opened: What, after all, is Plutarch's understanding of "justice" as it relates to man's relationship with other species? Our discussion of De sollertia animalium 963E–965F makes it clear that Plutarch's answer avoids the one-dimensionality that Sorabji felt mars most modern definitions of the concept and some ancient definitions as well, including that of the Stoics.[57] Plutarch's case makes an appeal to his proof for rationality in animals to the extent of arguing that creatures demonstrating traces of this rationality cannot be excluded from human moral consideration, but he advances beyond the confines of a reason-based argument to include the demands of fellow-feeling for other species that can be shown to suffer as do their human counterparts. Since animals are akin to humans both in their rationality and in their sentience, they share with humans that relationship called oikeiotês that the Stoics deny them. In modern terms, animals share interests with humans, including an interest in staying alive, and they are harmed if their interests are ignored or violated. Any definition of justice derived from Plutarch's animal treatises must include the idea of a regard for the interests of other species. Animals, like humans, seem in Plutarch's vision to experience distress and pain, and this fact in his view has moral relevance for human action. The nature of the pains and pleasures inherent in the animal estate is the subject of the chapter that follows.

4

FEELING BEASTLY

Pain, pleasure and the animal estate

what a strange thought.

> The question is not, Can they *reason?*, nor, Can they *talk*, but, Can they *suffer?*
> Jeremy Bentham, *An Introduction to the Principles of Morals and Legislation*

It has not always been obvious to scientists and philosophers that animals are capable of feeling pain. Nor has it always been acknowledged that the pain of animals, if it does indeed exist, might have moral claims on human sympathy. Sorabji notes that such considerations scarcely figured at all in classical discussions of animals and human relations, "The other side of the coin is how astonishingly late in the philosophical texts we find the first explicit statement that the pain and terror felt by animals is a reason for treating them justly."[1] In the Greco-Roman period, the question of whether animals can *reason* always far outweighed in importance any consideration of whether they can *feel*, a position in direct contrast to that expressed in the famous dictum of Bentham cited in the epigraph to this chapter. Moreover, for more than a millennium after the fall of the classical world, the issue of animal pain was regarded primarily as a religious problem among thinkers who grappled with the question of how suffering fits into God's plan for his creatures. The moralized version of Aristotelian zoology advanced by the Stoics, in which the reason of humans placed unreasoning animals forever below them, found a fertile breeding ground in early Christian writers who embraced the notion of human primacy based on the possession of reason.

In a discussion of the biblical injunction against killing, which he takes to include a prohibition against suicide, Augustine answers the objections of his Manichean opponents that perhaps the injunction should be extended to plants and animals too. This is absurd, Augustine contends, because a plant does not feel (*non sentiat, De civitate Dei* I. 20) and animals deserve no consideration because they do not belong with humans to the community of reason (*quia nulla nobis ratione socientur*, I. 20), the Stoic *oikeiotês* argument once again. While denying that plants can feel pain, Augustine avoids the issue of whether animals can, and concludes with the Aristotelian observation that God has justly decreed

66

that the lives of animals are subordinate to those of humans (*vita et mors eorum nostris usibus subditur*, I. 20).[2] The possibility that animals might feel pain simply does not matter to Augustine. This harsh view found its way into the thought of Christendom's greatest philosopher, Thomas Aquinas, who assures us that if the Scriptures seem to discourage us from being cruel to animals, as, for example, by killing a mother bird with her young, an act prohibited in Deuteronomy 22:6, this is only because such an action might lead us to be cruel to other humans (*Summa contra Gentiles* III. 112). This "indirect duty view" of man's obligation to animals remained for centuries the most that animals could hope for from humans, and it is reflected in the contractualist position on cruelty to animals. As Carruthers explains the issue, "Animals have indirect moral significance nevertheless, in virtue of the qualities of moral character they may invoke in us. Actions involving animals that are expressive of a bad moral character are thereby wrong."[3] Not wishing us to overvalue the potential suffering of animals, however, he concludes on the issue, "Because attitudes to animal and human suffering may be readily psychologically separated, however, the constraints so placed on our treatment of animals are minimal ones."[4]

Speculation on the problem of pain in animals reached its nadir in the work of Descartes, another philosopher whose position was influenced by his religious beliefs. Descartes sought to establish an absolute distinction between the natures of humans and of animals to discourage us from supposing that, if we are like animals, we too might be spared the punishments of the afterlife. This endeavor was itself inspired by another question of faith that troubled the philosopher. How, he wondered, could God countenance suffering in animals since they, unlike humans, were innocent of original sin which occasioned those punishments in the afterlife? His answer went well beyond anything found in even the most extreme pronouncements to be found in Greek philosophy. He concluded that animals are utterly devoid of conscious experiences, so that they are incapable of feelings, emotions or sensations, including that of pain. In his vision, animals scarcely seem to be living creatures at all, but are rather akin to machines. This belief led Descartes the scientist to become an ardent vivisectionist, and his experiments have become legendary for their cruelty. He pinned dogs to boards and cut them to observe the circulation of their blood, assuring his squeamish students that the shrieks they heard were merely the sound of the springs that operate the machinery of the animals. One contemporary observer of the animal experiments conducted by Descartes' pupils reported that they beat dogs mercilessly and mocked those who pitied the creatures that they mistakenly thought to be in pain.[5]

The mechanistic approach to the problem of animal pain manifested in Cartesianism enjoyed a rebirth starting in the 1910s in the work of behaviorist psychologists J. B. Watson and B. F. Skinner, whose influence on investigation into the mental states of animals can still be detected. According to behaviorist theory, the scientist must confine his observations solely to external influences and directly observable behaviors of animals, on the belief that all subjective mental states are ultimately unmeasurable, private phenomena which cannot profitably be commented upon by the scientist.[6] We are again confronted with Descartes' problem of consciousness. If the scientist cannot measure or observe consciousness, he cannot be sure that animals are in fact experiencing any conscious activity, including the sensation of pain. A strict adherence to behaviorism naturally absolves the investigator of concern for many of the moral issues that arise from a belief in animal consciousness. Behaviorists, whom biologist Rosemary Rodd aptly terms "the New Cartesians,"[7] were free to inflict any tortures upon animals, whose reactions were judged to be purely mechanical. If, with the behaviorist, we conclude that animals merely react to external stimuli and have no awareness of their surroundings, we can readily conclude that we have no duties toward them.

Much of current ethological polemic endeavors, at least by implication, to combat the specter of behaviorism that still hangs over research into animal psychology. Ethologist Donald R. Griffin, whose work has been instrumental in promoting the position that some animals are indeed capable of conscious mental experiences, observes of the current state of research into animal consciousness, "Students of animal behavior are still severely constrained by a guilty feeling that it is unscientific to inquire about subjective feelings and conscious thoughts. . . . Although ethologists have recognized more and more complexity and versatility in animal behavior, many have lagged behind the cognitive psychologists and try dutifully to fit all the new knowledge about animal behavior into the same old pigeon-holes that seemed sufficient years ago."[8] Recent discoveries in neurobiology have cast doubt on many of the comfortable assumptions of behaviorism that have countenanced much animal suffering. Rodd argues that the basic premise of behaviorism, that the scientist cannot tell if animals are suffering, is simply false. When chickens are debeaked, for example, pain receptors in the cut beaks become active, and the animals squawk and struggle at the procedure.[9] Similarly, Rollin notes that even earthworms release endorphins, hormones that act like morphine in humans to relieve pain, and he cites the research of British entomologists that suggests that insects experience pain when exposed to heat or shock.[10] The conclusion that Rollin draws from such evidence is compelling, "If animals feel pain at all, and feeling pain is legitimate grounds for entering the moral arena, then animals should be objects of moral concern."[11]

Scientists and philosophers are widely agreed that pain is a negative, if useful, sensation, and that creatures seek to avoid it. Nevertheless, laboratory scientists have not always considered the reduction of suffering in their animal subjects to be a duty incumbent upon them. Biologist Rosemary Rodd, who dedicates her work *Biology, Ethics and Animals* to an investigation of how factual discoveries in the life sciences influence attitudes toward the moral status of animals, begins with the premise that animals experience not merely painful and pleasant sensations but emotions as well which are prompted by conscious mental activity. For Rodd, study of the nervous systems of animals is of primary importance, and the criterion for determining how an animal should be treated by humans is its capacity to experience painful and pleasant sensations.[12] Some philosophers, including the contractualists, maintain that, even if animals do experience pain, the pain of humans matters more than does that of animals because humans, with their sophisticated consciousness, can anticipate pain and can appreciate its potential to endure or intensify. Clark, among others, rejects this argument as speciesist, arguing that humans cannot after all be sure that animals have no concept of futurity or indeed of death itself, and that we really cannot be sure that they feel pain to a lesser degree than do humans. Scientists obviously use expectation of pain, which suggests at least a shadowy understanding of futurity, to induce desired behaviors in animals.[13] Perhaps, in fact, the pain of animals is more intense because they cannot conceive of how they might escape it, and must therefore "live" it more acutely than do humans, with their sophisticated view of futurity.

Griffin contends that, while scientists frequently judge mammalian suffering to be more objectionable than that of invertebrates, they still know so little about either that every new piece of evidence gathered by ethologists will be crucial in enabling human beings to make decisions and what he terms "trade-offs" in life choices that affect animal lives. Will staunch vegetarians, for example, refuse vegetables if they were treated with insecticides that caused pain and death to insect pests?[14] Griffin's comments here hint at the extent to which scientific and philosophical inquiry into animal pain is colored by human interests. It is in the interest of humans to believe that animals do not feel pain or at least that their pain is morally irrelevant. Some writers have charged that this prejudice has rendered some investigators blind to common sense. In the early days of the modern animal rights movement, Brigid Brophy quipped, "If we are going to rear and kill animals for our food, I think we have a moral obligation to spare them pain and terror in both processes, simply because they are sentient. I can't *prove* they are sentient; but then I have no proof *you* are."[15] More recently, Masson and McCarthy lamented that scientists have become blind to the common-sense evidence before them that animals are capable of many sorts of feelings, and that they apparently have more direct access to their world of feelings than do humans. Consequently, they see a long road ahead for research into animal pain and other emotive states, "At the very least, this poses a matter for serious debate – a debate that has scarcely begun."[16]

If the issue of pain in animals remains at least contentious, the idea that animals experience pleasurable states is still largely taboo in much scientific and philosophical discourse. This is perhaps not surprising. While it is often relatively simple to determine that an animal is experiencing pain based upon its physical responses to negative stimuli, avoidance behaviors, grimaces, and vocalizations, it is more difficult to determine that an animal is experiencing positive feelings that we might identify as pleasure. Nor would it seem to be an easy task to decide what constitutes animal pleasures. This does not mean, however, that the potential pleasure of animals is without moral significance.

Ethicist Bernard Rollin argues that the issue of pain and pleasure in animals has moral relevance because it concerns the interests of animals, and it is incumbent upon us to take interests into account in dealing with other beings.[17] Neurobiology suggests that some animals have the neural apparatus to allow them to experience pleasurable states. DeGrazia observes on this point, "Neural pathways have been located in the brains of mammals, birds, and fish. In addition, animals certainly act as if they experience pleasure, although their apparent pleasure behavior becomes vastly more convincing as one moves up the phylogenetic scale."[18] Moreover, he maintains that since the function of pleasure is to attract a creature to that which is beneficial to it, it seems unreasonable to assume that animals do not experience some pleasure.

Fear of charges of blatant anthropomorphism still hinder many ethologists from giving voice to their suspicions that at least some species of animals inhabit a world in which pleasurable sensations figure. A purring cat, a tail-wagging dog, and a colt gamboling in a meadow certainly seem to be giving vent to such sensations. Masson and McCarthy note with some justice that even when scientists are willing to admit the possibility that some animals may feel emotions, they are often more ready to attribute to them pain-filled emotions like rage, hatred and jealousy than such pleasurable emotions as joy, love or compassion.[19] Some cautious ethologists reject this "common-sense" evidence as lacking in scientific objectivity. Dawkins, for example, feels that, in the final analysis, we have only an animal's actions to go on in judging its emotional state. What does an animal choose, if given a choice? Hens will choose to be around others of their kind over being alone, while pigs will choose access to more food over the companionship of other pigs. This sort of "domination" by a desire Dawkins considers to be a function of emotion, and the choices made would seem to suggest a higher level of pleasurable emotion achieved by the choices made.[20] Yet the issue remains highly speculative for her. Do animals feel as do humans? Are analogies with human feelings at all valid? She answers in the positive. We may at least assert that animals have a knowledge of pleasurable states of mind as much as they do of unpleasant emotional states, although we can still make few specific claims about animal pleasures.[21]

The investigations of ethologists, and the assertions of animal rights advocates who depend on their scientific revelations, suggest that the pains and pleasures of animals should matter to humans, and are not morally neutral. Biologist Rosemary Rodd adopts the stance of an animal rights philosopher when she argues that killing even minimally conscious beings is wrong because "selves" are thereby destroyed. For her, the factor that must guide human conduct is what she terms "continuity of consciousness," which even minimally conscious creatures possess. Killing is wrong because it disrupts this continuity.[22] She raises yet another objection to the infliction of pain upon animals by noting that sometimes the greatest pain is visited upon those who survive rather than upon those who are killed. It is well known that certain animal species actively seek and mourn their lost partners. Even if an animal cannot understand death, it may feel pain at separation.[23] As the level of consciousness in animal species increases, killing animals becomes increasingly objectionable from a moral standpoint. We have come full circle, as the present state of the argument on animal pain, in the view of many scientists and animal rightists, validates the utilitarian stance of Bentham. What matters is consciousness, or sentience, as the faculty is sometimes termed. Singer, Bentham's most prominent philosophical descendant, holds that intelligence is no more relevant than is skin color or gender in determining proper treatment of others, but that sentience is the criterion for moral consideration, in the case of humans and animals alike.[24] As Ryder, who agrees with Singer's position, puts the case, "It is because nonhumans can suffer that they have interests that must be considered."[25]

In contrast to the sometimes substantial contribution made by ancient writers to many of the issues that figure in our study, classical antiquity had relatively little to say on the subject of the pain and pleasures of animals. Only Plutarch, as far as we can judge from extant references to the topic, unequivocally raises the issue in formulating his case for better treatment of animals by human beings. Although he unfortunately scarcely elaborates his observation, Urs Dierauer is correct in observing that Plutarch alone of ancient thinkers argued that animals are capable of feeling pain and that therefore humans have no right to cause it to them.[26] Moreover, Sorabji notes that, even when animal pain and terror seem to be a source of concern in classical authors, the issue is seldom explicitly spelled out, and apparent references to the concept may in fact be prompted by some other consideration altogether.[27] He cites as evidence for this fact a passage in Lucretius in which the poet affectingly portrays the anguish of a mother cow wandering about in search of her calf that is led off to sacrifice (*De rerum natura* [*On the Nature of Things*] II. 349–366). Yet, Sorabji argues, the poet's point here is that a cow can recognize her offspring despite the similarities in appearance among cows, and, perhaps more importantly, that religion leads men to such cruel actions.[28] The animal's pain is quite incidental to Lucretius' diatribe against the excesses of religion. Whatever his motivation in the passage cited here, Lucretius possessed a genuine affection for animals and, it would appear, a belief that they are capable of simple pleasures, a position placing him at odds with the Epicurean school that shared the Stoic conviction that animals fall outside the sphere of human concern.[29] Scholars often call attention to Lucretius' charming portrait of a newborn calf frolicking on shaky legs while "drunk" on its mother's milk (*hinc nova proles/ artubus infirmis teneras lasciva per herbas/ ludit lacte mero mentes perculsa novellas, De rerum natura* I. 259–261). Cicero may have had this Lucretian passage in mind when he suggests that pleasure, the *summum bonum* of the Epicureans, should be left to the lower animals (*voluptatem bestiis concedamus, De finibus* II. 109). Some animals, he acknowledges, feel joy in running and roaming about (*partim cursu et peragratione laetantur, De finibus* II. 109), but despite their capacity for joy and their apparent ability to display affection for their offspring, they are hardly worthwhile models for human morality. For Cicero, the capacity of animals to experience pleasure of some order ends up providing a negative lesson for humans, as their simple joys become a thing to be shunned rather than to be celebrated. A motivation similar to that of Lucretius in his portrait of the bereaved mother cow may stand behind Pythagoras' intercession on behalf of a beaten dog, as Diogenes Laertius records the anecdote, derived from Xenophanes, in the course of his life of Pythagoras. Although Pythagoras is said to be moved to pity (ἐποικτῖραι, Diogenes Laertius VIII. 36) when he hears the animal's yelping, this is only because he recognizes the animal as a former friend of his.

Pythagoras' intercession here suggests that, as in so many ancient discussions of man's relations with animals, we may detect a hint of anthropocentrism in even the most apparently animal-friendly pronouncements. Vegetarians, who pursue what we would naturally assume to be the lifestyle least likely to cause pain to other creatures, were challenged by their ancient opponents to show how those who spare pain to animals might not be obligated to spare pain to plants as well, a proposition called in modern philosophical discourse the "slide argument" and mocked by Augustine, as we noted at the outset of this chapter.[30] Sorabji notes that Porphyry answered this challenge, in a passage which he judges to be "apparently drawn from a lost discussion by Plutarch,"[31] by arguing that the two life forms cannot be compared because, whereas animals by nature have perceptions, can feel pain, can experience fear, and can suffer injury, plants have no perceptions (τὰ μὲν γὰρ αἰσθάνεσθαι πέφυκε καὶ ἀλγεῖν καὶ φοβεῖσθαι καὶ βλάπτεσθαι . . . τοῖς δὲ οὐθέν ἐστιν αἰσθητόν, De abstinentia III. 19).[32] The Plutarchan source for Porphyry's argument may not be altogether lost, but may perhaps be detected behind his claim, made in the course of his proof for the rationality of animals, that it is absurd to call one tree less intelligent than another or one vegetable more cowardly than the next, when nature has not accorded them the faculty of thought (ἡ τοῦ φρονεῖν δύναμις, De sollertia animalium 963A) in any degree at all. The prospect of sentience in plants does not seem to have exercised Plutarch's imagination in his own defense of vegetarianism as it did that of Porphyry, since Plutarch attempts in De esu carnium to convince humans of the abundance of plant foods available to them that will allow them to spare animals the horrific pain and anguish that a carnivorous diet in humans entails.

Not surprisingly, De esu carnium contains the majority of Plutarch's pronouncements on animal pain. In our discussion of Plutarch's call for justice toward animals, we have already called attention to his deeply moving portrait of an animal about to be slaughtered pleading that humans reconsider their diet if its death will serve only to provide those humans a more elaborate meal.[33] Presumably, the cries and shrieks that the animal utters (ἃς φθέγγεται καὶ διατρίζει φωνάς, De esu carnium 994E) are a sign that the animal anticipates the pain that it is about to endure. Earlier in the treatise, Plutarch had lamented that it is a dreadful meal indeed (δεῖπνον ἀληθῶς τερατῶδες) when a human thinks of the meat he will devour while it is still alive and bellowing and shouting (τῶν μυκωμένων . . . ζώντων ἔτι καὶ λαλούντων, De esu carnium 993C).

The picture of animals anticipating the pain of slaughter seems to have haunted Plutarch since he refers to it with similar feeling in his volume of dinner-table conversation, the *Quaestionum convivalium libri*, where the interlocutor Lamprias observes that because humans breathe the same air and drink the same water as they do, humans have become ashamed at butchering animals despite their piteous cries (φωνὴν γοεράν, *Quaestionum convivalium libri* 669D). Shortly after his harrowing scene of an animal begging for justice at the point of being slaughtered, Plutarch relates an anecdote of an Athenian man who was punished for flaying a living ram, a reaction which he considers of doubtful value when one considers the possibility that torturing a live beast may be no worse than slaughtering it for food (996A). If humans must kill an animal for food, they should do so with a modicum of pity and sorrow, and not in a wanton and torturing manner (οὐχ ὑβρίζοντες οὐδὲ βασανίζοντες, *De esu carnium* 996F). Plutarch even charges that a lust for variety has led men to pass beyond what is necessary to secure food to a state in which they enjoy the cruelty involved in slaughtering an animal (997B). This dreadful eventuality leads Plutarch, who otherwise does not put much store in the Pythagorean doctrine of metempsychosis as a motive for avoiding a meat diet, to suggest, in an apparent allusion to the anecdote from Xenophanes that we noted above, that when someone urges us to slaughter a beast that stands before us with head bent back, we should perhaps heed the warning of others that the beast may be some former friend or relation, so that the pain that the animal is about to experience may in fact be felt by a human being in another guise (998F). Plutarch had already raised the disturbing possibility that humans actually enjoy inflicting pain upon animals in *De sollertia animalium*, in the discussion of hunting with which the treatise opens. Autobulus charges that now humans have become inured to the sight of the gore of animals, and take pleasure in their deaths (χαίρειν σφαττομένοις καὶ ἀποθνήσκουσιν, 959D).

Plutarch's rationale for concluding that animals are capable of experiencing pain, and that this fact has ethical consequences for human conduct, lies in his doctrine of animal rationality, a key component of which is perception by the senses (αἴσθησις). In the opening paragraphs of *De sollertia animalium*, Autobulus had argued that every creature born with soul is from birth endowed with that perception and is capable of mental representations (πᾶν τὸ ἔμψυχον αἰσθητικὸν εὐθὺς εἶναι καὶ φανταστικὸν πέφυκεν, 960D). Continuing from the Aristotelian position that nature does not create any sentient creature merely so that it can be sentient but always has some purpose for it, he asserts that the sensation (αἴσθησις) given to animals allows them to distinguish the harmful from the useful, and in consequence to flee from that which is hurtful and painful (τὰς ἑπομένας τῇ αἰσθήσει τῶν μὲν ὠφελίμων λήψεις καὶ διώξεις, διακρούσεις δὲ καὶ φυγὰς τῶν ὀλεθρίων καὶ λυπηρῶν, 960E). In the view of Autobulus, it would be preferable to remove all sensation from an animal if that sensation has no use, than to allow an animal to experience struggles, anxiety and pain without the means of removing these (αἰσθήσεώς τε πάσης καὶ φαντασίας τὸ χρώμενον οὐκ ἐχούσης ἀπηλλάχθαι βέλτιον ἢ πονεῖν καὶ λυπεῖσθαι καὶ ἀλγεῖν, ᾧ διακρούσεται ταῦτα μὴ παρόντος, 961A). Furthermore, this faculty of sensation appears, in Plutarch's analysis, to be capable of operating independently of intellect itself (ἔστω δὲ μὴ δεῖσθαι τοῦ νοῦ τήν αἴσθησιν πρὸς τὸ αὐτῆς ἔργον, 961B), but it is this intellect that allows the animal, once the sensation that has enabled it to distinguish between the harmful and the useful has faded, to recall in future the distinction and to fear the painful and to crave the useful (τί τὸ μνημονεῦόν ἐστιν ἤδη καὶ δεδιὸς τὰ λυποῦντα καὶ ποθοῦν τὰ ὠφέλιμα . . . μὴ παρόντων;, 961B).

Plutarch likewise countenances the possibility that animals are capable of experiencing simple pleasures, and his case is again directed against the views of the Stoics. While developing his case for rationality in animals, Plutarch observes that humans take advantage of the capacity of animals to feel pleasure to hunt and capture them successfully. In *De sollertia animalium*, Autobulus attributes to animals, in phraseology distinctly Stoic in inspiration, the pleasure apprehended by the sense of hearing that arouses in the hearer a sort of enchantment called κήλησις. In his life of Zeno, Diogenes Laertius tells us that the Stoics define pleasure (ἡδονή) as the irrational elation (ἄλογος ἔπαρσις, VII. 114) at the receipt of that which seems to be worthy of being chosen, one variety of which is this enchantment (κήλησις) which reaches the ears. Autobulus claims that crabs are enticed from their burrows by flute music, while fish are lured to the surface by singing (961E). This evidence leads Autobulus to conclude that those Stoics who foolishly maintain that animals do not in fact feel pleasure (οἱ δὲ περὶ τούτων ἀβελτέρως λέγοντες μήθ' ἤδεσθαι, 961E) but only "as it were" (ὡσανεί) do so, might as well say that animals only "as it were" live at all. In sharp contrast to Cicero's assertion (*De finibus* II. 109) that pleasures are best left to animals because they are shameful examples of excess, Plutarch argues in *Bruta animalia ratione uti* that the pleasures enjoyed by animals serve rather as lessons of modesty and continence for humans. Plutarch's philosophic pig Gryllus laments that humans instill a taste for unnatural pleasures (ἡδονῶν παρὰ φύσιν, 987E) in nestling birds and bears to foster docility in them and to tame them more easily. Yet the pleasures of animals in their natural state are simple and free of excess, unlike those of humans who covet precious gems and gold (989E–F). Animals, in contrast, enjoy pleasant fragrances and simple tastes, for the senses of animals admit only that which is proper to them and reject the inappropriate (τὸ μὲν οἰκεῖον εἴσω παρίησι τὸ δ' ἀλλότριον ἀπελαύνει, 990A), yet another assertion that animals live in accord with nature by recognizing that which is akin to them (οἰκεῖον) while rejecting that which is alien, an admirable arrangement that humans do not emulate.

Without benefit of the neuroscience which forms the underpinnings upon which biologists like Rodd and ethicists like Rollin build their cases for the capacity of animals to experience pains and pleasures, Plutarch develops here an argument whose key components and philosophical assumptions closely parallel those of modern theorists, and he arrives at the same conclusion reached by Rollin that the pains and pleasures of animals should matter to humans who seek to act justly. Plutarch had argued in *De sollertia animalium* that rationality is a continuum from which animalkind is not excluded, and he would agree with Rodd's concept of "continuity of consciousness" in the universe of living creatures as a principle that must guide human conduct. Animals share with humans the capacity for sensation (αἴσθησις), as they do the capacity for memory and feelings. Plutarch would disagree heartily with Augustine that animals do not share in the community of reason with humans and therefore cannot claim to have their pleasures and pains taken into account in human actions. Plutarch may be no more certain than is Rollin on what constitutes the pleasures of animals, but he would back him in maintaining that, whatever those pleasures may be, they are not morally neutral. Free of fears of charges of anthropomorphism that render the assertions of many ethologists so tentative and circumspect, Plutarch would agree with Masson and McCarthy that, like people, animals feel joy merely at being alive. "The evidence is good," they observe, "that animals as well as people do feel such pure joy."[34] One remarkable type of behavior that both ancient and modern investigators have isolated in some animal species that one might, at least at first glance, suspect to derive from such joy at being alive, is that of helping others, whether those of one's own species or those of other species. The following chapter explores the phenomena of cooperation, altruism and philanthropy in animals.

5

BEAUTY IN THE BEAST

Cooperation, altruism and philanthropy
among animals

It is because we are animals, warm-blooded and mammalian, that we
display parental and familial care, pity the weak and give our lives up
for our friends.

Stephen R. L. Clark, *The Moral Status of Animals*

One of the most charming tales in Herodotus is that of the dithyrambic poet
Arion of Methymna on Lesbos who, on returning from a lucrative singing tour
in Italy and Sicily, was compelled to jump overboard by greedy sailors who
hatched a plot to seize his earnings while conducting him back to the court of
Periander at Corinth. When he was adrift, Herodotus recounts, a dolphin was
said to have picked him up and carried him safely back to Taenarum in Laconia
(τὸν δὲ δελφῖνα λέγουσι ὑπολαβόντα ἐξενεῖκαὶ ἐπὶ Ταίναρον, Herodotus I. 24).
Herodotus makes no further comment on this extraordinary incident other than
to remark that a small statue of a man astride a dolphin could still be seen in
his day in a temple in Taenarum (I. 24). In view of his fondness for pointing out
the moral lessons to be learned from the anecdotes that he retails, it is curious
that Herodotus passed up the opportunity that this inscription, which he may
well have seen, might have afforded him. In his version of the anecdote, however,
Aelian at least hints at such a moral reading of the tale. According to Aelian,
who quotes the inscription in Taenarum (*De natura animalium* XII. 45) and who
implies at times that more than one dolphin was involved in the rescue, the
verses recorded that the animal depicted in the statue had been sent by the gods
and had rescued the poet (ἐκ Σικελοῦ πελάγους σῶσεν ὄχημα τόδε). He quotes
in turn the hymn that Arion composed as a sort of payment of a reward for this
rescue by the dolphins (οἱονεὶ καὶ τούτοις ζωάγρια ἐκτίνων ὁ Ἀρίων ἔγραψε,
De natura animalium XII. 45). In the hymn, Arion contrasts the actions of the
dolphins who supported him upon their arched backs with the actions of the
treacherous men (φῶτες δόλιοι) who cast him into the water. Since the general
context in which Aelian's retelling of the anecdote of Arion is found deals with
love of music in animals, it is possible to understand Aelian's tale to mean that

76

the dolphins were "repaying" Arion for the enjoyment that his music had afforded them.[1]

More than a century ago, in an intriguing work devoted to Greek tales of "gratitude" in animals, August Marx observed that no species was more revered in classical literature for this virtue than was the dolphin.[2] Tales of encounters between humans and dolphins in ancient literature, according to Marx, typically involved a dolphin being helped by a human while in some distressful situation, after which the same animal would reciprocate by aiding the same human when that person found himself in distress. Although in Herodotus' version of the tale of Arion the action of the dolphin is not prompted by any prior act of human kindness and this idea is perhaps only slightly felt in Aelian's retelling, ancient stories of dolphin rescues have caught the attention of animal rightists who otherwise seldom take account of ancient exempla that corroborate modern scientific claims about animal behaviors. In their chapter on compassion, rescuing behavior, and what they term the "altruism debate," Masson and McCarthy allude to "ancient tales of dolphins saving humans from drowning," tales on which they comment dismissively, "although some of these are plausible, none are documented."[3] The sort of helping action in animals that is in evidence in the anecdote of Arion is, as Masson and McCarthy's reference to the "altruism debate" makes clear, a phenomenon that is currently the object of close scrutiny in scientific and philosophic circles as scholars weigh in on the question of whether non-human animals are capable of genuinely altruistic behaviors that might entail cooperation with conspecifics, and might even suggest evidence of "philanthropic" tendencies in animals, as seems to be hinted at in the actions of Arion's rescuers.

Even ethologists who are willing to accept the possibility that some non-human species may experience emotions like love, joy, friendship and hope draw the line when the issue of altruistic behavior in non-human animals is raised, often on the grounds that the sort of selfless aiding behavior that altruism presupposes is potentially detrimental to the survival of the aiding creature, and contradicts the tendency of evolution to preserve the genetic material of a species. Scientists who take this position believe that the animal world is ruled by self-interest and that generous behavior is, genetically speaking, potentially suicidal. Biologist Richard Dawkins developed the concept of the "selfish gene" that, at least metaphorically, seeks to survive and reproduce, and in his view, all behavior, however altruistic it may appear, is ultimately selfish.[4] Carried to its logical conclusion, this would demand that all seemingly ethical conduct be merely a function of survival mechanisms. No creature would help another unless it benefited itself from its action. Common sense and everyday observation of animal interactions seem to refute Dawkins' thesis. Well-documented tales abound, for example, of cats who adopt and nurse orphaned puppies, of rats who adopt baby mice and even baby rabbits, and of elephants who slow their pace if one of their fellows is injured.[5] Such actions hardly seem to be gene-serving. Rodd notes that animals that are normally predatory toward other species often do not exhibit such tendencies when they are raised together with their normal prey, which suggests that gene-serving behavior is not likely here.[6]

Other issues, cognitive in nature, have been raised by some scientists and philosophers who question the possibility of helping behavior in non-human animals. Other than humans, only certain species of cetaceans have been documented to help other species in distress. In the case of humans, this behavior arises from the recognition that another individual is in distress, which itself depends upon an understanding of what constitutes distress for other individuals. If cetaceans aid other animal species in distress, might we conclude therefrom that they possess the same understanding of what distress is for others that motivates human aiding interventions? Should we read the anecdote of Arion to mean that the dolphin understood that, in the case of a human, being left adrift at sea constitutes distress that requires some aiding behavior? As scientists and philosophers frame the question, is apparently altruistic action in animals *intentional*, as it clearly is in the case of humans, and does it in fact need to be? The point at issue here, as is so often the case in the debate on the moral status of animals, is that of whether animals are moral agents, as intentional aiding behavior would suggest them to be. Once again, a positive answer to this question would have profound implications for human treatment of non-human animals. The aiding behavior that is the tangible manifestation of altruism would seem to require a degree of identification on the part of the aiding creature with the needs of another creature. As deWaal states the matter, some cognitive abilities are necessary for a complete identification, including a well-developed sense of self and an ability to assume the perspective of another creature. "Perspective-taking," deWaal maintains, "revolutionizes helpful behavior, turning it into *cognitive altruism*, that is, altruism with the other's interests explicitly in mind."[7]

A creature whose aiding behavior evidences such a perspective is clearly operating as a moral being, that is, as one capable of acting morally, but some philosophers have questioned whether the moral worth of aiding behavior is lessened if that behavior is carried out without accompanying cognitive action. Philosopher Steve Sapontzis notes, for example, that seeing-eye dogs perform actions which, if performed by humans, we would not hesitate to declare moral.[8] If morality were solely a behavioral issue, we would have to conclude that such actions were moral. Yet, Sapontzis observes, some deny that animals can be moral beings because, in their view, morality depends upon the possession of reason and, if we judge animals to be irrational, their actions cannot be moral. The actions of animals, whether good or bad, will after all remain morally neutral. Those who demand rationality for moral action hold that an action becomes moral only if the doer recognizes it as such, and only rational beings can do so. Sapontzis challenges this position by asking why rationality is necessary for morality and by questioning the premise that animals are in fact irrational.

A second premise of the rationality argument maintains that only beings that are free to choose their actions can act morally, and again only rational beings are thus free. Sapontzis counters that examples can be cited from nature that suggest that animals do perform courageous and compassionate actions that are not mechanical or chemical responses to instincts, and he offers an example that closely parallels the ancient tale of Arion's rescue. "The case of porpoises helping drowning sailors," he argues, "must be spontaneous acts of kindness. There is no reason to believe that porpoises have developed an instinct for saving humans, and they certainly have not been conditioned to perform such acts through training or repetition."[9] It seems, he concludes, that animals respond on some level to the moral goods and evils of situations. In Sapontzis' view, it does not matter whether animals recognize that they act in accord with morality any more than humans need to be moral philosophers to act morally. The argument that only rational beings can act morally is ultimately false since a being can act morally without espousing a moral theory. Nevertheless, Sapontzis argues, moral action is motivated by a desire to do what is required to bring about an honorable way of life, and altruistic actions in animals do not seem to be the sort of actions that are so motivated. Hence, Sapontzis concludes that animals are after all not moral beings even when their actions are in themselves moral because "they seem to lack the ability to lead a dedicated moral life."[10] Still, a being is worthy of human respect if its actions are virtuous even if it cannot decide to act virtuously, and in Sapontzis' view, humans have certain obligations toward such beings. "They are beings who must be accorded rights to life, dignity, and a fulfilling life by those who are concerned to create a more virtuous world, i.e. by moral beings."[11] Through their acts of altruism, animals become moral *recipients* who naturally fall within the purview of human moral concern.

As we noted above, in his analysis of ancient tales of aiding behaviors in dolphins, August Marx pointed out that these behaviors frequently involve a sort of "pay back" in which the animal returns some favor by helping a human who had previously benefited the animal in some way.[12] Ethologists who have studied altruistic behaviors in animals have isolated what they term "reciprocal altruism," a kind of system of repayment which deWaal has characterized as "a complex mechanism based on the remembrance of favors given and received."[13] Reciprocal altruism has been observed to operate among some primate species that share food when they have previously been offered food even by individuals who are not their own kin. deWaal places great weight on the operation of reciprocity among animals on the grounds that morality is impossible without reciprocity, in which "the first hints of moral obligation and indebtedness are already observable."[14]

Ethologists distinguish reciprocal altruism from the sort of aiding behavior that they term cooperation. In the former, the aiding animal may not derive any immediate benefit from his pay-back behavior, whereas in the latter more immediate benefit is realized. Examples of cooperative behaviors in nature are legion, and are most readily observed in cases of hunting of prey by packs of conspecific animals.[15] Some primate species form alliances to catch prey more effectively, as do dolphins, cats and dogs.[16] Griffin notes as well that dolphins engage in such cooperative aiding behaviors if they observe that fellow-dolphins are sick or injured. "If a dolphin is visibly weak and sinks below the surface, its companions may swim down and push it from below, lifting it to the surface so that it can breathe air."[17] His conclusion on this behavior is striking. "Some conscious thoughts," he maintains, "seem likely to accompany this aiding behavior."[18] Griffin notes as well instances of dolphins lifting human swimmers from below, an action which he speculates derives "presumably from similar behavior."[19] That is, dolphins may consciously choose to aid humans in the same manner that they do ailing conspecifics, in which case we would have to label their behavior genuinely "philanthropic" if a deliberate choice is made to help humans in distress. However that may be, cooperative behavior is in itself not without ethical ramifications since it involves considerations of loyalty, trust and friendships of at least temporary duration.

There are few areas in which ancient and modern discussions of animal behavior intersect so strikingly as in the case of the sort of aiding actions in non-human species that we have outlined in the opening pages of the present chapter, to such an extent that some philosophers and animal rights advocates seem to be aware that ancient writers noted the same sorts of behavior in the same species that have formed the subject of their study in recent decades, although some modern writers tend to be somewhat dismissive of ancient interpretations of apparent instances of altruistic behaviors in other species. Plutarch had much to say, in the course of the comparative chapters in *De sollertia animalium* and elsewhere in the *Moralia*, on altruistic actions, cooperation and even philanthropic tendencies in non-human animals, and his conclusions on these issues seem to anticipate modern views more fully than do those of his Greek and Roman colleagues. Specifically, he appears to be more eager than either Pliny or Aelian to explore the moral dimensions of altruistic behaviors in animals.

Plutarch's discussion of aiding behaviors in dolphins caught the attention of Barrow, who unfortunately does not elaborate his intriguing observation on the subject. Referring apparently to the anecdotes related in *De sollertia animalium* 984A–F, Barrow writes, "The long section given to the dolphin as the most intelligent of animals (the only one which takes the initiative in becoming friendly with man) anticipates in small compass what is now being written about this animal."[20] Surprisingly, Arion, the mortal whose encounter with dolphins so captivated the ancients, is alluded to only in passing in these paragraphs of *De sollertia animalium*. It is in Plutarch's symposiac dialogue *Septem sapientium convivium* (*Banquet of the Seven Sages*) that Plutarch offers his take on antiquity's most famous meeting between man and dolphin. The topic is easily integrated into the conversation since the dramatic setting of the dialogue is the court of Arion's patron, Periander of Corinth. Periander's brother Gordus enters, having just returned from Taenarum where he has taken part in a night-time religious ceremony at the water's edge and has witnessed a school of dolphins bearing a man to shore (160F–161A). Plutarch's dependence upon

Herodotus' telling of the incident is evident in certain external details: Gordus alludes to the plot of the greedy sailors, he describes Arion's intention of jumping overboard in full artistic costume, and he details the circumstances of the capture of the sailors whose false tale of Arion's safe journey is refuted when the singer appears before them at Periander's court (161C–162B). At the same time, the ethical reading of the incident in evidence in Plutarch's account of Arion's rescue owes very little to any literary predecessors. Gordus relates that Arion, who was initially frightened by the appearance of the dolphins around him in the water, was reassured and comforted when he noted their friendly demeanor and realized that they seemed to sense that rescuing him was a sort of duty obligatory for them in which it was necessary that they all participate (πολλοὺς ἑώρα ἀθροιζομένους περὶ αὐτὸν εὐμένως καὶ διαδεχομένους ὡς ἀναγκαῖον ἐν μέρει λειτούργημα καὶ προσῆκον πᾶσιν, 161D–E).

Slightly later in the same dialogue, Solon the wise man, another participant at Periander's apocryphal banquet, relates a second anecdote of dolphins with a developed sense of morality. The poet Hesiod, according to Solon's account, was murdered by the brothers of a woman when they had falsely accused him of concealing knowledge about an affair which a friend of the poet was conducting with their sister. They had no sooner thrown the murdered poet's body into the sea than a school of dolphins conveyed it back to land, and when the astonished onlookers beheld the action, they immediately investigated the murder and punished the wrongdoers. Solon's interpretation of the behavior of the dolphins again emphasizes the potential ethical dimension of the action of the animals when he concludes that, if dolphins take such "philanthropic" interest in dead humans, one can scarcely wonder if they show still more care for living humans (εἴπερ οὖν οὕτως ἔχουσιν οἰκείως καὶ φιλανθρώπως πρὸς τοὺς ἀποθανόντας, ἔτι μᾶλλον εἰκός ἐστι τοῖς ζῴοι βοηθεῖν, 162F).

The aiding behavior of animals inspired greater admiration in Plutarch than did almost any other aspect of animal conduct, if we may judge by the elaborate treatment accorded the topic in the comparative chapters of *De sollertia animalium*. It is surely no coincidence that Plutarch leaves dolphins to last in Phaedimus' defense of the superiority of sea-dwellers over land-dwellers, as if they supported his case most effectively. Immediately after his presentation on the aiding behavior of dolphins, the participants in the dialogue are invited to cast their votes for those creatures whose behavior seems in the final analysis more "clever" to them (985C). Phaedimus declares that the dolphin is the only creature that loves human beings for themselves (μόνος γὰρ ἄνθρωπον ἀσπάζεται, καθ' ὃ ἄνθρωπός ἐστι, 984C). Some animal species avoid human contact, he explains, while others befriend humans only because they feed them, but dolphins offer what philosophers seek: friendship without advantage (τῷ δὲ δελφῖνι παρὰ πάντα καὶ μόνῳ τὸ ζητούμενον ὑπὸ τῶν ἀρίστων φιλοσόφων ἐκεῖνο, τὸ φιλεῖν ἄνευ χρείας, 984D).

In our discussion in Chapter 3 of the possibility of a sense of justice in animals, we already touched upon Plutarch's anecdote of a dolphin who enjoyed swimming with a boy who rode upon the back of the animal.[21] When the boy fell off and drowned, the dolphin beached himself and lay beside the dead boy because the animal thought it only just to share in the death that he had caused (δικαιώσας μετασχεῖν ἧς συναίτιος ἔδοξε γεγονέναι τελευτῆς, De sollertia animalium 984F). Plutarch is not unique in relating tales of dolphins who sacrifice themselves when they have caused the death of a human being whom they have carried. Pliny tells of a dolphin who beached himself as a means of confessing that he had allowed a human passenger to fall from his back in the course of a storm (delphinum causam se leti fatentem non reversum in maria atque in sicco expirasse, Naturalis historia IX. 27).[22] Later, Aelian told of a dolphin who deliberately (ἑκών) beached himself because he had accidentally pricked his human passenger with his dorsal fin (De natura animalium VI. 15). While the anecdotes of Pliny and Aelian might equally well be considered illustrative of a sense of reciprocal justice in animals, only Plutarch, both in Septem sapientium convivium and in De sollertia animalium, specifically draws his reader's attention to the ethical dimension inherent in the behavior of the dolphins by his employment of words with such a coloring (ἀναγκαῖον, προσῆκον, εἰκός ... βοηθεῖν, δικαιώσας, συναίτιος). Plutarch is not unaware of the notion, fairly prominent in both Pliny's and Aelian's accounts, that dolphins are prompted to help humans because of a love of music. He allows Gordus to remark that we can scarcely wonder that dolphins show tender care for humans if they have been charmed by the music of their flutes and songs (κηληθέντας αὐλοῖς ἤ τισι μέλεσι, Septem sapientium convivium 162F). Plutarch likewise shows himself to be aware of the belief that some divine inspiration may be involved in the aiding behavior of dolphins since their "philanthropy" has elicited the affection of the gods (ἀλλὰ μᾶλλον ἔοικε τὸ φιλάνθρωπον αὐτοῦ θεοφιλὲς εἶναι, De sollertia animalium 984C). Yet these ideas, however much they influenced the presentations of Pliny and Aelian, scarcely figure in Plutarch's account of aiding behavior in dolphins. Neither the notion that dolphins aid humans in reaction to human music nor that their behavior is divinely inspired is developed at all in Plutarch, whose choice of vocabulary in accounting for this behavior suggests that his interest in the phenomenon lies elsewhere. His interest in animal altruism arises from the consequences for human morality that instances of apparently purposeful interventions on behalf of human beings carried out by non-human animals may have.

While the phenomenon of animals aiding other animals, whether conspecifics or members of other species, does not inspire the admiration of Plutarch so much as does that of animals aiding humans, perhaps because he viewed it as having less direct bearing on his theme of the moral dimension of interaction between human and animal, he does take note of such behaviors. He records, for example, that Juba, the scholarly king of Mauretania, had written that, when one of their fellows has fallen into a pit designed by humans to entrap the creatures, other elephants will drop wood and stones into the pit to enable their trapped comrade to walk out, an action which Juba took as an illustration of how intelligence and community spirit are united in elephants (τό γε μὴν κοινώνικον μετὰ τοῦ συνετοῦ τοὺς ἐλέφαντας ἀποδείκνυσθαί φησιν ὁ Ἰόβας, *De sollertia animalium* 972B). Similarly, fishes are credited with freeing their comrades when they are hooked by fishermen by swimming around their comrades and nibbling at the hook, an action which Phaedimus declares, in language remarkably similar to that used of Juba's account of elephants, to be an illustration of the community spirit and mutual affection that some fishes display along with their intelligence (ἄλλα δ᾽ ἐπιδείκνυται μετὰ τοῦ συνετοῦ τὸ κοινωνικὸν καὶ τὸ φιλάλληλον, *De sollertia animalium* 977C). Plovers are said to ward off attackers from crocodiles, in return for which the crocodiles, otherwise the most unsociable of animals (τὸ πάντων ἀμικτότατον, *De sollertia animalium* 980D), allow the birds to walk safely inside their mouths to remove food scraps for themselves. Plutarch does not otherwise develop these examples of animals aiding animals or offer observations on their moral ramifications.

In his *Politics*, Aristotle argued that one of the factors that distinguishes man from other animals is his unique possession of a sense of justice (τοῦτο γὰρ πρὸς τἆλλα ζῷα τοῖς ἀνθρώποις ἴδιον, τὸ μόνον ἀγαθοῦ καὶ κακοῦ καὶ τῶν ἄλλων αἴσθησιν ἔχειν, *Politica* 1253a11–14). This is attributable, according to Aristotle, to man's unique possession of language since only humans can communicate to others what constitutes the nature of good and evil.[23] Plutarch's portrait of aiding behavior in dolphins suggests that he would disagree with his predecessor on this point. The vocabulary that he uses to describe the approach of dolphins to humans in distress shows him willing to countenance the belief that dolphins, at least among animal species, have some sense of justice and regularly act upon it, even when their actions are not prompted by prior acts of kindness on the part of the humans whom they aid. In his view, dolphins have a sense of what deWaal calls reciprocal altruism, but, uniquely among animals, in Plutarch's judgment, they will aid humans simply because they are humans (*De sollertia animalium* 984A). Although one could hardly claim that Plutarch even contemplated the notion that dolphins, or any other species of animals, are out to create what Sapontzis terms a more virtuous world, he does seem to hold that dolphins act morally and even somehow have a sense of morality that causes them to feel that aiding behavior is incumbent upon them. Plutarch's dolphins are capable of the sort of "perspective taking" that deWaal maintains will turn helpful behavior into cognitive altruism, that is, behavior that has the interests of another in mind. Plutarch's dolphins fulfill Sapontzis' requirements for moral beings: they act in a manner that we would recognize as moral if humans acted so. Sapontzis had questioned the demand of other philosophers that animals exhibit rationality if they are to be understood as acting morally, although we might keep in mind that Griffin had speculated that the sort of aiding behavior evidenced in dolphins seems in itself to involve some conscious thoughts. Plutarch, a strong believer in rationality in animals, only once in the course of his discussion of aiding behavior in sea-dwellers overtly connects this behavior with animal intelligence, and in that instance not specifically in connection with dolphins, when he allows Phaedimus to mock Juba's tale of altruistic elephants and to declare that, even if it is true, it shows no more than that sea-dwellers are in no way inferior to land-dwellers in these qualities of intelligence and community spirit (ἀληθὴς δ' οὖσα πολλὰ δείκνυσι τῶν ἐνάλων μηδὲν ἀπολειπόμενα τῷ κοινωνικῷ καὶ συνετῷ τοῦ σοφωτάτου τῶν χερσαίων, *De sollertia animalium* 977E). Although he does not develop the intellect–altruism connection to the extent that we might expect, Plutarch's conclusions on the consequences for human morality that arise from apparent altruistic behavior in animals that is directed to humans would accord fully with Sapontzis' take on the issue: if animals display virtuous actions, humans have obligations toward them. These animals fall within the sphere of human moral concern, as examples of what modern philosophy calls moral recipients, as clearly as do animals whose actions can be concluded to arise from an exercise of reason. By employing morally charged vocabulary to describe the actions of dolphins toward humans, Plutarch has made a case that animals can act altruistically toward humans because of some prompting of morality within them, and he would agree with Sapontzis that humans who seek to create a more virtuous world owe consideration to other creatures who demonstrate such behavior.

Unquestionably the greatest mark of respect that humans interested in creating a more virtuous world can show to other moral creatures is not to eat them. Plutarch's arguments in defense of the vegetarian lifestyle are examined in the following chapter.

6

ANIMAL APPETITES
Vegetarianism and human morality

The most mischievous effect of the practice of flesh-eating, in its influence on the study of animals' rights at the present time, is that it so stultifies and debases the very *raison d'être* of countless myriads of beings – it brings them into life for no better reason than to deny their right to live.
Henry S. Salt, *Animals' Rights Considered in Relation to Social Progress*

Since antiquity, much of philosophical speculation and a good deal of scientific investigation into the nature of animalkind and the relationship between humans and animals has had, as a more or less hidden agenda, the justification of or, conversely, the rejection of man's appetite for animal flesh. If animals are senseless, mindless, speechless brutes with no understanding of what goes on around them and no capacity to feel pain, then humans need have no compunction at slaying them for food, and history has been well supplied with philosophers, scientists and theologians eager to convince us that this is indeed the case. Those who have held that animals are to a lesser or greater degree sentient and therefore capable of experiencing pain, and that it is therefore morally unjustifiable to confine them in darkness, to deprive them of the company of their offspring and of others of their own kind, to restrict their movement, and ultimately to slaughter them for human consumption, have found themselves branded by such thinkers as churlish opponents of human progress if not as hopelessly insane. In a sense, all the topics broached in the previous chapters of this volume, including the question of whether animals are rational, of whether human beings can stand in any relationship of justice with them, of whether they are capable of experiencing pains and pleasures, and whether their actions, toward each other and toward human beings, have a moral dimension, culminate in the topic with which this chapter deals. Are humans, after all, justified in eating other animals, or is vegetarianism a lifestyle that is either preferable or obligatory for humans? As has been the case with subjects treated in earlier chapters, there is scarcely an argument for or against abstention from meat eating that appears in modern philosophical and scientific literature that was not anticipated in ancient sources, and, with the exception of Porphyry, no ancient author argued so broadly or so passionately for the necessity of vegetarianism on aesthetic, hygienic, spiritual and ethical grounds as did Plutarch.

Although ancient literature is well supplied with references to individuals who apparently followed a vegetarian regimen, and with arguments in defense of abstention, ancient vegetarianism is a surprisingly complex topic involving motivations that are frequently difficult to sort out, since seemingly animal-friendly pronouncements may mask selfish motives. The two treatises that make up Plutarch's *De esu carnium* constitute, after Porphyry's *De abstinentia* which makes abundant use of its predecessor's arguments, the most extensive defense of abstention from a meat diet that survives from antiquity, but some critics have doubted the sincerity of Plutarch's commitment to the vegetarian lifestyle. Even critics who are willing to entertain the notion that *De esu carnium* may reflect its author's lifestyle at times conclude that vegetarianism was a passing fancy that Plutarch outgrew or "got over" as he matured and came to his senses. In the Introduction to his Loeb edition of the treatises, for example, William C. Helmbold suggests that they "probably depict faithfully a foible of Plutarch's early manhood," but that "there is little trace of this in his later life."[1] This remark is doubly interesting in view of the fact that the treatises contained in the *Moralia* are largely undatable. In his study of religious themes in Plutarch, Frederick E. Brenk goes a step further than had Helmbold in mocking Plutarch's advocacy of vegetarianism, branding it a sign of his "youthful sincerity and idealism and the appeal of the heart over the head."[2] On Plutarch's concern for animals in general, Brenk observes, in language now charmingly quaint, "The young Plutarch is not too far removed from the youth communes of today, the flower children, and the hippies, at least insofar as these are concerned with a more primitive way of life which makes fewer incursions upon nature and its animals."[3] More recently, in a study of Plutarch's treatise *De tuenda sanitate praecepta* (*Advice on Keeping Well*), Aldo Tirelli complained of Plutarch's unreasonable adherence to a Pythagorean vegetarianism in his youth.[4] Fortunately, he continues, Plutarch eventually allowed the consumption of meat, which shows, in Tirelli's view, the triumph of good sense.[5]

It is perhaps not surprising to find Plutarch's advocacy of a meat-free lifestyle viewed askance if not actually mocked in modern critical literature when we consider how strong and pervasive anti-vegetarian sentiment remains in modern culture. The consumption of meat, some argue, has a significance that extends far beyond mere nourishment, into a complex of symbolic meanings that hint at concerns with power, dominance and even sexuality. In his fascinating work *Meat: A Natural Symbol*, anthropologist Nick Fiddes explores some of the non-nutritional meanings of meat eating. Because it is a food difficult and expensive to produce, he notes, meat often symbolizes prosperity and dominance. As Britain industrialized in the nineteenth century, for example, meat consumption increased as a diet rich in meat came to symbolize conquest over the environment.[6] Fiddes likewise connects meat eating with sexual gratification as activities both pleasurable and linked to the survival of the species.[7] Along similar lines, men are traditionally viewed as hunters who provide nourishment to women through the killing of animals and men are generally supplied with larger portions of meat than are women. Vegetarianism is sometimes branded as "womanish" in modern societies, a sort of activity rejected by "real men," and advocacy of abstention from meat is mocked as akin to such other "progressive" causes as feminism and ecological awareness.[8]

Even if we are tempted to judge these symbolic meanings of meat, which Fiddes terms "meatologies," to be far-fetched, it is obvious that those who have a vested interest in ensuring that an appetite for animal flesh continues in modern society take every step to disassociate meat eating from the abuse and killing of animals. The very names of meat products are so devised as to disguise their exact animal origins, as is seen in the designations "beef," "veal," "pork" and "poultry," and meats are sold on plastic trays that virtually obliterate all trace of animality from the purchaser's consciousness. The modern meat industry is eager to convince consumers that meat is what humans *should* eat. It is not difficult to sense in these modern practices the intellectual legacy of Stoicism, with its doctrine that animals are intended for man's use and can have no claim on human sympathy. Ironically, even the most stalwart defenders of animal rights argue that, in some cases, the claims of those who maltreat animals for profit cannot be dismissed out of hand. Tom Regan, for example, counters the argument of Singer that the interests of meat producers are trivial in comparison to the suffering they cause to countless animals by pointing out that meat producers hardly consider their interests trivial, not to mention the fact that more persons seek to perpetuate current treatment of animals than to reform it. It is not at all obvious, in Regan's estimation, that the overall situation of all involved in the transition from meat eating to universal vegetarianism would improve.[9]

When we recall that, despite their differences in approach, Singer and Regan both consider a vegetarian lifestyle to be incumbent upon all persons, it becomes obvious how complex the issue of abstention can prove. This is especially true in the case of those whose practices seem to be in conflict with their pronouncements. Perhaps the most famous lover of animals, the gentle St. Francis of Assisi, who, as Dombrowski puts it, is widely viewed as a "syrupy nature lover,"[10] and who preached to the birds as to his brothers, does not seem to have practiced vegetarianism. Dombrowski remarks tartly of this much-admired figure, "St. Francis is one of the more famous 'animal lovers' who showed his love by eating them!"[11] Another individual who, like Francis, is often assumed to have been vegetarian because of his work, but whose practice and preaching seem equally conflicted, is Charles Darwin. In his history of speciesism, that prejudice of humans to value their own species over others, Ryder has called Darwin "the prime example of humankind's inconsistency in relation to nonhumans."[12] Although he pointed out the kinship between humans and other animals, and personally abhorred cruelty to animals, he ended up supporting the vivisectionists of his time and never adopted the vegetarian lifestyle that his own discoveries might reasonably have recommended to him. Perhaps the greatest disappointment to advocates of vegetarianism is the moral philosopher Jeremy Bentham, whose statement on the importance of taking into account the sufferings of animals is often approvingly cited in animal rights literature, not least in defenses of vegetarianism.[13] While Bentham downplayed the significance of reason as a determining factor in interspecies relations and personally opposed sports like hunting and fishing on the grounds that they cause pain to animals, he stopped short of advocating vegetarianism and satisfied himself with recommending that food animals be killed as swiftly and painlessly as possible.

Despite the impassioned tone and broad knowledge of ancient arguments in defense of vegetarianism that *De esu carnium* demonstrates, Plutarch's own commitment to vegetarianism has been called into question by critics, largely on the basis of passages sprinkled through the treatises of the *Moralia* that appear to condone the consumption of meat that he condemns in *De esu carnium*. Barigazzi, for example, noting Plutarch's surprisingly lukewarm support for Pythagoreanism, doubts that he was a vegetarian in the first place.[14] Moreover, the highly wrought rhetoric of the vegetarian treatises has contributed to the notion that they are merely youthful exercises that might not reflect their author's own practices. Helmbold, for example, speaks of the "exaggerated and calculated rhetoric" of the treatises, despite which, he admits, Plutarch might have believed in what he was writing, at least in his callow youth.[15]

Because of the difficulty involved in attempting to date the treatises of the *Moralia* on internal grounds owing to their scarcity of allusions to datable historical events and recognizable personalities, it is necessary to seek some other explanation for the apparent contradictions in Plutarch's pronouncements on vegetarianism.[16] The vast majority of his seemingly meat-friendly statements are found in the nine books of his rambling collection of dinner table conversations, the *Quaestionum convivalium libri* (*Table Talk*), wherein Plutarch and some friends and family members tackle various light-hearted topics appropriate to the context of a cultivated banquet setting. These topics are formally proposed and then commented upon by the participants, in something resembling the form of a loose lecture. In at least some of these discussions, Plutarch is himself an interlocutor. Not surprisingly, given the nature of the work, a number of these topics relate to the eating of meat. In one section, for example, the diners debate the issue of whether the sea provides tastier eatables than does the land (667C–669E), a discussion followed immediately by speculation on why the Jews abstain from eating pork and other meats (669F–671C). In yet another, the interlocutor Patrocleas, a relative of Plutarch, offers an explanation for why the meat of sheep becomes sweeter when they have been bitten by wolves (642C). On occasion, issues relating to the ethics of meat eating do surface in the treatise. In a statement that echoes argumentation in *De sollertia animalium* (975E–F), the interlocutor Lamprias notes that human beings have historically felt greater shame at slaughtering land animals for food than those from the sea because of the pitiful groans (φωνὴν γοεράν, 669D) that land animals emit at slaughter, and have felt more at ease in eating sea creatures because they live a style of life remote from that of human beings and do not so move us by their appearance (669D–E). Later, the participants speculate on why the early Pythagoreans avoided the consumption of fish more strictly than of land animals, and it is noteworthy that here Plutarch depicts himself as offering the explanation, speculating that this may have been from a concern for justice (ἕνεκα τοῦ δικαίου, 729E), since fish cause humans no harm and provide us with no excuse to injure them. He laments that, while necessity may originally have forced men to adopt a carnivorous diet, it is now a difficult task to break the habit of meat eating because it is now perceived as pleasurable (ἤδη καὶ δι' ἡδονὴν ἔργον ἐστὶ παῦσαι τὴν σαρκοφαγίαν, 730A). Although some critics have questioned the strength of Plutarch's commitment to abstention because the eating of meat is approvingly discussed in the *Quaestionum convivalium libri*, it is significant that the strongest condemnation of meat eating in that treatise is put into the mouth of Plutarch himself, and his remarks here are entirely consistent with his position elsewhere.

Certain pronouncements in Plutarch's dialogue *De tuenda sanitate praecepta* have likewise prompted some critics to see inconsistencies in his position on vegetarianism and have led them to conclude that he actually recommends consumption of meat for a healthy diet. In this treatise, the interlocutor Zeuxippus relates the contents of a lecture on healthy living that he has heard, some elements of which pertain to proper diet. What Tirelli judges to be a more accepting attitude toward meat eating in the work might more reasonably be considered to reflect Plutarch's recognition of the realities of life.[17] The vast majority of persons are after all not likely to practice or adopt a vegetarian lifestyle, and Plutarch is not so much giving in to the practice as pointing to the dangers involved in a lifestyle prevalent in his day. The habit of meat eating is called a kind of unnatural second nature (τὸ ἔθος τρόπον τινὰ φύσις τοῦ παρὰ φύσιν γέγονεν, 132A), and humans should resort to it only as a kind of support in the diet (οἷον ὑπέρεισμα καὶ διάζωμα τῆς τροφῆς), while we should rely predominantly on foods more in accord with nature (ἃ καὶ τῷ σώματι μᾶλλόν ἐστι κατὰ φύσιν, 132A), and less dangerous to the function of the reason. Slightly earlier, the speaker had warned about indigestion arising from meat eating and advised against eating it on those grounds (κράτιστον μὲν ἐθίσαι τὸ σῶμα μηδεμιᾶς προσδεῖσθαι σαρκοφαγίας, 131F). This is in no sense an endorsement of meat eating, as Tirelli seems to understand it, but rather a warning to those who cannot renounce their unhealthy carnivorous ways to keep their consumption of meat to a minimum. Plutarch here (131F) makes the point, repeated at *De esu carnium* 993D and *Bruta animalia ratione uti* 991C, that the earth produces its fruits in such abundance that the consumption of animal flesh is unnecessary and unjustifiable.[18]

The contradictions which critics have claimed to detect in Plutarch's statements on meat eating prove to be more apparent than real, if our analysis of these passages is correct, but critics are in any case correct in calling attention to the complexity involved in attempting to understand the positions taken and motivations involved in ancient vegetarian philosophy. Just as it is virtually impossible to determine who followed a vegetarian regimen even among those who appear to have advocated it in their writings, so it is equally challenging to ascertain the grounds on which those who advocated it did so. Plutarch's own motivations have been variously assessed, as one scholar has downplayed an argument that another has judged to be central to Plutarch's position, and has found his allegiance to abstention to lie in some other explanation altogether.

Some scholars of Plutarch's animal-related treatises have concluded, perhaps not unreasonably, that Plutarch's position on vegetarianism was developed under the influence of Pythagoreanism. Although, as we noted above,[19] the grounds for Pythagoras' abstention are not easy to determine from statements in ancient sources, he is widely considered to be the foremost advocate of vegetarianism in classical antiquity, and it is only logical to assume that later advocates of abstention were heavily influenced by Pythagorean doctrine. Already Haussleiter had declared an adherence to Pythagorean metempsychosis to have been the primary influence on Plutarch's own position.[20] Babut agreed with Haussleiter, citing De esu carnium 998C in defense of his view.[21] Brenk saw a similar fascination with Pythagorean palingenesis in Plutarch, and he detected in De esu carnium a "preoccupation with Dionysiac legend and reincarnation which is the basis of the vegetarianism in it."[22] The text of Plutarch seems, however, to belie this claim. In the opening sentence of De esu carnium, Plutarch dismisses Pythagoras out of hand, and says he would rather investigate what led man in the first place to put gory animal flesh into his mouth (ἀλλὰ σὺ μὲν ἐρωτᾷς τίνι λόγῳ Πυθαγόρας ἀπείχειτο σαρκοφαγίας, ἐγὼ δὲ θαυμάζω καὶ τίνι πάθει καὶ ποίᾳ ψυχῇ ὁ πρῶτος ἄνθρωπος ἥψατο φόνου στόματι, 993A). Later in the work, he notes in passing that both Pythagoras and Empedocles attempted to accustom humans to acting justly toward animals (997E), but he nowhere implies, there or elsewhere, that he had himself adopted their position on transmigration of souls. The passage upon which Babut based his assertion of Plutarch's allegiance to Pythagoreanism, De esu carnium 998C, does not bear out his claim. There, Plutarch states that unless someone were to prove that souls in the process of palingenesis employ common bodies, persons may not be expected to cease filling their bodies with disease and heaviness through meat eating (ἐὰν μὴ προσαποδείξῃ τις, ὅτι χρῶνται κοινοῖς αἱ ψυχαὶ σώμασιν ἐν ταῖς παλιγγενεσίαις . . . ταῦτ' οὐκ ἀποτρέψει . . . τὸ καὶ σώματι νόσους καὶ βαρύτητας ἐμποιοῦν, 998C). The implication here is that no one has yet proved this doctrine. Plutarch's most generous endorsement of Pythagoras is his following observation that, although the doctrine of transmigration of souls remains unproven, it should at least give us pause when contemplating mistreatment of animals (καίτοι τῆς λεγομένης ταῖς ψυχαῖς εἰς σώματα πάλιν μεταβολῆς εἰ μὴ πίστεως ἄξιον τὸ ἀποδεικνύμενον, ἀλλ' εὐλαβίας γε μεγάλης καὶ δέους τὸ ἀμφίβολον, 998D). There even surfaces in the text of Plutarch some doubt as to whether Pythagoras' ban on flesh extended to all sorts of animal foods.[23] One of the discussions in the *Quaestionum convivalium libri* asks whether the Pythagoreans did not in fact allow the consumption of some meat while demanding a more strict abstention from fish (μάλιστα τῶν ἰχθύων ἀπείχοντο, 728D). Such passages do not suggest that Plutarch was an enthusiastic follower of Pythagoras or that his own vegetarian philosophy owed much to his great predecessor.[24]

In a recent study of Plutarch's vegetarian philosophy, Montserrat Jufresa has emphasized what might be considered the hygienic or scientific side of his case for abstention, citing his argument (*De esu carnium* 994F–995A) that meat eating is against nature for human beings, whose dental anatomy does not allow them to tear animal flesh readily.[25] In addition, she calls attention to Plutarch's doubts about Pythagorean metempsychosis, and she likewise notes his concern that meat eating involves ethical problems for humans. Barigazzi had expressed a similar view that Plutarch largely discounted Pythagorean metempsychosis in formulating his position on abstention while making room for rational arguments, but he does not develop these observations in any detail.[26]

The most exhaustive modern analysis of Plutarch's vegetarian philosophy was published by Damianos Tsekourakis, who incidentally showed how contradictory ancient testimonies on Pythagoras' own rationale for abstention prove to be. He concludes that Pythagoras' concern for justice toward animals, to the extent that it figured at all in his system, arose as a corollary to his concern for the welfare of the human soul throughout its successive transformations, rather than from any direct sympathy for animals as suffering creatures.[27] He concludes that metempsychosis as a rationale for abstention held little attraction for Plutarch, and he underlines rather the effect of Plutarch's own humane sensibilities on his vegetarian stance, noting, "Being himself a man of charitable character he felt very sympathetic towards animals and also felt pity for them when they were mistreated."[28] Tsekourakis leans toward Jufresa's position, however, in concluding that, despite Plutarch's obvious interest in questions of justice toward animals, his primary motivation in advocating vegetarianism was a concern for human health. The belief that meat eating is dangerous to human health and actually unnatural to humans figured heavily in Plutarch's own philosophy, according to Tsekourakis, who cites Plutarch's observation that meat eating is contrary to nature (παρὰ φύσιν, *De esu carnium* 993E) and his claim (*De esu carnium* 994F–995A) that humans cannot readily digest animal flesh. He concludes that Plutarch's primary influences were the Academics with their relatively sympathetic attitudes toward animals, and the medical writers of Greece, along with physicians of his own day.[29]

In her Introduction to the recent edition and commentary on *De esu carnium* that she and Inglese produced, Giuseppina Santese concludes that Plutarch had no strong religious motivation for advocating abstention, in the manner of Pythagoras. She feels rather that he developed his own position as a sort of corollary to his strongly felt belief in the necessity for control and restraint in dealing with all human passions, not least in the case of control of the appetite. More than a concern for kindness toward animals was involved, in Santese's estimation.[30] She stresses the rational side of Plutarchan abstention, and points out how his desire to counter Stoic attitudes toward animals led him to advocate better treatment of animals in all respects.

This brief survey of recent scholarship on Plutarch's vegetarian philosophy allows us to draw several conclusions. It is obvious that scholars still do not agree on the grounds for his support for abstention, and that some critics doubt that he advocated abstention at all in his adulthood. In light of his numerous expressions of doubt and even mockery of the doctrine of metempsychosis, it seems safe to conclude that Plutarch was not attracted to abstention from any allegiance to Pythagoreanism. It is equally clear that he was conversant with every type of argument adduced in ancient philosophy in support of the vegetarian stance, even if some arguments figure less prominently in his writings. Tsekourakis and Santese at least draw attention to Plutarch's innate sympathy for animals as a contributing factor in his case for abstention from meat eating. Yet even their relatively elaborate discussions of Plutarch's vegetarian philosophy call little attention to the place of animals themselves in his arguments, perhaps from their realization that ancient vegetarianism remained, in the great majority of arguments in support of it, starkly anthropocentric. No modern critic has taken sufficient account of the part played in Plutarch's advocacy of abstention by his belief in the rationality and concomitant sentience of animals. Human consumption of animal flesh was in his view morally wrong because it destroyed creatures that shared the reason that distinguishes humankind and because it visits suffering upon creatures possessing the intellectual capacities that allow them to be cognizant of their own suffering. Plutarch's conviction that animals are to some degree rational led him to formulate, as part of his case for abstention, a series of arguments to which the assumption of rationality and sentience in animals is central and which figure now, in sophisticated formulations, in the case for the moral necessity of abstention from animal flesh that we encounter in modern animal rights literature. These arguments, found in embryonic form in Plutarch, include Peter Singer's Argument from Equality of Interests, elaborated in his groundbreaking treatise *Animal Liberation* in 1975, and Tom Regan's Harm as Deprivation Argument developed in his work *The Case for Animal Rights*, published in 1984. We had occasion earlier to call attention to the Plutarchan passages in which these anticipations are found because of their bearing on his case for according justice to animals, but their full significance emerges when we see that in them, Plutarch makes a clear connection between unjustifiable harm to animals and human dietary choices.[31]

The philosophical basis of Singer's Argument from Equality of Interests is the principle that no creature can be left out of the sphere of human moral concern if it can be shown that it has interests that humans should take into account in dealing with it. For centuries, humans have dismissed out of hand the possibility that non-human animals may have interests on the grounds that they are incapable of suffering in the manner that humans do, a position akin to Descartes' view that animals cannot suffer at all because they are senseless automata. While it may be true that a young animal cannot suffer from the knowledge that it will live only a few months before being slaughtered for food, it can, in Singer's view, suffer in other ways, as, for example, from electric shock or from confinement. Yet all signs that indicate suffering in humans, including grimacing, writhing, vocalizations, and attempts to avoid the source of pain, are observable in animals as well. Moreover, the nervous systems of animals react in the same ways to pain stimuli as do the nervous systems of humans, with fluctuations in blood pressure and dilation of the eyes in the same manner as is observable in humans. Singer's conclusion from these data is compelling, "If a being suffers there can be no moral justification for refusing to take that suffering into consideration. No matter what the nature of the being, the principle of equality requires that its suffering be counted equally with the like suffering – in so far as rough comparison can be made – of any other being."[32] Sentience, that is, in Singer's definition, the capacity to suffer, is in Singer's estimation "the only defensible boundary of concern for the interests of others."[33] Animals, as sentient creatures, have interests in the same way as do humans, and, as in the case of humans, animals have an interest in avoiding suffering. Like humans, other animals have an interest in being alive, and that interest is obviously violated when animals are slaughtered for food. Hence, for Singer, vegetarianism is a moral imperative for the person who wishes to live an ethical life.

Equally convinced that vegetarianism is incumbent upon all ethical humans, Tom Regan rejects the argument of those who maintain that neither animals themselves nor their interests would suffer if they could be killed painlessly for food. He argues, in contrast, that suffering is not the sole harm that humans can inflict upon animals, but that they can be harmed merely by being deprived of those preferences that animals would seek to exercise if given the opportunity, as, for example, the desire of a calf to play beside its mother. The central ideological component of this Harm as Deprivation Argument of Regan is the position that killing an animal for food necessarily robs it of the satisfaction of any future preference that it might seek to exercise. Obviously, death is the most profound deprivation that one being can visit upon another. "Once dead," Regan argues, "the individual who had preferences, who could find satisfaction in this or that, who could exercise preference autonomy, can do this no more. Death is the ultimate harm because it is the ultimate loss – the loss of life itself."[34] Toward the end of his treatise, Regan applies the Harm as Deprivation Argument to prove that vegetarianism is obligatory for human beings. Because animals may, in his view, be legitimately harmed by humans only when they pose harm to us or are used as innocent shields by humans who pose danger to other humans, it is morally unjustifiable to harm animals for food use inasmuch as animals have, in Regan's system, the right not to be harmed otherwise.[35] The counter-arguments of human carnivores as, for example, the claim that meat is tasty or convenient or even necessary to human nutrition, carry insufficient weight when set against the overriding right of animals not to be harmed, and since death is the ultimate harm, vegetarianism is obligatory for humans.

In *De esu carnium*, Plutarch confronts the reader with grueling scenes involving the torture and slaughter of animals destined for the human dinner table, in which the issues of animal sentience and the harm of depriving sentient animals of their lives take center stage. The most developed of these passages is that in which Plutarch pictures an animal at slaughter begging for justice (δικαιολογίας ἑκάστου λέγοντος, 994E). The animal is willing to be slain if its death will prevent humans from going hungry altogether, but he asks to be spared if his death provides merely a richer diet to humans. The wrong perpetrated here by humans is that, for the sake of a little meat, humans are content to deprive animals of the simple pleasures of their lives, the light of the sun and that space of life which are a kind of birthright to them (σαρκιδίου μικροῦ χάριν ἀφαιρούμεθα ψυχήν, ἡλίου φῶς, τὸν τοῦ βίου χρόνον, ἐφ᾽ ᾇ γέγονε καὶ πέφυκεν, 994E). Humans in the process ignore the fact that these beasts display remarkable intellectual gifts (περιττὸν ἐν συνέσει, 994E). At the core of Plutarch's argument here is the notion that what humans are visiting upon animals is wrong precisely because animals are sentient and understand their situation to some degree, and because in the process we unjustifiably *deprive* (ἀφαιρούμεθα) them of those simple pleasures to which they are by birth entitled, the issue that is central to Regan's Harm as Deprivation Argument.

The animal's indignant demand that it be sacrificed only if humans will otherwise go hungry remarkably foreshadows Regan's discussion of which animal after all, the human or the slaughtered food animal, will endure the greatest deprivation if the animal is sacrificed or spared, "We are not being asked to choose between eating and cooking with meat *or* harming ourselves by depriving ourselves of opportunities for the pleasure of the palate and the pride of having prepared good food well. And if *we* are not being asked *to harm ourselves* by depriving ourselves in these ways, then we cannot justify supporting those who harm animals because of any harm we would have to endure, as a result of loss of taste or culinary rewards, if we stopped supporting them."[36] Shortly before this scene, Plutarch had raised the point, also made by Regan, that humans do not eat predators, that is, those animals that seek to do harm to humans, but rather only defenseless beasts (τὰ δ᾽ ἀβλαβῆ καὶ χειροήθη καὶ ἄκεντρα καὶ νωδὰ πρὸς τὸ δακεῖν συλλαμβάνοντες ἀποκτιννύομεν, 994B). Already in the opening paragraph of *De esu carnium*, Plutarch had made the connection between animal sentience and the unendurable horror which a meat diet in humans entails when he asks indignantly how the first human carnivore was able to touch to his lips the gore from a dead animal (ἐγὼ δὲ θαυμάζω καὶ τίνι πάθει... ὁ πρῶτος ἄνθρωπος ἥψατο φόνου στόματι καὶ τεθνηκότος ζῴου χείλεσι προσήψατο σαρκός, 993B), devouring parts of an animal that had, precisely because the animal had sensed the horror that awaited it at slaughter, bellowed and cried moments ago (ἔμπροσθεν βρυχώμενα μέρη καὶ φθέγγοντα, 993B). Similarly, toward the end of the second treatise of *De esu carnium*, Plutarch asserts that every meal is expensive that costs a living creature its life, because each animal possesses some degree of sentience, intelligence and perception from nature (αἰσθήσεώς γε μετέχουσαν, ὄψεως ἀκοῆς, φαντασίας συνέσεως, . . . παρὰ τῆς φύσεως ἕκαστον εἴληχε, 997E). Plutarch's arguments here are distinguished from those of other ancient advocates of vegetarianism by their close focus upon and concern for the suffering of animals used for human consumption, and in this respect, he betrays an attitude toward the issue of human diet strikingly similar to that in evidence in the defenses of vegetarianism found in the works of modern animal rights advocates, including, as we have seen, those of Singer and Regan.

Toward the beginning of the second treatise of *De esu carnium*, in a passage that must resonate powerfully with animal advocates who decry the excesses of modern factory farming, Plutarch evokes yet another wrenching scene of mistreatment of food animals that appeals, at least by implication, to the concepts of animal sentience and the injustice of deprivation visited upon animals. Plutarch notes that humans thrust red hot irons down the throats of pigs to render their flesh more tender, and jump on the udders of pregnant sows, kicking them to mingle blood and milk in order to enable themselves to eat the most inflamed part of the poor beasts (ἵνα . . . φάγωσι τοῦ ζῴου τὸ μάλιστα φλεγμαῖνον, 997A).[37] Other humans sew up the eyes of cranes and swans, and lock them in darkness while fattening them for pâtés (ἄλλοι γεράνων ὄμματα καὶ κύκνων ἀπορράψαντες ἐν σκότει πιαίνουσιν, 997A). Plutarch offers here a stark example of how humans deprive animals of their birthright of the light of day for the sake of a bit of meat, and that a mere luxury. Such argumentation would be at home in current animal rights literature that condemns "agribusiness" that treats animals as "production units" rather than as sentient creatures, and is content to visit any horror upon them that will increase profits, including separation from their mothers at birth, confinement in darkness, and kicking and prodding of so-called "downers," animals so weakened by mistreatment that they cannot walk to slaughter on their own. Animals raised for human consumption in such conditions are regularly deprived of light in the belief that light stimulates aggression while darkness promotes a desirable passivity. In his work *Inhumane Society*, a powerful indictment of animal exploitation in all forms, veterinarian and animal advocate Michael W. Fox writes of modern "farms," "Rows of sows are housed indoors, often in semidarkness, on concrete slats without bedding."[38] Similarly, Matthew Scully, in words that recall Plutarch's description, has condemned the production of liver pâté, "all of it obtained by forcing a metal pipe down the ducks' throats and pumping pounds of food until their livers are grotesquely enlarged. . . ."[39]

One of the most remarkable aspects of Plutarch's defense of vegetarianism on grounds of animal sentience is his suspicion that animals are sufficiently sentient to appreciate the danger they face at the moment of slaughter and to attempt to communicate the level of their terror to their human tormentors. When his animal begs for consideration from its slaughterers, they ignore its squeals and shrieks (ἃς φθέγγεται καὶ διατρίζει φωνάς, *De esu carnium* 994E) that are inspired by terror and informed by some rational consciousness. Conversely, we recall that Lamprias, an interlocutor in Plutarch's collection of dinner conversations, the *Quaestionum convivalium libri*, had lamented that humans themselves felt shame at the pitiable cries that animals give forth at slaughter (σφάττοντες ἐδυσωποῦντο φωνὴν ἀφιέντα γοεράν, 669D). Scarcely any modern treatise advocating the rights of animals fails to include descriptions of the horrors of the last moments in the lives of animals facing slaughter. Recently, Matthew Scully has written of workers in an American slaughterhouse whose reaction to their own handiwork recalls the comment of Lamprias, "The electrocutors, stabbers, and carvers who work on the floor wear earplugs to muffle the screaming."[40] Many animals, he continues, must be forced to the electrical bolt or knives that will end their lives because their trembling and shaking renders them incapable of moving on their own. Even so, he notes, the animals fight what they see approaching. "At this point," Scully writes, "you'd almost expect that some mighty instinct would make them charge the throat slasher, the sooner to escape a world that never gave them anything but hurt, but they don't, they still want to live. . . ."[41] The language of Plutarch's depiction of the horrors felt by sentient creatures at the point of slaughter, unique in extant ancient literature relating to animals, eerily foreshadows Scully's glimpse of an industry which, excepting the increased sophistication of its methods, seems hardly to differ from Plutarch's vision of it.

Viewed in the context of his overarching goal of demonstrating that animals are rational and sentient, Plutarch's portrayal of the horrors visited upon food animals serves as a sobering reminder of the arguments he had made in developing his case for the necessity of justice toward animals. Just as he had maintained, against the Stoics, that humans are after all not without moral obligations toward non-human species, so his case for rationality in animals has as its corollary the position that using animals for food is morally unjustifiable because animals, as rational beings, share that *oikeiotês* with humans that Stoicism denied them. Using the technical terminology of the Stoics, as he often does, to controvert their stances, Plutarch maintains that humans will not attain the often-mentioned Stoic goal of living "in accord with nature" if they pursue a carnivorous lifestyle because meat eating is contrary to nature.[42] As in the treatise *De tuenda sanitate* Plutarch had condemned meat eating as a custom that reflected a sort of "nature against nature" (ἔθος τρόπον τινὰ φύσις τοῦ παρὰ φύσιν γέγονεν, 132A), so he on five occasions in *De esu carnium* labels meat eating "contrary to nature" (παρὰ φύσιν): those who first adopted a meat diet led a life παρὰ φύσιν (993D); even when the earth had difficulty supplying her own produce for human consumption, resorting to meat was παρὰ φύσιν (993E); devouring that which itself possesses animal life is παρὰ φύσιν (995B); meat eating is not only intrinsically παρὰ φύσιν for human beings, but it coarsens their souls (995E); humans care more about acts that are contrary to law than about those that, like violence to animals, are παρὰ φύσιν (996B).

The sorts of arguments that Plutarch adduces to prove that the eating of flesh is "contrary to nature" for human beings have been variously labeled hygienic, aesthetic, and even spiritual by students of Plutarch's vegetarian philosophy, as we have noted in our survey of recent scholarship on *De esu carnium.*[43] Unlike his unique anticipations of Singer's Argument from Equality of Interests and of Regan's Harm as Deprivation Argument, the sorts of arguments that Plutarch advances of a hygienic or aesthetic nature can be paralleled elsewhere in ancient defenses of abstention, and some of them still make an appearance in modern defenses of vegetarianism. In *De esu carnium*, Plutarch introduces his attack on meat eating based on hygienic and aesthetic considerations with the observation, in effect the mirror image of his repeated assertions that meat eating is "contrary to nature," that the very structure of the human body proves that the practice is "not in accord with nature" in the case of human beings (ὅτι γὰρ οὐκ ἔστιν ἀνθρώπῳ κατὰ φύσιν τὸ σαρκοφαγεῖν, πρῶτον μὲν ἀπὸ τῶν σωμάτων δηλοῦται τῆς κατασκευῆς, 994F), because humans do not possess the hooked talons, sharp teeth and claws characteristic of true carnivores. Nor can they easily digest a heavy meat diet (995A). Nature itself, he declares, argues against a carnivorous regimen in humans (ἡ φύσις . . . ἐξόμνυται τήν σαρκοφαγεῖν, 995A).[44] Humans cannot by nature tear the flesh that they consume, but require axes and knives (995A), and we cannot bear to eat dead animals without so altering them through cooking and spicing that our nature can finally accept what is foreign to it by being deceived by such alterations (ἵν' ἡ γεῦσις ἐξαπατηθεῖσα προσδέξηται τὸ ἀλλότριον, 995B).[45] Humans must, in a sense, predigest their meat by mixing it with oils and spices, as if preparing a corpse for burial (ὥσπερ ὄντως νέκρον ἐνταφιάζοντες, 995C), for only by thus softening it can mortals avoid indigestion and stomach pain. From such hygienic arguments Plutarch easily directs the reader's attention to the aesthetics of meat eating in an attempt to suggest that a carnivorous diet, besides being unnatural and difficult for a human being, is in itself disgusting and repulsive. At the outset of *De esu carnium* he expresses astonishment that the first human carnivores were able to bring themselves to touch their lips to a food that reeks from its own corruption (πῶς ἡ ὄσφρησις ἤνεγκε τὴν ἀποφοράν, 993B), and could bear to come into contact with pollution from the wounds of other creatures (πῶς τὴν γεῦσιν οὐκ ἀπέστρεψεν ὁ μολυσμὸς ἕλκων ψαύουσαν ἀλλοτρίων, 993B).

In the first book of his *De abstinentia*, Porphyry demonstrates that the sort of hygienic argument for abstention we have noted in Plutarch had been advanced as well by the Epicureans, a school that otherwise placed little value upon animals *per se* and agreed with the Stoics that they can lay claim to no covenant of justice with human beings.[46] The Epicureans, as Porphyry explains their position, opposed the eating of meat because not only does it fail to remove any troubles from the human constitution, but it actually provides only a sort of violent satisfaction mingled with its opposite (τό γε τῆς σαρκοφαγίας οὔτ᾽ ἔλυέν τι ὀχληρὸν τῆς φύσεως . . . τὴν δὲ χάριν βιαίαν εἶχεν καὶ ταχὺ τῷ ἐναντίῳ μιγνυμένην, De abstinentia I. 51). This is because meat does not intrinsically aid human health but rather impedes it (ἔτι δὲ οὐδὲ πρὸς ὑγείαν τὰ κρέα συντελεῖ, ἀλλὰ μᾶλλον τῇ ὑγείᾳ ἐμποδίζει, I. 52). Health, therefore, is guaranteed, in the estimation of the Epicureans, by a simple and meatless diet. Porphyry is correct in understanding that the Epicurean objection to meat eating arises from the school's doctrine that a simple regimen contributes to the release from disturbance that constitutes the happy life for the Epicurean, for, as they see it, nature requires few things toward its maintenance (ὧν καὶ χωρὶς οὐκ ἂν ὑπομένειεν, βραχέα παντάπασίν ἐστι, I. 51).

Slightly earlier, and apparently reflecting his own views, Porphyry had observed that no person intent upon living a long life would maintain that a meat diet is easy on the human digestion (δειξάτω τοίνυν ἡμῖν τις ἀνήρ, σπεύδων ἔνι μάλιστα ζῆν κατὰ νοῦν καὶ εὐπορότερα ἐκ τῶν κατὰ τὸ σῶμα παθῶν εἶναι . . . ὡς . . . ἡ κρεοφαγία . . . κουφοτέρα δὲ ἐν ταῖς πέμψεσιν τῆς ἑτέρας κἂν ταῖς ἀναδόσεσιν ταῖς εἰς τὸ σῶμα ταχυτέρα τῆς ἐκ λαχάνων ἀναδόσεως, I. 46). Still, although he here cites the hygienic perils of meat eating and quotes Epicurean views on the matter at length, Porphyry's central objection to a meat diet is the damage it does, in his thinking as a Neoplatonist, to the welfare of the human soul, a type of argument made with particular frequency in ancient cases for abstention and more than once mentioned in Plutarch, who, as we have seen, at the same time agrees with the Epicureans on the dangers of a meat diet to the physical body.

The concept of human "health" understood as a spiritual metaphor rather than as a literal function of bodily digestion, as it appears both in the Epicureans and in the passages from Plutarch discussed above, can be traced already in the doctrines of Pythagoras. As Tsekourakis has remarked, "We have seen so far that, according to Pythagoras and the early Pythagoreans, the motives for abstinence from animal flesh were mystical and religious."[47] Again, Porphyry is a helpful source on earlier Greek views on abstention. He informs us that Pythagoras believed that no man concerned with piety would sacrifice any living thing to the gods (οἶδεν δὲ ὁ τῆς εὐσεβείας φροντίζων ὡς θεοῖς μὲν οὐ θύεται ἔμψυχον οὐδέν, De abstinentia II. 36). Along similar lines, Porphyry recalls (III. 27) that Pythagoras had taught that no man who wishes to become godlike will harm either human beings or other animals, sparing even plants to the extent possible. Porphyry develops Pythagoras' injunctions here to conclude that the just man, through practice of bodily control, which includes abstention from animal food, will improve his inner goodness, which consists of his likeness to the divinity (αὔξεται γὰρ τῇ τούτου παιδαγωγίᾳ καὶ ἐγκρατείᾳ τὸ ἐντὸς ἀγαθόν, τοῦτ᾽ ἔστιν ἡ πρὸς θεὸν ὁμοίωσις, III. 26).

98

Although, as we argued above,[48] the text of Plutarch does not appear to bear out the claim of some recent critics that he was substantively influenced by Pythagorean doctrines in the formulation of his own case for abstention, he is not willing to reject any argument that might lend support to his own case, acknowledging that, even if the theory of transmigration of souls has not yet been proven, enough doubt still remains on the issue that we should be cautious in undertaking to mistreat animals (*De esu carnium* 998D). In a previous paragraph, Plutarch had apparently cited several verses from Empedocles, now missing from Plutarch's text, that had maintained that the eating of animals constitutes cannibalism because human souls are imprisoned in mortal bodies as a punishment for murder (996B), an idea somewhat reflective of Pythagorean transmigration of souls. He similarly argues that the consumption of flesh renders human souls dull from fullness and surfeit (αἱ κρεοφαγίαι . . . τὰς ψυχὰς ὑπὸ πλησμονῆς καὶ κόρου παχύνουσιν, *De esu carnium* 995E). When the human body is glutted with food improper to it, the light of the soul is necessarily dulled and confused (οὕτω δὴ καὶ διὰ σώματος θολεροῦ καὶ διακόρου καὶ βαρυνομένου τροφαῖς ἀσυμφύλοις πᾶσ᾽ ἀνάγκη τὸ γάνωμα τῆς ψυχῆς καὶ τὸ φέγγος ἀμβλύτητα καὶ σύγχυσιν ἔχειν, 995E–F). In this line of argument, not otherwise prominent in Plutarch's defense of abstention, he seems to have taken a hint from Plato's doctrine of the necessity for liberation from the bonds and demands of the body toward achieving spiritual advancement.[49] He mentions Pythagoras and Empedocles together in an approving manner when he reminds the reader that both had recommended a meat-free diet on the belief that kindness toward animals will lead to kindness toward humans, whether or not we accept the notion that animals may contain the spirits of humans, and in so doing they both sought to encourage us to act justly toward other species (Πυθαγόρας καὶ Ἐμπεδοκλῆς ἐθίζοντες εἶναι καὶ πρὸς τὰ ἀλλογενῆ δικαίους, 997E). Plutarch here attributes to his predecessors a line of argument that would in later ages come to be known as an indirect duty view of human obligation toward non-human species, according to which animals are judged to have value only in so far as what happens to them has an impact on human interests. To mistreat animals might encourage us to mistreat humans and, conversely, to treat animals kindly might encourage us to treat other humans kindly.[50]

Regrettably, the text of the second treatise of *De esu carnium* breaks off at the point at which Plutarch seems to have been about to take up the question of the connection between dietary choices and human justice, an issue at least touched upon earlier in the two treatises and implicit in the discussion of Pythagoras and Empedocles cited above. The topic of justice is rather formally introduced at this point, as if Plutarch wishes us to understand that a new phase in his argument is being taken up (Οὐ μὴν ἀλλὰ καὶ τοῦτ᾽ ἤδη σκεψώμεθα, τὸ μηδὲν εἶναι πρὸς τὰ ζῷα δίκαιον ἡμῖν, 999B). Perhaps he wished to indicate that the arguments from hygienic, aesthetic and spiritual welfare that he had borrowed from his predecessors are being set aside now as he undertook, in the latter pages of *De esu carnium*, to forge a still stronger link between his case for justice toward non-human species and the sort of arguments for rationality and sentience in animals that are developed at length in *De sollertia animalium* and are applied to the question of human dietary choices in *De esu carnium*, in a manner that, as we have argued earlier in this chapter, strikingly anticipates arguments found in modern treatises of animal rights and, in its focus on ethical considerations, constitutes Plutarch's most significant contribution to the historical development of vegetarian philosophy. While the mutilated state of the second treatise of *De esu carnium* makes it impossible to know how Plutarch's argument would have developed, we can in any case draw some conclusions from his statements heretofore in that treatise, which can be supplemented with statements drawn from other treatises in the *Moralia*, as to what sort of moral action the choice of a vegetarian lifestyle constitutes in Plutarch's animal philosophy.

In *The Philosophy of Vegetarianism*, his historical survey of ancient philosophical attitudes toward abstention, Daniel Dombrowski identifies four types of moral actions that philosophers are wont to distinguish: some actions are morally neutral and consequently allowable; some others are morally wrong and impermissible; still others are actions that we ought to perform; and the remaining actions are above and beyond the call of duty. These latter praiseworthy actions are called supererogatory.[51] Dombrowski concludes his volume with a discussion of how vegetarianism is classified with respect to its proper status as a moral action in the thought of several contemporary moral philosophers, and he touches upon the question of how abstention would be classified in ancient authors, including Plutarch, without, however, including any citations from the text of Plutarch in support of his observations. We noted earlier in this chapter that both Singer and Regan judge abstention to be incumbent upon all persons because of certain qualities that animals possess by nature. Singer argues that animals are entitled to equal consideration of their interests with those of other beings who are sentient and can suffer, while Regan maintains that creatures who are subjects of a life entailing preferences have a natural right not to be harmed.[52] For some philosophers, including Singer, the issue of animal sentience and mentation matters more than it does for some others, including Regan, but both would agree that, since abstention is morally incumbent upon all human beings, it cannot be classified as supererogatory.

Plutarch's position on the moral value of abstention is in one sense more firmly grounded in the realities of life in his own age than the positions of Singer and Regan reflect the realities of life in the twenty-first century, since Plutarch recognizes that the vast majority of human beings will never be convinced to adopt a vegetarian lifestyle, while the ethically minded individual may be judged to be bound to do so. Plutarch would agree with Singer and Regan that vegetarianism is a lifestyle that is incumbent upon the philosopher, but he considers it supererogatory for the majority of human beings. He clearly articulates this position in a number of his pronouncements on meat eating in the treatises of the *Moralia*. In *De tuenda sanitate praecepta*, Plutarch had reluctantly concluded that since the consumption of meat has become for humans a sort of unnatural second nature (τὸ ἔθος τρόπον τινὰ φύσις τοῦ παρὰ φύσιν γέγονεν, 132A), it can be countenanced, if only as a support to the diet (ὑπέρεισμα καὶ διάζωμα τῆς τροφῆς, 132A), while the greater part of the human diet must consist of foods more in accord with nature (ἃ καὶ τῷ σώματι μᾶλλόν ἐστι κατὰ φύσιν, 132A). In one of the discussions included in the *Quaestionum convivalium libri*, Plutarch remarks, in his own person, that while necessity introduced the custom of meat eating, the pleasure that it entails now makes the practice difficult to eradicate (διὸ τῆς ἀνάγκης ἐπαγούσης τὸ πρῶτον, ἤδη καὶ δι' ἡδονὴν ἔργον ἐστὶν παῦσαι τὴν σαρκοφαγίαν, 730A). In the *Septem sapientium convivium*, Plutarch portrays the wise Solon arguing that all human nourishment entails by its nature some injustice because it involves the taking of life, be that animal or plant life, and since no man can exercise complete justice in the matter of diet except by total abstention from food, the next best solution is to cease to crave superfluous foods and to live on the simplest foods, since the desire for unnecessary things quickly becomes a habit (ὁ γὰρ τῶν περιττῶν ζῆλος εὐθὺς ἀκολουθεῖ καὶ συνοικίζεται τῇ χρείᾳ τῶν ἀναγκαίων, *Septem sapientium convivium* 159E). Plutarch's most telling pronouncement on the lamentable effects of "custom" on human diet is found at the beginning of the second treatise of *De esu carnium*, where he maintains that if humans cannot after all be free of error in their dietary choices because of their familiarity with meat eating, they should resort to flesh only with a sense of the shamefulness of the act, and only out of hunger and not from a desire for luxury (οὐ μὴν ἀλλ' εἰ καὶ ἀδύνατον ἤδη διὰ τὴν συνήθειαν τὸ ἀναμάρτητον, αἰσχυνόμενοι τῷ ἁμαρτάνοντι χρησόμεθα διὰ τὸν λόγον, ἐδόμεθα σάρκας, ἀλλὰ πεινῶντες οὐ τρυφῶντες, 996E–F).

Plutarch supplies an "out" for those humans who cannot break free from the bounds of convention, counseling them to wean themselves from their carnivorous ways to the extent possible while acknowledging that, for the mass of humanity, adoption of a meat-free diet is unlikely. For most humans, vegetarianism must be classed as a supererogatory ethical action. Plutarch realized, as do at least some modern advocates of abstention, that individuals who eat meat from birth are not likely to heed the call to a higher ethic. The texts of Plutarch which we have cited above serve to bear out Dombrowski's tentative pronouncement, which he does not support with citations, on Plutarch's position, "Both Porphyry and Regan (perhaps also Plutarch) imply that vegetarianism is a duty for philosophers, but supererogatory for the multitude."[53] Despite his grudging approval of Plutarch's apparent position, Dombrowski faults both Plutarch and his successor Porphyry for countenancing what amounts to a two-tiered position on the ethical value of abstention, charging, "The problem with this dichotomy is not that it expects too much from the philosopher, but that it expects too little from the multitude."[54] In raising this objection, Dombrowski fails to take into account that Plutarch had developed a case for vegetarianism that depends upon arguments for rationality and sentience in animals, and in so doing had advanced a case that not even most ancient philosophers would accept. Throughout his animal treatises, and in passages in other works that make casual mention of animals, Plutarch has provided arguments intended to convince the person of developed ethical convictions that vegetarianism is a matter of justice and an aspect of the moderate lifestyle to which the thoughtful person should aspire.

There are indications, in the final extant paragraph of the second treatise of *De esu carnium*, that Plutarch was about to take up this very issue of the necessity for abstention in the true philosopher, and the arguments he would raise, and the opponents he would single out, are ones familiar to readers of the animal treatises. While, as we have seen, he does not embrace with enthusiasm their doctrine of metempsychosis, Plutarch still reminds the reader that both Pythagoras and Empedocles enjoined us to act justly toward other living creatures (997E). Even if we cannot accept their notion that an animal may be the current home of our parent, child or friend, we can at least be sure that animals possess some degree of perception, sight, hearing, imagination and intelligence which enable them to seek what is akin to them and avoid that which is alien, a power that an animal receives from nature itself (ἀλλ᾽ αἰσθήσεώς γε μετέχουσαν, ὄψεως ἀκοῆς, φαντασίας συνέσεως, ἣν ἐπὶ κτήσει τοῦ οἰκείου καὶ φυγῇ τοῦ ἀλλοτρίου παρὰ τῆς φύσεως ἕκαστον εἴληχε, 997E). In the final sentences of the treatise, his old nemesis, the Stoics, are one last time singled out for attack as his discussion of justice toward animals intersects with his discussion of the mental faculties of animals. The Stoics, he reminds us, maintain that we have no kinship with irrational creatures (ναί, φησιν, οὐδὲν γὰρ ἡμῖν πρὸς τὰ ἄλογα οἰκεῖον ἔστιν, 999A). One last time, the issue of kinship (*oikeiotês*) is raised. Yet in his mention of Pythagoras and Empedocles, Plutarch had just reiterated his conviction that an animal "shares" (μετέχουσαν) with us those mental faculties that make it incumbent upon us to take its interests into consideration. In the last pages of *De esu carnium*, Plutarch employs the same term, "share," that he had used in the first pages of *De sollertia animalium* when he had initially taken up the issue of our mental kinship with other species, a position that he would argue at length in that treatise. In that initial discussion, Autobulus had reminded his fellow discussants that he had proposed the idea that all animals "share" in reason and understanding (ἀποφηνάμενοι γὰρ ἐχθές, ὡς οἶσθα, μετέχειν ἁμωσγέπως πάντα τὰ ζῷα διανοίας καὶ λογισμοῦ, 960A). Proving that humans and other animal species share in sentience and reason had been the central goal of Plutarch's animal philosophy, and he would have wished that the true philosopher, the true lover of wisdom, would take account of that kinship in all the actions of his own life, including compassionate choices in diet. For the human being who accepts Plutarch's position that we are, along with animals, part of a community of consciousness, sparing the lives of our partners in thought and feeling is not a heroic action, but merely the rational thing to do.

102

7

CONCLUSION

or human social convention.

There are moments when you do not need doctrines, when even rights become irrelevant, when life demands some basic response of fellow-feeling and mercy and love.

> Matthew Scully, *Dominion: The Power of Man,*
> *the Suffering of Animals, and the Call to Mercy*

In the opening pages of his work *Animal Revolution: Changing Attitudes towards Speciesism*, Richard D. Ryder gives a brief history of the animal rights movement in Britain, a movement which he describes as spearheaded to a remarkable degree by professional philosophers like himself. His characterization of the central intellectual tenets guiding that movement deserves to be quoted in full:

> Our moral argument is that species is not a valid criterion for cruel discrimination. Like race or sex, species denotes some physical and other differences but in no way does it nullify the great similarity among all sentients – our capacity for suffering. Where it is wrong to inflict pain upon a human animal it is probably wrong to do so to a nonhuman sentient. The actual killing of a nonhuman animal may also be wrong if it causes suffering or, more contentiously, if it deprives the nonhuman of future pleasures. The logic is very simple.[1]

In the chapters of this book, I have attempted to show that not a single idea in Ryder's manifesto of the modern animal rights movement as it relates to the moral stance which humans must adopt toward other animal species fails to appear in Plutarch's animal philosophy, in some cases apparently uniquely in Plutarch among extant ancient texts. He certainly stands alone in advocating, as Ryder seems to here, a style of argument in which an appeal to the mind and an appeal to the heart are not to be viewed as incompatible. For this reason, I have adopted a manner of presentation in which ancient texts and modern texts interweave in a kind of dialogue which suggests a level of continuity between ancient and modern thought usually denied or ignored by investigators who chart the troubled history of man's treatment of other species. While I have nowhere suggested that Plutarch was an animal rights advocate in any modern sense of the term, or that his work exercised any influence on the complex modern formulations of the arguments that he sets forth, I have sought to demonstrate that a number of the central arguments developed by animal rights philosophers relating to intellect and sentience in non-human animals and to the part such considerations play in conditioning human ethical responses toward other animals, are at least adumbrated in Plutarch, and that his philosophical stance is based upon the conviction, again prominent in the work of modern animal rightists, that the points of likeness which other species share with human beings carry infinitely greater ethical weight than does any point of unlikeness that may separate them. For Plutarch, the intellectual faculties of humans and of other species differ in quantity rather than in quality.

Animals, in Plutarch's philosophy, do not merit human moral consideration any less because their intellectual faculties are not so highly developed as are those of human beings, but must be included in the purview of human morality because they share these faculties if only to a slight degree: all sentient creatures, he maintains, are fit objects of human moral concern. Some modern animal rights theorists have suggested that it is precisely because other species have less highly developed intellectual capacities that humans have a special debt to them. Philosopher Stephen R. L. Clark expresses this principle eloquently when he argues that, even if other species cannot reason so effectively as can humans or have fewer desires or less sophisticated interests than do humans, still, "it does not follow that animals deserve no respect at all – those that are weak deserve our especial care."[2] Plutarch would agree.

NOTES

1 INTRODUCTION

1 Richard Sorabji, *Animal Minds and Human Morals: The Origins of the Western Debate* (Ithaca: Cornell University Press, 1993).

2 Sorabji 208–219.

3 For example, Sorabji notes, 52, that Plutarch challenged the Stoic downplaying of animal accomplishments. Exceptionally, he does allow, 125, of Plutarch's claim that humans may owe benevolence to animals, "I have not found this argument anywhere else." At the same time, more typical is the fact that, while he acknowledges, 176, that anticipations of the so-called "harm as deprivation argument" observable in modern animal literature are traceable in such writers as Theophrastus, he does not note that it can be seen as well in Plutarch; see Stephen T. Newmyer, "Plutarch on the Moral Grounds for Vegetarianism," *Classical Outlook* 72, 2 (1995) 41–43, for Plutarch's anticipation of this modern argument.

4 Sorabji 156–157. Porphyry, *De abstinentia* III. 20–24 is lifted wholesale, with slight verbal changes, from Plutarch, *De sollertia animalium* 959E–963F.

5 C. J. Giankaris, *Plutarch* (New York: Twayne, 1970) 119–122.

6 D. A. Russell, *Plutarch* (London: Duckworth, 1972) 13–14. Similarly, Robert Lamberton, *Plutarch* (New Haven: Yale University Press, 2001) 188 makes the tantalizing comment, without further elaboration, that a number of themes that would have an "unexpected afterlife" appear for the first time in Plutarch, among which he numbers "philosophical vegetarianism and animal rights."

7 Francesco Becchi, "Istinto e Intelligenza negli Scritti Zoopsicologici di Plutarco," in *Scritti in Memoria di Dino Pieraccioni*, ed. Michele Bandini and Federico G. Pericoli (Florence: Istituto Papirologico G. Vitelli, 1993) 60, "Gli scritti sulla psicologia animale sono tra quelli che hanno sinora riscosso un interesse assai limitato da parte della critica . . ."

8 Becchi, "Istinto e Intelligenza" 81–82.

9 A notable exception is the famous passage in *Cato Maior* (339A–B) on the proper treatment of worn-out slaves and farm animals. For a discussion of the relation of this passage to Plutarch's thought on animals, see Stephen T. Newmyer, "Plutarch on the Treatment of Animals: The Argument from Marginal Cases," *Between the Species* 12 (1996) 43. In the opening paragraph of his life of Pericles (152B–C), Plutarch mentions, without editorial comment, that Augustus Caesar chastised foreign visitors to Rome for lavishing a degree of affectionate attention upon pets that should belong only to fellow-humans. More distinctly negative is his comment, in his life of Solon (81F–82A), that men have been plunged into excessive grief at the death of horses or dogs, while others have borne the death of

sons without unacceptable levels of grief. These latter comments may be taken rather as reflections on weakness in human conduct than as negative reflections on the intrinsic value of animal life.

10 *De sollertia animalium* 960A, 962B, and 985C. Presumably, the treatise entitled εἰ λόγον ἔχει τὰ ζῷα, listed as number 135 in the so-called Catalogue of Lamprias of Plutarch's works that is attributed to a son of Plutarch by that name, who is in fact not historically attested, would have dealt with the question of the intellectual capacities of animals. The loss of this treatise is much to be lamented by students of Plutarch's animal psychology.

11 For a recent discussion of this treatise, see Stephen T. Newmyer, "Of Pigs and People: Plutarch and the French Beast Fable," *Ploutarchos* 13, 1 (1996) 15–22.

12 See Stephen T. Newmyer, "Plutarch on the Moral Grounds for Vegetarianism," *Classical Outlook* 72 (1995) 41–43.

13 *De amore prolis* 493F–494A.

14 Especially noteworthy are Adelmo Barigazzi, "Implicanze Morali nella Polemica Plutarchea sulla Psicologia degli Animali," in *Plutarco e le Scienze*, ed. Italo Gallo (Genoa: Sagep Editrice, 1992) 297–315; Giovanni Indelli, "Plutarco, *Bruta Animalia Ratione Uti*: Qualche Reflessione," in Gallo, *Plutarco e le Scienze* 317–352; Becchi, "Istinto e Intelligenza" and "Irrazionalità e Razionalità degli Animali," *Prometheus* 26 (2000) 205–225; Giuseppina Santese, "Animali e Razionalità in Plutarco," in *Filosofi e Animali nel Mondo Antico*, ed. S. Castignone and G. Lanata (Pisa: Edizioni ETS, 1994) 141–170; Giovanni Indelli, ed. and trans., *Plutarco: Le Bestie Sono Esseri Razionali* (Corpus Plutarchi Moralium 22) (Naples: D'Auria, 1995); and Lionello Inglese and Giuseppina Santese, ed. and trans., *Plutarco: Il Cibarsi di Carne* (Corpus Plutarchi Moralium 31) (Naples: D'Auria, 1999).

15 Sorabji 156–157. In contrast, some contemporary writers on ancient attitudes toward environmental issues see parallels to modern thought in almost every ancient pronouncement on the natural world. It is certainly an exaggeration to maintain, for example, as does J. Donald Hughes, *Pan's Travail: Environmental Problems of the Ancient Greeks and Romans* (Baltimore: Johns Hopkins University Press, 1994) 110, "An ancient animal rights movement, if so one may term it, existed among writers, mostly of Pythagorean bent, who honored the sanctity of all forms of life and maintained that animals possess rational souls," or, 111, that Plutarch was "an early defender of animal rights."

16 I use the term "animal" in this volume to refer to non-human animals, the sense in which the word is generally understood. Some philosophers of the animal rights movement object to the use of the word because of the negative connotations of beastliness and savagery that the word has taken on. Richard D. Ryder, for example, is troubled by this semantic difficulty when he observes, *Animal Revolution: Changing Attitudes towards Speciesism* (Oxford: Blackwell, 1989) 2, "Using the word 'animal' in opposition to the word 'human' is clearly an expression of prejudice." One need hardly note the connotations of the common designation "dumb animals."

17 On the term "ethology," zoologist Frans deWaal, *Good Natured: The Origins of Right and Wrong in Humans and Other Animals* (Cambridge, Mass.: Harvard University Press, 1996) 35, observes, "When ethology later reached Great Britain, the term gained its current status in Webster's as 'the scientific study of the characteristic behavior patterns of animals' (although most ethologists would probably change 'scientific' to 'naturalistic')." That is to say, ethology is currently understood as the study of animal behavior in nature rather than in the context of controlled laboratory experiments. An important and controversial branch of the science is that termed cognitive ethology, whose adherents seek to investigate

whether animals have conscious mental experiences. Philosopher David DeGrazia, *Taking Animals Seriously: Mental Life and Moral Status* (Cambridge: Cambridge University Press, 1997) 85, defines cognitive ethology as that branch which investigates the cognitive states and processes which animals may possess, including beliefs, desires and such affective states as fear, pain and distress.

18 It is instructive to observe that, while many of these horrors would have been unfamiliar to classical antiquity, Plutarch does note, *De esu carnium* 997A, the existence of such practices as fattening food animals in the dark, thrusting hot irons into the throats of pigs to render their flesh more tender, and jumping on the udders of pregnant sows and kicking them to blend their milk with their blood, horrific actions that bear disturbing similarities to the practices of modern intensive factory farming; see, for example, Jim Mason and Peter Singer, *Animal Factories* (New York: Harmony Books, 1990) and Michael W. Fox, *Inhumane Society: The American Way of Exploiting Animals* (New York: St. Martin's Press, 1990) 24–46.

19 There are noteworthy exceptions to this statement. Daniel A. Dombrowski, in his book *The Philosophy of Vegetarianism* (Amherst: University of Massachusetts Press, 1984), uses the insights of ancient defenders and opponents of the vegetarian lifestyle to throw light on the current status of the argument among philosophers. Of those who erroneously consider the philosophical defense of vegetarianism to be an exclusively modern position, Dombrowski notes, 2, "Those with the most occlusive blinders think that the issues surrounding this idea were created *ex nihilo*, or perhaps out of the environmental movement of the 1960s." While Dombrowski concerns himself in this book exclusively with the question of vegetarianism, his appreciation of the classical precedents of contemporary arguments is illuminating and refreshing. Dombrowski has himself taken some hints from the work of philosopher Stephen R. L. Clark, who claims, *The Moral Status of Animals* (Oxford: Clarendon Press, 1977) 4–5, that his own position owes something to the Aristotelian, Sceptic and Neoplatonist traditions, with an admixture of Buddhism. Andrew Linzey, in such works as *Animal Theology* (Urbana: University of Illinois Press, 1995), discusses ancient Christian notions of the moral status of animals.

20 Ryder 2.

21 Ryder 23.

22 Ryder 3. Some contemporary philosophers contend that a concern for the potential rights of animals is misguided when the rights of human beings are not universally acknowledged. Peter Carruthers, a vocal opponent of animal rights, remarks, *The Animals Issue: Moral Theory in Practice* (Cambridge: Cambridge University Press, 1992), xi–xii, "Just as Nero fiddled while Rome burned, many in the West agonise over the fate of seal pups and cormorants while human beings elsewhere starve or are enslaved. . . . The philosophical gurus of the animal rights movement have managed to seize the high moral ground, charging those who oppose them with inconsistency or morally arbitrary speciesism."

23 This phrase is found in Charles R. Magel, *Keyguide to Information Sources in Animal Rights* (Jefferson, NC: McFarland, 1989) 103.

24 Peter Singer, *Animal Liberation: A New Ethics for Our Treatment of Animals* (New York: Avon, 1975) 1, 200. These observations reappear unchanged in the revised edition of Singer's book (New York: Avon, 1990) 1, 193.

25 Henry S. Salt, *Animals' Rights Considered in Relation to Social Progress* (Clarks Summit, Pa.: Society for Animal Rights, 1980; reprint of the edition of 1892) vii.

26 Ryder 5. See Brigid Brophy, "The Rights of Animals," *Sunday Times*, October 10, 1965; reprinted in Brigid Brophy, *Don't Never Forget: Collected Views and Reviews* (New York: Holt, Rinehart and Winston, 1966) 15–21.

27 Brophy, *Don't Never Forget* 16.

28 Ryder 3. The "welfarist" stance holds that animals should be treated humanely and spared unnecessary suffering, while the "animal rightist" stance maintains that animals are like humans in having inherent value that humans must respect. Rightists assert that animals cannot be the property of humans and cannot be experimented on or eaten because such activities violate the obligation of justice that humans owe to animals. The tensions between the two positions in the United States is well delineated in Gary L. Francione, *Rain without Thunder: The Ideology of the Animal Rights Movement* (Philadelphia: Temple University Press, 1996).

29 DeGrazia 2.

30 See, for example, Max Schuster, *Untersuchungen zu Plutarchs Dialog De Sollertia Animalium, mit besonderer Berücksichtigung der Lehrtätigkeit Plutarchs* (Dissertation: Munich) (Augsburg: Hammer, 1917) 76, "Wir haben Grund anzunehmen, dass die Polemik, die im ersten Teile unseres Dialoges sehr stark zum Durchbruch kommt, sich in der Hauptsache gegen die Stoa der älteren Zeit wendet." The classic study of Plutarch's reaction to Stoicism remains that of Daniel Babut, *Plutarque et le Stoïcisme* (Paris: Presses Universitaires de France, 1969). On Plutarch's views of Stoic notions about animals, see Babut 54–65. Some recent scholars have contended that the anti-Stoic polemic of Plutarch's animal treatises has been overemphasized as a motivating factor in his pronouncements on animals. See, for example, the edition of *Bruta animalia ratione uti* by Giovanni Indelli, *Plutarco: Le Bestie Sono Esseri Razionali*, introduzione, testo critico, traduzione e commento a cura di Giovanni Indelli (Naples: D'Auria, 1995) 21, where Indelli asserts that the little work is not directed against any specific philosophical school but is rather intended to give Plutarch's own ideas on animals in a manner more charming and less arid than would be possible in a standard treatise. Jackson P. Hershbell, "Plutarch and Stoicism," *Aufstieg und Niedergang der römischen Welt* II, 36, 5 (1992) 3336–3352, reexamines the issue of Plutarch's stance toward the school and concludes that he probably studied at least Chrysippus, the Stoic most frequently cited in Plutarch's corpus, and may have prepared notebooks (ὑπομνήματα) from his readings for citations in his own works. He feels that Plutarch was less likely to have read Cleanthes since he never refers to specific works of his. Hershbell believes that Plutarch was consistently anti-Stoic in his philosophical outlook, but that it is difficult to estimate how fair he was in representing the ideas of the school.

31 R. H. Barrow, *Plutarch and His Times* (London: Chatto and Windus, 1967) 74. Almost a century ago, Schuster had branded Plutarch a thinker satisfied to look backward and to nourish himself on earlier times. His final assessment is damning, 65, "Auch Plutarch war nur ein Hüter, kein Mehrer alter Schätze."

32 *De sanitate tuenda* 132A.

33 Juan Francisco Martos Montiel, "*Sophrosyne o Akrasía*: Los Animales como Modelo de Comportamiento en los *Moralia* de Plutarco," in *Estudios sobre Plutarco: Aspectos Formales*, ed. José Antonio Fernández Delgado and Francisca Pordomingo Pardo (Madrid: Ediciones Clásicas, 1996) 205–210.

34 *De fortuna* 98C; *De fraterno amore* 478E.

35 For recent attempts to reconcile Plutarch's self-contradictions, see, for example, Jorge Bergua Cavero, "Cinismo, Ironía y Retorica en el *Bruta Ratione Uti* de Plutarco," in *Estudios sobre Plutarco: Paisaje y Naturaleza*, ed. José García López and Esteban Calderón Dorda (Madrid: Ediciones Clásicas, 1991) 13–19; Santese, "Animali e Razionalità in Plutarco" 165–168 and her Introduction to Inglese and Santese, *Plutarco: Il Cibarsi di Carne* 8, 50–51 and 59–61; and Becchi,

"Irrazionalità" 208–225. See Chapter 2, p. 39 and note 109, for Becchi's argument that Plutarch does not in fact argue against rationality in animals in *De amore prolis*.

36 Adolf Dyroff, *Die Tierpsychologie des Plutarchos von Chaironeia* (Würzburg: Bonitas-Bauer, 1897) 56. Dyroff complains here that Plutarch does not adequately distinguish between the technical meanings of σύνεσις, φρόνησις and διανόησις as these pertain to the psychology of animals.

37 Dyroff, 55, chastises Plutarch for misrepresenting Stoic technical terms and ideas like λογικός, although he declares him in general clever at attacking the Stoics using their own weapons. More recently, Barrow, 103, has charged that Plutarch's greatest shortcoming as a thinker was his failure to understand Stoicism, maintaining that Plutarch was too literal-minded and not subtle enough to grasp the system totally.

38 Philosophers who seek to accord moral status to animals remain highly sensitive to charges of anthropomorphism, as can be seen, for example, in DeGrazia's meticulous investigation of evidence for the mental capacities of animals, *Taking Animals Seriously* 75–210. Ethologist Alexander F. Skutch, *The Minds of Birds* (College Station: Texas A&M University Press, 1996) xvi, offers an intriguing formulation of an ethologist's dread of these charges, "In my student days, anthropomorphism was one of the most flagrant of scientific heresies, only a little less heinous than the unforgivable sin of falsifying one's observations or data." Donald R. Griffin, an expert in animal cognition, provides a useful rejoinder to such charges in his work *Animal Minds* (Chicago: University of Chicago Press, 1992) 24, "When one carefully examines such charges of anthropomorphism, it turns out that they entail the implicit assumption that whatever it is suggested the animal might do, or think, really *is* a uniquely human attribute. Such an assumption begs the question being asked because it presupposes a negative answer and is thus literally a confession of prejudgment or prejudice." The problem of anthropomorphism and animals is studied in the essays included in Robert W. Mitchell, Nicholas S. Thompson and H. Lyn Miles, ed. *Anthropomorphism, Anecdotes, and Animals* (Albany: State University of New York Press, 1997). The recognition of the tendency toward anthropomorphism in Plutarch's animal treatises dates back to Dyroff, *Die Tierpsychologie des Plutarchos*, who observes, 46, that it is extremely characteristic of ancient psychological research to humanize animal behaviors. He finds examples of such argumentation in Plutarch to be "überall zahlreich" (48).

39 Sherwood Owen Dickerman, "Some Stock Illustrations of Animal Intelligence in Greek Psychology," *Transactions and Proceedings of the American Philological Association* 42 (1911) 123–130. A few recent scholars, however, have been more willing to countenance the belief that some of Plutarch's pronouncements on animals may be derived from personal observation. For example, Sven-Tage Teodorsson, "Plutarco Naturalista attraverso le *Questioni Conviviali*," in Gallo, *Plutarco e le Scienze*, 199, observes, "Sappiamo molto bene che Plutarco non era un ricercatore come Aristotele o Teofrasto. D'altra parte non è giusto chiamarlo un dilettante. Le sue conoscenze delle cose naturali erano, veramente, e vaste e profonde. Anche independenza e originalità non ne troviamo meno in lui che in altri intellettuali della sua epoca. . . . Abbiamo dunque ragione di aspettare de lui almeno alcune idee nuove."

40 Dyroff 46.

41 Dyroff 56–58.

2 THE NATURE OF THE BEAST

1 The poetry of Hesiod contains what is widely considered to constitute the earliest pronouncement in Greek literature on the moral status of animals, as Hesiod maintains (*Opera et dies* 276–279) that Zeus gave justice to men but not to animals. On this passage, see Chapter 3, p. 55. Robert Renehan, "The Greek Anthropocentric View of Man," *Harvard Studies in Classical Philology* 85 (1981) 254–255 sees Hesiod's pronouncement as an early manifestation of what he calls the Greek "man alone of animals" prejudice against other species that seeks to identify characteristics possessed by man but not by other species, thereby justifying man in holding himself above the rest of creation, an attitude that came to full flower in the work of Aristotle. We might note as well that Homer comments favorably on the tender care of animal parents for their offspring, an observation that would figure in later Greek observations on man's moral obligations toward other species whose behavior is apparently worthy of moral consideration. On Homer's views on animals, see Urs Dierauer, "Das Verhältnis von Mensch und Tier im griechisch-römischen Denken," in *Tiere und Menschen: Geschichte und Aktualität eines prekären Verhältnisses*, ed. Paul Münch and Rainer Walz (Paderborn: Schöningh, 1998) 37–39.

2 Mary Midgley, *Animals and Why They Matter* (Athens: University of Georgia Press, 1984) 9.

3 Carruthers xi.

4 For a discussion of the question of the interests of animals, see the classic work of philosopher Tom Regan, *The Case for Animal Rights* (Berkeley: University of California Press, 1983) 87–88, 223; DeGrazia 39–40; and Chapter 3, pp. 49–50.

5 An excellent example of the application of scientific techniques to questions of the moral status of animals is the work of Rosemary Rodd, *Biology, Ethics and Animals* (Oxford: Clarendon Press, 1992). Rodd, 1, describes her book as a "philosophical examination of the significance of theories and factual discoveries from the life sciences for the development of ideas about the moral standing of animals." DeGrazia, 8, remarks approvingly of Rodd's approach to animal issues, "Combining competence in both philosophy and biology, Rodd explores animal ethics equipped with something the other authors lack: a superior scientific understanding of animals generally (in terms of evolutionary theory and scientific methodology) and of different species of animals. This allows her, for example, to rebut effectively various sceptical claims about animal mentation, comment knowledgeably about the animal-communication debate, and cast serious doubt on the assumed human monopoly on self-awareness and moral agency." Of Carruthers' work, in contrast, DeGrazia contends, 9, "Discussions (in several chapters) of animals' mental capacities are vitiated by very little engagement with relevant empirical literature (in stark contrast to Rodd's work, for example)."

6 Peter Singer, *Animal Liberation* 178–179, struggles with this issue in his discussion of which creatures humans must avoid eating if they seek to spare sentient beings, "Those who want to be absolutely certain that they are not causing suffering will not eat mollusks either; but somewhere between a shrimp and an oyster seems as good a place to draw the line as any, and better than most."

7 On this controversial issue see Steve F. Sapontzis, *Morals, Reason, and Animals* (Philadelphia: Temple University Press, 1987) 47–70; Rodd 251–255; and DeGrazia 265–266.

8 Jeremy Bentham, *An Introduction to the Principles of Morals and Legislation*, ed. J. H. Burns and H. L. A. Hart (Oxford: Clarendon Press, 1996) 283n. Bentham is quoted at length and discussed in Regan, *The Case for Animal Rights* 95–96.

9 Bernard E. Rollin, *Animal Rights and Human Morality* (Buffalo: Prometheus Books 1992) 70–71.

10 Sapontzis, *Morals, Reason, and Animals* xii–xiv, 43–44.

11 Marian Stamp Dawkins, *Through Our Eyes Only? The Search for Animal Consciousness* (Oxford: Freeman, 1993) ix.

12 Dawkins, *Through Our Eyes Only* 24. Ethologist Lesley J. Rogers, *Minds of Their Own: Thinking and Awareness in Animals* (Boulder: Westview Press, 1997) 38–39 points out that vervet monkeys also employ different sounds to indicate the presence of various types of predators. When a monkey utters the "leopard warning sound," other vervet monkeys run up trees, but if a monkey utters the "snake warning sound," other monkeys stand erect and inspect the grasses. Rogers observes, 39, on this pattern of behavior, "The monkeys certainly seem to be responding as if they know the meaning of the calls." In his fascinating work *Wild Minds: What Animals Really Think* (New York: Henry Holt, 2000), animal cognition specialist Marc D. Hauser, a scientist who expresses an unusual degree of caution against making claims about the mental capacities of animals that might contain hidden instances of anthropomorphization, discusses the calls of vervet monkeys in some detail, 185–191, and concludes that vervet calls resemble human speech in containing utterances that have, like human words, an arbitrary relationship between the referent and the utterance; that is, calls warning of eagles, for example, do not sound like eagles. While Hauser hesitates to call these utterances "words," he would certainly allow that vervet monkeys show adaptability to circumstances in the utterances they make.

13 Dawkins, *Through Our Eyes Only* 133. Examples of deception among roosters, chimpanzees, and other species are discussed in Hauser 141–172.

14 Dawkins, *Through Our Eyes Only* 178. Hauser 45–63 maintains that the ability to assess number is part of the universal mental "tool kit" of animals, although we still know little about how animals represent number in their heads.

15 Rodd 64. On self-recognition in chimpanzees, see also Hauser 100–106.

16 See the instructive comment of Rogers, 129, "We know of no single structure in the brain that is unique to humans, despite continual claims that have been made to this effect at one time or another. . . . So far, however, searching for the key to 'humanness' in brain structure has served more to dash illusions about our superiority, or simply difference, than to provide confirmation of them."

17 Griffin, *Animal Minds* 6.

18 Griffin, *Animal Minds* 121–122.

19 Griffin, *Animal Minds* 257.

20 deWaal, 18, makes the interesting observation about the ethologist's dilemma, "If animals do show tolerance or altruism, these terms are often placed in quotation marks lest their author be judged hopelessly romantic or naive. To avoid an overload of quotation marks, positive inclinations tend to receive negative labels. Preferential treatment of kin, for instance, instead of being called 'love of kin,' is sometimes known as 'nepotism.'"

21 deWaal 1.

22 This point is make by Jeffrey Moussaieff Masson and Susan McCarthy in their work of "popular ethology", *When Elephants Weep: The Emotional Lives of Animals* (New York: Delacorte Press, 1995) xx, "If chimpanzees can experience loneliness and mental anguish, it is obviously wrong to use them for experiments in which they are isolated and anticipate daily pain. At the very least, this poses a matter for serious debate – a debate that has scarcely begun." More recently, in another work of popular ethology, *The Pig Who Sang to the Moon: The Emotional Lives of Farm Animals* (New York: Ballantine, 2003), Masson argued that pigs, sheep, chickens, goats, cows and ducks live complex emotional lives characterized by friendships, joys, fears, depressions, and a host of other emotional states. Marc D.

Hauser has come out strongly against such claims of animal emotions that fill Masson and McCarthy's book and other works of popular ethology, charging, 8, "We are seduced by appearance. If there are familiar cues or signals, we tend to ascribe similar emotional experiences and thoughts." Hauser is willing to ascribe anger and fear to animals, but he reserves other emotive states to human beings exclusively. Hauser offers scientific grounds for doubting that animals can experience some emotive states, 211–253; see especially 224–227.

23 Masson and McCarthy 75.

24 Masson and McCarthy 154–155.

25 deWaal 12. Masson and McCarthy 167–168 discuss instances of apparent cross-species rescues at sea. On such apparent "animal altruism," see below, Chapter 5.

26 deWaal 218. He draws an intriguing conclusion from these data, 218, "We seem to be reaching a point where science can wrest morality from the hands of philosophers."

27 See Donald R. Griffin, *The Question of Animal Awareness: Evolutionary Continuity of Mental Experience*, revised and enlarged edition (Los Altos: William Kaufmann, 1981) 99–116. Animal rights philosopher Tom Regan, 19, observes, "Thus, given evolutionary theory and given the demonstration of the survival value of consciousness the human case provides, we have every reason to suppose that the members of other species are also conscious."

28 Bernard E. Rollin, 29, states this case pointedly, "There are innumerable differences that obtain between people and animals. The question is, do these differences serve to justify a *moral* difference? After all, there are innumerable differences between humans. I have curly hair; some men have no hair. But surely no one would accept my excluding bald men from the province of my moral deliberations simply on the grounds of baldness."

29 See Genesis 1:26–28. Scarcely a writer on either side of the animal rights debate has failed to weigh in on the thorny problem of the meaning of "dominion." While some have seen it as a sanction to man to subject animals to any abuse they choose, others have taken it to mean rather such notions as custody or stewardship. Ryder, 28, makes the interesting observation, "It is worth noting that the same word for dominion was used to describe God's relationship to humankind." On this contentious issue, see also Rollin 30–31; Linzey 33–36; and Singer 192–196. More recently, Matthew Scully, *Dominion: The Power of Man, the Suffering of Animals, and the Call to Mercy* (New York: St. Martin's Press, 2002) argues persuasively that "dominion" does indeed mean stewardship, a concept which he envisions as a feeling of compassion and concern for non-human species joined with a profound sense of responsibility to respect life. See especially 117–120 and 130–131.

30 Renehan, 240, sees this line of argument as a classical invention, "The pronounced dichotomy, wherein man is rigidly opposed to other animals, has scarcely any rival as a characteristically Greek concept."

31 Griffin, *Animal Minds* 106, 113.

32 Rogers 84. On tool use and making by animals, see Griffin, *Animal Minds* 101–114; deWaal 72–73; Rogers 81–89; and Hauser 33–39. For a discussion of ancient observations on tool use in animals and how these anticipate the findings of modern biology, see Stephen T. Newmyer, "Tool Use in Animals: Ancient Insights and Moral Consequences," forthcoming in *Scholia: Studies in Classical Antiquity*.

33 Joseph Mortenson, *Whale Songs and Wasp Maps: The Mystery of Animal Thinking* (New York: Dutton, 1987) 113. It is worth noting that Griffin, *The Question of Animal Awareness*, includes a chapter provocatively entitled "Is Man Language?" (73–85).

34 R. G. Frey, *Interests and Rights: The Case against Animals* (Oxford: Clarendon Press, 1980) 86–100.

35 See, for example, Regan 38–49 and DeGrazia 3–4.

36 Frey 169.

37 See Carruthers 98–169 for an overview of the contractualist stance on animal issues. Moral philosopher David Gauthier gives eloquent expression to the contractualist position on non-humans and other classes of individuals whose intellectual capacities exclude them from moral consideration when he explains, *Morals by Agreement* (Oxford: Clarendon Press, 1986) 268, "Animals, the unborn, the congenitally handicapped and defective, fall beyond the pale of a morality tied to mutuality," and later, 285, "In grounding morality in rational choice, we exclude relations with non-human creatures from the sphere of moral constraint." For a critique of Carruthers' position, see DeGrazia 53–56.

38 Kant's position on animals is examined in Regan 174–185 and Rollin 40–46. The idea that the manner in which one treats animals influences one's treatment of humans is adumbrated in ancient sources; see for example Ovid, *Metamorphoses* XV. 463–469 and Plutarch, *De esu carnium* 996A and 998B.

39 For a discussion of Chomsky's theories as they relate to animals, see Carruthers 141 and 144.

40 On "cueing," see DeGrazia 185–187; and Roger Fouts and Stephen Tukel Mills, *Next of Kin: What Chimpanzees Have Taught Me about Who We Are* (New York: William Morrow, 1997) 98–99. Fouts' work contains much fascinating discussion of the linguistic attainments of Washoe, whose language training Fouts supervised.

41 DeGrazia 180–181.

42 Carruthers 141–142.

43 Vittorio d'Agostino, "Sulla Zoopsicologia di Plutarco," *Archivio Italiano di Psicologia* 11 (1931) 30.

44 Barrow 112.

45 Jacqueline de Romilly, *La Douceur dans la Pensée Grecque* (Paris: Les Belles Lettres, 1979) 300. In de Romilly's understanding of the term, *douceur* encompasses the qualities of mildness, gentleness and goodnaturedness, and is opposed to the qualities of harshness, cruelty and violence (1).

46 Damianos Tsekourakis, "Pythagoreanism or Platonism and Ancient Medicine? The Reasons for Vegetarianism in Plutarch's 'Moralia'," *Aufstieg und Niedergang der römischen Welt* II, 36, 1 (1987) 383.

47 William Edward Hartpole Lecky, *History of European Morals from Augustus to Charlemagne* (New York: George Braziller, 1955; reprint of the edition of 1867) I, 244. A similar idea was expressed recently by Rod Freece and Lorna Cunningham, *Animal Welfare and Human Values* (Waterloo, Ont.: Wilfred Laurier University Press, 1993) 16, "The Greek Plutarch (A. D. 46–120) was the first to advocate ethical treatment for animals as ends in themselves rather than merely because they may be a repository of human souls (as Pythagoras had argued)."

48 Clark, *The Moral Status of Animals* 17.

49 Matt Cartmill, *A View to a Death in the Morning: Hunting and Nature through History* (Cambridge, Mass.: Harvard University Press, 1993) 44.

50 The Greek text of the animal treatises of Plutarch cited in this volume is that of the Teubner edition, *Plutarchi Moralia* VI. 1, ed. C. Hubert (Leipzig: Teubner, 1969). In addition, I have consulted the useful Loeb edition, *Plutarch's Moralia* XII, ed. Harold Cherniss and William C. Helmbold (Cambridge, Mass., and London: Harvard and Heinemann, 1957; reprinted 1968 and 1984). Available now in the series Corpus Plutarchi Moralium, with freshly edited texts, are *Gryllus*, under the title *Plutarco: Le Bestie Sono Esseri Razionali*, Introduzione, testo

critico, traduzione e commento a cura di Giovanni Indelli (Corpus Plutarchi Moralium 22) (Naples: D'Auria, 1995); and *De esu carnium*, under the title *Plutarco: Il Cibarsi di Carne*, Introduzione, testo critico, traduzione e commento a cura di Lionello Inglese e Giuseppina Santese (Corpus Plutarchi Moralium 31) (Naples: D'Auria, 1999).

51 Pliny, *Naturalis historia* VIII. 21, *missa fugae spe misericordiam vulgi inennarabili habitu quaerentes supplicavere quadam sese lamentatione complorantes, tanto populi dolore ut oblitus imperatoris ac munificentiae honori suo exquisitae flens universus consurgeret dirasque Pompeio quas ille mox luit inprecaretur*. Cicero, otherwise no champion of animals, expresses sympathy for the animals mistreated on this occasion, and includes an uncharacteristic assertion of kinship between humans and animals (*Epistulae ad familiares* VII. 1. 3), *Quin etiam misericordia quaedam consecuta est atque opinio eiusmodi, esse quamdam illi beluae cum genere humano societatem*. In contrast, Seneca, in his report on the incident in Pompey's theater (*De brevitate vitae* 13. 6–7), merely expresses disgust that Pompey, a leader known for his kind heart (*princeps civitatis . . . bonitatis eximiae*), thought it a suitable entertainment for humans to be crushed by huge animals (*ingenti mole animalium exterantur*). J. M. C. Toynbee, *Animals in Roman Life and Art* (Ithaca: Cornell University Press, 1973) 21 considers it "one of the outstanding paradoxes of the Roman mind – that a people that was so much alive to the interest and beauty of the animal kingdom . . . should yet have taken pleasure in the often hideous suffering and agonizing deaths of quantities of magnificent and noble creatures." Robert Francis West, 'Animal Suffering in Roman Literature' (Thesis: University of Calgary, 1997) takes the incident in Pompey's theater as the starting point for an exploration of the possibility that the Romans were not so callous toward animals as is sometimes supposed, as in Toynbee. West cites evidence from Lucretius, Vergil, Ovid, Statius and Martial in defense of his thesis that at least some Roman poets believed that the sufferings of animals should excite pity because of their kinship with human beings.

52 Urs Dierauer noted recently that ancient philosophers in general seldom felt moved to come out against arena sports, "Das Verhältnis von Mensch und Tier in griechisch-römischen Denken," 80, "Es ist eigenartig, wie selten sich Philosophen gegen diese Kämpfe äußerten." On the overall lack of effect that ancient thinkers had on the betterment of the lot of animals, see the pointed comment of Liliane Bodson, "Attitudes Toward Animals in Greco-Roman Antiquity," *International Journal for the Study of Animal Problems* 4 (1983) 314, "Yet, the most open-minded among the ancient philosophers and moralists never brought the question of animal rights beyond the speculative level and individual applications. There is no clue of their discussions being influential enough even at some local scale to stir up the radical changes that the mishandling of animals, such as in the games organized by authorities in the Roman empire, . . . would have justified."

53 Hughes 111.

54 Dierauer 82, "Plutarch ist auch jener antike Philosoph, der praktisch als einziger auf die Leiden der Tiere hinwies und fand, man dürfte ihnen keinen Schmerz zufügen."

55 For a recent analysis of Ovid's portrait of Pythagoreanism, see Stephen T. Newmyer, "Ovid on the Moral Grounds for Vegetarianism," in *Ovid: Werk und Wirkung*, ed. Werner Schubert (Frankfurt: Peter Lang, 1999) I, 477–486.

56 Sorabji, 173, cites Iamblichus, *Life of Pythagoras* 5. 25, as holding that the "Pythagoras" who allowed athletes to consume meat as actually another man by that name!

57 Regan 100. Sorabji, 176, alludes to Theophrastus' anticipation of the "harm as deprivation argument," but does not associate it there with Regan. For a

discussion of Regan's Harm as Deprivation Argument, see below, Chapter 6, pp. 92–94.

58 Franz Dirlmeier, "Die Oikeiosis-Lehre Theophrasts," *Philologus Supplementband* 30 (1937) 1–100 argued for the Theophrastean origin of the doctrine of οἰκειότης. For recent discussions of the doctrine, see C. O. Brink, "Οἰκείωσις and Οἰκειότης: Theophrastus and Zeno on Nature in Moral Theory," *Phronesis* 1 (1955–56) 123–145; S. J. Pembroke, "Oikeiôsis," in *Problems in Stoicism*, ed. A. A. Long (London: Athlone, 1971) 114–149; Gisela Striker, "The Role of *Oikeiosis* in Stoic Ethics," *Oxford Studies in Ancient Philosophy* 1 (1983) 145–167; Dirk Obbink, "The Origins of Greek Sacrifice: Theophrastus on Religion and Cultural History," in *Theophrastean Studies on Natural Science, Physics and Metaphysics, Ethics, Religion and Rhetoric*, ed. William W. Fortenbaugh and Robert W. Sharples (New Brunswick: Transaction Books, 1988) 272–295; and Francesco Becchi, "Biopsicologia e Giustizia verso gli Animali in Teofrasto e Plutarco," *Prometheus* 27 (2001) 119–135. Striker, 145, has conveniently defined οἰκείωσις as "recognition and appreciation of something as belonging to one." The term οἰκειότης was used by Theophrastus and the Stoics to indicate the actual relationship of belonging, in the sense of being a member of the same household, while οἰκείωσις denoted the process of welcoming perceived kindred individuals into the household or community; see Brink *passim*; Sorabji 122–133; and Becchi, "Biopsicologia" 127–135.

59 Useful discussions of Porphyry's treatise are offered in Dombrowski, *Philosophy of Vegetarianism*, 107–119, and in his article "Porphyry and Vegetarianism: A Contemporary Philosophical Approach," *Aufstieg und Niedergang der römischen Welt* II, 36, 2 (1987) 774–791; and, with special attention to his doctrine of animal rationality, in Anthony Preus, "Biological Theory in Porphyry's *De abstinentia*," *Ancient Philosophy* 3 (1983) 149–159. Porphyry's treatise has recently been translated, with extensive commentary, in *Porphyry: On Abstinence from Killing Animals*, trans. Gillian Clark (Ithaca: Cornell University Press, 2000).

60 In her Introduction to Inglese and Santese, *Il Cibarsi di Carne*, Santese considers the establishment of a juridical relationship between humans and animals to be the real innovation of Theophrastus' animal philosophy, 79, "È da sottolineare, per concludere, che le reflessioni sul diritto rappresentano, a quanto ne sappiamo, la vera innovazione teofrastea."

61 Sorabji 7ff. He argues, 9–11, that Plato had laid the groundwork for the philosophical crisis by maintaining (*Theaetetus* 186b–c) that animals can perceive sensations (αἰσθάνεσθαι) already at birth, while reflections (ἀναλογίσματα) about such perceptions can be achieved only with difficulty through education (παιδεία). Socrates does not here indicate whether he believes animals capable of such education, nor does he state that no animals are capable of reflection. Sorabji concludes that this passage was not sufficient to precipitate the crisis.

62 In her Introduction to *Il Cibarsi di Carne*, Santese states this idea succinctly, 79, "Mentre nei trattati zoologici, infatti, sembra concedere di piú al λόγος degli animali, in quelle opere dove oggetto di indagine è l'uomo, . . . l'uomo in relazione alla divinità, all'Essere, alla vita associata, la differenza si accentua e φρόνησις e λόγος diventano suo esclusivo privilegio."

63 Sorabji, 2, "Aristotle, I believe, was driven almost entirely by scientific interest in reaching his decision that animals lack reason." A useful general introduction to Aristotle's zoological treatises can be found in Roger French, *Ancient Natural History: Histories of Nature* (London: Routledge, 1994) 6–82.

64 On the generally unsympathetic attitude of Christianity toward animals throughout history, see, for example, Clark, *The Moral Status of Animals* 195–198; Singer 197–205; Ryder 30–42; Linzey 9–12; and Sorabji 195–207. Christopher

Manes, *Other Creations: Rediscovering the Spirituality of Animals* (New York: Doubleday, 1997) offers fascinating insight into how Christianity has, since the Middle Ages, marginalized animals from the religious consciousness of the faithful, and has caused believers to forget almost totally the rich religious symbolism of animals in the early Church. He laments, 216, "Many of our religious institutions have become monologues about humanity without a mention of the animal world that inspired our sacred texts."

65 The question of whether animals exercise conscious mental activity in their behaviors, that is, whether they can exercise *choice*, remains at the center of the contemporary debate on the moral status of animals, with opponents of according rights to animals maintaining that language is necessary to conscious action; this position is defended, for example, by Carruthers 127–131. While some ethologists still attribute animal behavior to simple stimulus-response actions, others consider animal behavior to be purposeful and motivated by exercise of conscious mental processes. On the present state of the debate, see Rogers 1–14 and Hauser xiii–xx.

66 On Aristotle's "man alone of animals" doctrine and its influence on subsequent speculation on the status of animals, see in particular Renehan; the subject is discussed as well in Dierauer 53–55, and in Sorabji 89–93. For a discussion of the "man alone of animals" argument as it pertains to the possibility of an under-standing of the divine in animals, see Stephen T. Newmyer, "Paws to Reflect: Ancients and Moderns on the Religious Sensibilities of Animals," *Quaderni Urbinati di Cultura Classica* NS 75, 3 (2003) 111–129. On this manner of argumentation, Sorabji, 93, remarks justly, "My own impression on attempts to draw a boundary between humans and animals is that it is very easy to find things well beyond the compass of animals, like advanced mathematics, but very difficult to find the supposed border itself." For other Aristotelian denials of reason to animals, see, for example, *Ethica Nicomachea* 1098a3–4; *Metaphysica* 980b28; *Politica* 1332b5–6; and *Ethica Eudemia* 1224a26–27. Aristotle's doctrine of συνέχεια, biological gradualism, has been seen as the philosopher's attempt to exclude intellect from the stages through which animals might pass on their road toward proximity to higher beings. On this, see Sorabji 13, "Even Aristotle's gradualism in biology is carefully qualified so that it allows for a sharp intellectual distinction between animals and man." The doctrine of συνέχεια was an important contributing element to the philosophical concept of the *scala naturae*, or Great Chain of Being. Aristotle's contribution to this concept is assessed in the classic work of Arthur O. Lovejoy, *The Great Chain of Being* (Cambridge, Mass.: Harvard University Press, 1936) 55–59.

67 Becchi, "Istinto e Intelligenza" 80, has observed that scholars have almost entirely ignored the importance which Aristotle's zoological treatises have for understanding Plutarch's animal philosophy, attributing this situation largely to a belief that Plutarch's treatises can be adequately understood as an attack upon Stoic doctrines. The fact that Plutarch does seem to direct his polemic against the Stoics may be due to his objection to the *moral* conclusions which the Stoics drew from Aristotle's zoological doctrines. The notion that man can have no debt of justice toward non-rational beings, a position which drew fire from Plutarch, is an important instance of the Stoic moralization of Aristotelian zoology.

68 See p. 21 of the present chapter and note 58.

69 Sorabji 100 notes that the denial of soul to plants, found in some Pythagoreans (Diogenes Laertius VIII. 28), Philo (*De animalibus* 94) and the Epicureans, did not extend to animals, although Porphyry's successors Iamblichus and Proclus leaned toward that position.

70 The subsequent discussion of Stoic animal psychology is expanded from the treatment of the subject in my article, "Speaking of Beasts: The Stoics and Plutarch on Animal Reason and the Modern Case against Animals," *Quaderni Urbinati di Cultura Classica* NS 63, 3 (1999) 99–110.

71 Aetius, *Placita* 4. 21 (=*Stoicorum Veterum Fragmenta* II. 827), Οἱ Στοϊκοὶ ἐξ ὀκτὼ μερῶν φασι συνεστάναι (τὴν ψυχήν), πέντε τῶν αἰσθητικῶν ὁρατικοῦ ἀκουστικοῦ ὀσφαντικοῦ γευστικοῦ ἁπτικοῦ, ἕκτου δὲ φωνητικοῦ, ἑβδόμου δὲ σπερματικοῦ, ὀγδόου δὲ αὐτοῦ τοῦ ἡγεμονικοῦ, ἀφ' οὗ ταῦτα πάντα ἐπιτέταται. Sorabji, 42, defines the animal ἡγεμονικόν as a sort of "command centre" that consists of an animal's life, sensation and impulse, but does not entail reason.

72 Diogenes Laertius, in his life of Zeno, explains the Stoic notion of animal impulse as a function of self-interestedness (VII. 85 =*Stoicorum Veterum Fragmenta* III. 178), Τὴν δὲ πρώτην ὁρμήν φασι τὸ ζῷον ἴσχειν ἐπὶ τὸ τηρεῖν ἑαυτό. Thereby it avoids danger and approaches that which is akin to it, οὕτω γὰρ τὰ βλάπτοντα διωθεῖται καὶ τὰ οἰκεῖα προσίεται. In contrast, Clement of Alexandria, Stromata IV. 18 (=*Stoicorum Veterum Fragmenta* III. 442) tells us that ὄρεξις is a rational impulse (λογικήν . . . κίνησιν).

73 See above, p. 16.

74 Porphyry, *De abstinentia* III. 20, καὶ τῇ σαρκὶ τὴν ψυχὴν ὁ θεὸς οἷον ἅλας ἐνέμιξεν, εὐοφίαν ἡμῖν μηχανώμενος. At this point, Porphyry takes the Stoic argument to its logical conclusion, asking, if certain species of animals were created solely to be eaten by humans, how humans can be sure that they were not themselves created solely to be eaten by such animals as crocodiles, whales and snakes!

75 On the λόγος ἐνδιάθετος/λόγος προφορικός dichotomy, see the classic study of M. Mühl, "Der λόγος ἐνδιάθετος und προφορικός von der älteren Stoa bis zur Synode von Sirmium 351," *Archiv für Begriffsgeschichte* 17 (1962) 7–56, especially 7–16 on the Stoics. On Philo's defense of the Stoic position on animal rationality, see Stephen T. Newmyer, "Philo on Animal Psychology: Sources and Moral Implications," in *From Athens to Jerusalem: Medicine in Hellenized Jewish Lore and in Early Christian Literature*, ed. Samuel Kottek and Manfred Horstmanshoff (Rotterdam: Erasmus, 2000) 143–155. Philo's *De animalibus*, which survives only in an Armenian translation, has been translated into English with a valuable commentary in Abraham Terian, *Philonis Alexandrini de Animalibus: The Armenian Text with an Introduction, Translation, and Commentary* (Chico: Scholars Press, 1981). On Philo's discussion of the two λόγοι, see Terian 125–126 and 203–205.

76 Sorabji 112–113.

77 On "moral agents" and "moral patients," see, for example, Regan 151–156 and DeGrazia 65–71.

78 Regan 295–296. Regan does allow that humans may be justified in doing harm to moral innocents, be they human or animal, if they pose an innocent threat to humans, as for example in the case of a rabid dog or a human or animal used as an innocent shield by a terrorist.

79 DeGrazia 65–66.

80 DeGrazia 70–71.

81 Rollin 34.

82 Rollin 36.

83 See above, p. 25.

84 Sorabji, 59, notes that the later Stoic Posidonius taught that the emotions arose from the irrational parts of the soul, thereby opening the door to possession of emotions by animals.

85 Seneca, *De ira* I. 3. 4–5 denies emotions to animals on the grounds that emotions are a function of reason, *Sed dicendum est feras ira carere et omnia animalia praeter*

hominem; nam cum sit inimica rationi, nusquam tamen nascitur, nisi ubi rationi locus est. . . . Muta animalia humanis affectibus carent, habent autem similes illis quosdam impulsus.

86 Clark, *The Moral Status of Animals* 34–35.

87 Ibid. viii.

88 Ibid. 15.

89 Ibid. 18.

90 Even the Greek titles customarily given to the treatises included in the *Moralia* may not be original with the author. The Latin titles vary among ancient authors who cite them, among manuscripts, and in modern editions. See Russell, *Plutarch* 164 and Lamberton 196–197 on the titles of Plutarch's works.

91 See Schuster 4, "Nach alledem gehen wir in der Behauptung nicht zu weit, daß sich in Chäronea eine kleine Hochschule befand. Plutarch, der selbst in Athen studiert hatte, hat in seiner Vaterstadt eine Filiale der Akademie errichtet." More recently, Lamberton, 44–52, offers some useful observations on Plutarch's activities as teacher.

92 Hubert Martin, "Plutarch's *De sollertia animalium* 959B–C: The Encomium on Hunting," *American Journal of Philology* 100 (1979) 100, notes that a number of scholars have felt that this allusion may be a reference to the lost treatise Περὶ κυνηγετικῆς listed as number 216 in the Lamprias catalogue of Plutarch's works, but he concludes, 105, that Plutarch did not intend his readers to consider him a hunting enthusiast. For a recent presentation of the case that Plutarch opposed hunting, see Francisco-Javier Tovar Paz, "El Motivo de la 'Caza' en *De Sollertia Animalium* de Plutarco," in *Estudios sobre Plutarco: Aspectos Formales*, ed. Jose Antonio Fernández Delgado and Francisca Pordomingo Pardo (Salamanca: Ediciones Clásicas, 1996) 211–217. If, however, Plutarch is in fact the author of the "encomium on hunting" alluded to at the opening of *De sollertia animalium*, his own attitude toward the practice may ultimately have been as conflicted as that of many modern persons.

93 For ancient expressions of this attitude, see p. 26 of this chapter and note 74.

94 An anonymous commentator on Aristotle's *Nicomachean Ethics* tells us, for example, that the Stoics located the virtues in this ἀπάθεια (*Stoicorum Veterum Fragmenta* III. 201), ἰστέον δὲ ὅτι καὶ πρὸ τῶν Στωϊκῶν ἦν ἡ δόξα αὕτη, ἡ τὰς ἀρετὰς ἐν ἀπαθείᾳ τιθεῖσα.

95 Sorabji 125.

96 Cartmill 243–244.

97 On Stoic teaching on the relationship between language and reason, see above, p. 26.

98 The bracketed words are found in manuscripts of Porphyry's *De abstinentia* (III. 23), at a point where Porphyry has incorporated large tracts of *De sollertia animalium* into his own text.

99 Becchi, "Irrazionalità" 207, "Plutarco . . . procede ad una comparazione tra la psicologia animale e quella umana rilevando accanto a differenze secondo il più e il meno, quantitative più che qualitative." This point had been made slightly earlier by Santese, in Inglese and Santese 58, "La differenza che separa la razionalità da quella animale non è di sostanza ma di grado, non è qualitativa ma quantitativa."

100 For testimonies illustrating the Chrysippean theory of opposites, see *Stoicorum Veterum Fragmenta* II. 172–180.

101 On the Stoic theory of soul, see above, pp. 24–25.

102 The extraordinarily complex Stoic theory of the perceptual content of the animal mind is treated in Sorabji 20–28.

103 On the Stoic theory of emotion, see above, pp. 28–29 and the useful discussion in Sorabji 58–61.

104 On ὄρεξις as a rational impulse, see above, p. 25 and Sorabji 114.

105 The possibility of a debt of justice toward animals on the part of human beings is treated in Chapter 3, below.

106 See above, p. 23.

107 Scully 228.

108 On οἰκειότης and οἰκείωσις, see pp. 21–22 above. Raúl Caballero, "ΟΙΚΕΙΩΣΙΣ en Plutarco," in A. Pérez Jiménez, J. García López and R. Ma. Aguilar, ed. *Plutarco, Platón y Aristoteles* (Madrid: Ediciones Clásicas, 1999) 549–566 correctly points out that in Plutarch, the borders between human and animal psychology are more blurred than in the thought of other theorists on the nature of animals.

109 Since the publication of Dyroff's treatise *Die Tierpsychologie des Plutarchos von Chaironeia* in 1897, scholars have argued that Plutarch's position on animal rationality contains troublesome contradictions since in *De amore prolis*, he seems to hold that animals are irrational (ἄλογα ζῷα), while in *De sollertia animalium*, he lays out an elaborate case for rationality in animals. Some, including Dyroff, have seen this as evidence that Plutarch used Stoic sources in *De amore prolis* that he would repudiate in *De sollertia animalium* (Dyroff 36–39). From this contradiction, one might conclude that Plutarch at one time agreed with the Stoics, but at another rejected them. Babut, in contrast, sees the apparent contradiction not as evidence that Plutarch shifted his philosophical loyalties, but rather that his sources themselves diverged on the position of the relative intellectual powers of humans and animals, so that the explanation for the difference is "purement rhétorique" (Babut 82), a matter of the genre of the source from which Plutarch was deriving his material at a given time. Comparison of *De amore prolis* 493 with Plutarch's argument in *De sollertia animalium* suggests, however, that the thesis of a deeply contradictory position on Plutarch's part on the question of animal rationality is largely illusory, since in both treatises he advances the position that animals have some degree of reason. Becchi has argued convincingly, "Istinto e Intelligenza" 60–70 and "Irrazionalità" 205–215, that Plutarch's position is in fact unitary, and that the question at issue in Plutarch is one of degree of rationality, rather than of possession or non-possession of rationality in animals. Santese, "Animali e Razionalità" 161 argued, on the other hand, that animals are held in *De amore prolis* to be irrational, but in one respect to be superior to humans in living closer to their nature. Our examination of the text suggests that Plutarch accords some degree of reason to animals even in *De amore prolis* and that Becchi's interpretation is preferable. Becchi judges Plutarch's apparently less generous pronouncements on animal rationality scattered about the treatises of the *Moralia* as arising not from any desire to denigrate animal intellect but from his belief that humans, because they are endowed with more developed rational faculties, are more liable to negative outside influences that include unnatural and unnecessary passions, to which animals, because of their inferior degree of rationality, are immune. These "contradictions" arise therefore rather from Plutarch's intention to chastise human frailty than from any desire to downplay animal intellect. Becchi, "Irrazionalità" 215, similarly explains Plutarch's somewhat more troubling assertion (*De fortuna* 98C) that humans would not differ at all from beasts were it not for their possession of νοῦς and λόγος by arguing that Plutarch does not mean that animals have no traces of rationality but rather that, again, human rationality is superior, allowing them to control even fierce beasts.

110 On the possible sources of Plutarch's borrowings, see Chapter 1, note 39.

111 Dyroff 6, note 1, "Diese Unterscheidung . . . ist recht primitiv, war aber damals trotz der Autorität des Aristoteles populär, wie Plinius zeigt."

112 Schuster 57–58. Lamberton, 65, has recently expressed a similar dissatisfaction with Plutarch's use of the σύγκρισις in the *Lives*, "Plutarch's comparisons (*synkriseis*), where we have them, are generally unsatisfying. . . . Factitious though they may be, they allow the massive juxtaposition to stand, asserting a parallelism that exists only as a function of Plutarch's idiosyncratic imagination."

113 Schuster 62, "Eine richterliche Entscheidung am Schlusse fällt weg: Das Ganze war ja nur ein Spiel; das Schulthema hat nur den Zweck die rednerische Fertigkeit zu üben."

114 Dickerman 123–124. On ants, see, besides Plutarch, *De sollertia animalium* 967D–968B and 981B: Aristotle, *Historia animalium* 622b20–27; Philo, *De animalibus* 42; and Pliny the Elder, *Naturalis historia* XI. 108–110; on swallows, see Plutarch, *De sollertia animalium* 966D and 982F, and Aristotle, *Historia animalium* 612b21–31; Philo, *De animalibus* 22; and Aelian, *De natura animalium* III. 24–25.

115 See note 113 above.

116 Tim Duff, *Plutarch's Lives: Exploring Virtue and Vice* (Oxford: Clarendon Press, 1999) 245.

117 Duff 246.

118 Sorabji 21, 26.

119 For ancient testimonies on Chrysippus' dog, see *Stoicorum Veterum Fragmenta* II. 726–727. In Philo's dialogue *De animalibus* 45, the interlocutor Alexander cites this anecdote in defense of his thesis that animals are rational. See the useful discussion of Chrysippus' dog in ancient philosophy in Terian 156–157.

120 Griffin 122.

121 See above, p. 15.

122 Rogers 86.

123 Hauser 35.

124 Hauser 36.

125 See above, p. 16.

126 For further discussion of Stoic theory on language and Plutarch's response to it, see Stephen T. Newmyer, "Speaking of Beasts: The Stoics and Plutarch on Animal Reason and the Modern Case against Animals," *Quaderni Urbinati di Cultura Classica* NS 63, 3 (1999) 102–103.

3 JUST BEASTS

1 On Frey and Carruthers, see Chapter 2, pp. 15–17. Strictly speaking, the position that Newman espouses represents a brand of Stoicism filtered through the teaching of Augustine and Thomas Aquinas who endorsed the strictures against animals that they encountered in Stoic philosophy and incorporated into their own systems of thought, with borrowings from Aristotle. The attitude of Christianity toward animals has in general not been one of great sympathy. Sorabji remarks, 204, "By and large, despite some opposing tendencies, my impression is that the emphasis of Western Christianity was on one half, the anti-animal half, of a more wide-ranging and vigorous ancient Greek debate." Ryder, 36, offers an enlightening historical example of the sort of attitude that Sorabji isolates, "As late as the nineteenth century, Pope Pius IX refused to allow the foundation of a society to protect animals in Rome on the grounds that human beings had no duties towards lower creation."

2 DeGrazia 36–49.

3 Singer 5.
4 DeGrazia 48
5 Singer 17.
6 DeGrazia, 3, numbers among those who take Singer to task for ignoring the possibility that the lives of humans may be more valuable than those of animals.
7 Singer's ethical thinking, in *Animal Liberation* and his subsequent works, is subjected to a searching critique by Scully, 20–23, who reminds us that Singer has been dubbed "Professor Death" because of his apparent sanctioning of euthanasia in the cases of many types of handicapped individuals.
8 Sorabji 211.
9 Regan 235.
10 Regan 243.
11 Regan 96–99. On the application which Regan makes of this harm principle to defend vegetarianism as obligatory for humans, see below, Chapter 6, pp. 93–94.
12 Clark 29.
13 Clark 34.
14 Clark 34.
15 Clark 57.
16 Rollin 33.
17 Rollin 36.
18 Rollin 74.
19 Rollin 83.
20 Rodd 131.
21 Rodd 251.
22 On Chomsky, see above, Chapter 2, p. 16. In the course of his argument against language capacity in non-humans, Carruthers, 141, cites Chomsky approvingly, "For as Noam Chomsky and others have forcefully argued, the human capacity for language is very likely an innately determined aspect of our cognition."
23 Herbert Terrace, *Nim* (New York: Knopf, 1979) 114. Masson and McCarthy, alluding both to the case of Nim and to the sort of anecdotal material that fills ancient works on animal behavior, including Plutarch's treatises, observe, 214, "The stories of crow parliaments that hold trials and pass judgment on their members are fantasy, but less organized manifestations of what may be a sense of justice exist in many stories of righteously indignant chimps, for example."
24 deWaal 97.
25 deWaal 218. He notes along this line, 217, "Morality is as firmly grounded in neurobiology as anything else we do or are."
26 Steven M. Wise, *Drawing the Line: Science and the Case for Animal Rights* (Cambridge, Mass.: Perseus, 2002) 32–34.
27 Wise 240.
28 Sorabji 208–219.
29 Sorabji 211, 216.
30 Sorabji 214.
31 Sorabji 215.
32 Sorabji 118.
33 Sorabji 118.
34 Dierauer, *Tier und Mensch* 15, justly calls this Hesiodic passage "die erste prinzipielle Abgrenzung von Menschen und Tieren."
35 Sorabji, 120n76, argues that this passage from Epicurus can be made to yield this meaning only if one accepts an emendation by Usener which Sorabji himself rejects. The wording of *Kuriai Doxai* 32 clearly recalls the Stoic doctrine of οἰκειότης. Sorabji has demonstrated, 117 and 162, that the Epicureans, in particular Epicurus' successor Hermarchus, espoused a theory of "kinship" that,

as in Stoic doctrine, required a contract (συνθήκη in Epicurean parlance) for according justice to others, so that animals, as irrational beings, were excluded from human moral consideration. Jo-Ann Shelton, "Contracts with Animals," *Between the Species* 11 (1995) 115–121, has argued that Lucretius maintains that human beings can attain Epicurean "pleasure" by forming contracts of a mutually beneficial kind with some animal species while separating themselves from other species, a position that places the Roman poet somewhat outside the mainstream of Epicurean ethical theory.

36 Sorabji 119.

37 Sorabji 118. On the concept of the "just war" that humans wage against animals used as a defense for meat eating, see Porphyry I. 14, discussed above, Chapter 2, p. 32. Ancient opponents of meat eating pointed out, however, that humans eat not those animals that are potentially dangerous to them, like wolves and lions, but rather those that are completely tame and harmless; for this argument, see Plutarch, *De esu carnium* 994B.

38 See Chapter 2, pp. 20–21.

39 Sorabji, otherwise cautious in attributing a belief in "animal rights" to ancient thinkers, goes so far as to assert, 156, "Talk of animal rights, in the case of Pythagoras, Empedocles and Theophrastus may not be totally out of place". Empedocles believed, with Pythagoras, in reincarnation, and in his work *Katharmoi* (*Purifications*), he taught that man should avoid meat eating and the slaughter of animals since by these practices humans are devouring each other (fr. 136–137 DK). Aristotle, *Rhetoric* 1373b6–17, tells us that Empedocles forbade the killing of any living creature on the grounds that it was unjust for humans to do so. Again the issue of kinship between humans and non-human animals would seem to have figured in Empedocles' case against harming animals.

40 On Stoic teaching on the ἡγεμονικόν, see Chapter 2, p. 25. Since, according to Stoic theory, children reach a state of rationality either at age seven, as Aetius says Chrysippus held (*Stoicorum Veterum Fragmenta* II. 83) or at age fourteen, as Diogenes Laertius reports in his life of Zeno (VII. 55), the Stoics encountered a problem in accounting for how humans could extend this "kinship" to children. They solved it by arguing that children are born with the potential and propensity for the acquisition of rationality, as Seneca explains (Ep. 49. 11), *dociles natura nos edidit et rationem dedit imperfectam, sed quae perfici posset.* Hence children can be admitted to the kinship of humans from birth.

41 Schuster 76, "Wir haben Grund anzunehmen, dass die Polemik, die im ersten Teile unseres Dialoges sehr stark zum Durchbruch kommt, sich in die Hauptsache gegen die älteren Stoa wendet."

42 Barrow 103. Along these same lines, Barrow, 105, maintains that Plutarch's grasp of the subtleties of Stoicism was so tenuous and literal as to render his treatise on the contradictions inherent in the system, the *De Stoicorum repugnantiis*, totally worthless.

43 Hershbell 3350.

44 Hershbell 3341–3342.

45 Citations drawn from testimonia relating to Posidonius are taken from *Posidonius*, I: *The Fragments*, ed. L. Edelstein and I. G. Kidd (Cambridge: Cambridge University Press, 1972).

46 Dierauer, *Tier und Mensch* 234. Dierauer judges Posidonius' position on non-rational elements of the soul to be a movement toward a more Platonic conception of soul.

47 Seneca, *De ira* I. 3. 4–5. See Chapter 2, p. 29.

48 Dombrowski, *Philosophy of Vegetarianism* 80.

49 The topic of justice is not discussed in the extant portion of *Bruta animalia ratione uti* beyond the philosophic pig Gryllus' comment (986F) that Odysseus assumes that humans excel animals in such virtues as justice, wisdom and courage. The pig's discussion of human diet choices might be said to imply that he considers carnivorous humans to be unjust, but the subject is not specifically broached. Since Gryllus then proceeds to show Odysseus that animals in fact excel humans in courage, wisdom and temperance, it is possible that justice was taken up at that point in the text (991D) where a lacuna is posited by scholars after the other animal virtues have been discussed.

50 The so-called Catalogue of Lamprias of the works of Plutarch lists eight titles that mention Epicurus by name. Among the lost treatises are titles that address the contradictions in the school's teachings, on the paradoxes involved in the system, and on their mistaken theories concerning free will and the gods. In the case of the animal-related treatises of Plutarch, source hunters have at times declared *Bruta animalia ratione uti* to be an attack on Epicureanism because of the dialogue's discussion of desires put into the mouth of a pig; see Indelli, *Le Bestie Sono Esseri Razionali* 22–25.

51 See Chapter 2, p. 39 and note 109.

52 Caballero, 552, for example, calls *De amore prolis* "una acusación contra la maldad de la especie humana."

53 For a discussion of the place which the passage under discussion here holds in Plutarch's philosophy of vegetarianism, and of how it anticipates modern arguments in defense of vegetarianism, see below, Chapter 6, p. 94. For a full discussion of issues relating to Plutarch's ideas on the sense of justice in animals, see Stephen T. Newmyer, "Just Beasts? Plutarch and Modern Science on the Sense of Fair Play in Animals," *Classical Outlook* 74, 3 (1997) 85–88.

54 See above, Chapter 3, p. 52.

55 This tale is told, with variations, by Aelian, *De natura animalium* VI.15, and by Philo, *De animalibus* 67.

56 Sorabji 119–120.

57 Sorabji 215.

4 FEELING BEASTLY

1 Sorabji 208. On the widespread lack of sympathy for the sufferings of animals in evidence in classical culture, see above, Chapter 2, p. 19.

2 Aristotle, *Politica* 1256b16–18, states that animals are created for the sake of man: δῆλον ὅτι ... οἰητέον εἶναι καὶ τἆλλα ζῷα τῶν ἀνθρώπων χάριν.

3 Carruthers 165.

4 Carruthers 165.

5 This observation by Nicholas Fontaine (1625–1709) is discussed in Ryder 57. Useful treatments of Descartes' position on animals may be found in Singer 207–210; Regan 3–9; Dombrowski, *Philosophy of Vegetarianism* 11–14; and Ryder 55–57.

6 For a helpful summary of behaviorist doctrine on animal consciousness and a critique of its assumptions, see Griffin, *Animal Minds* 19–24.

7 Rodd 42.

8 Griffin, *Animal Minds* 21.

9 Rodd 62.

10 Rollin 64.

11 Rollin 66.

12 Rodd 41.

13 Clark, *The Moral Status of Animals* 41.

14 Griffin, *Animal Minds* 246.

15 Brophy, *Don't Never Forget* 18.

16 Masson and McCarthy xx.

17 Rollin 71–72.

18 DeGrazia 126.

19 Masson and McCarthy 26–27.

20 Dawkins, *Through Our Eyes Only* 154–159.

21 Ibid. 164.

22 Rodd 129.

23 Rodd 132. On mourning behavior in animals, see Masson and McCarthy 92–97 and deWaal 53–56.

24 Singer 9.

25 Ryder 325.

26 Dierauer "Das Verhältnis" 82, "Plutarch ist auch jener antike Philosoph, der praktisch als einziger auf die Leiden der Tiere hinwies und fand, man dürfte ihnen keinen Schmerz zufügen."

27 Sorabji 208.

28 Regan would interpret the anguish of the cow as an instance of harm visited upon her because she is deprived of her calf, and would view the removal of the calf as morally indefensible.

29 On Epicurean attitudes toward animals, see above, Chapter 3, p. 55 and note 35.

30 See above, p. 66.

31 Sorabji 208; see also Sorabji 102.

32 In this assertion, the Neoplatonist Porphyry does not agree with his master's statement (*Timaeus* 77a) that plants, which do not share in opinion or reasoning, do experience sensations, both pleasant and painful (αἰσθήσεως δὲ ἡδείας καὶ ἀλγεινῆς). The possibility that plants may be sentient still haunts philosophers who would defend the vegetarian lifestyle against those who argue that if we spare animals, perhaps we are obligated to spare plants as well. Stephen R. L. Clark, for example, argues, 171, "Some plants may feel. I say nothing against such research as has been done on this point, except that the interpretation of galvanic twitches as *distress*-signals seems much more dubious than the experimenters allow (whom are the plants signaling to?)."

33 See above, Chapter 3, p. 62.

34 Masson and McCarthy 112.

5 BEAUTY IN THE BEAST

1 In the course of a lengthy account of "dolphin wonders," Pliny (*Naturalis historia* IX. 20–33), who acknowledges that the dolphin is partial both to humans and to music (*delphinus non homini tantum amicum animal verum et musicae arti, Naturalis historia* IX. 24), only briefly alludes to the tale of Arion (IX. 28), remarking merely that his rescuers were drawn by the sound of his music and that the tale is in itself probable because of other instances of friendships between boys and dolphins.

2 August Marx, *Griechische Märchen von dankbaren Tieren und Verwandtes* (Stuttgart: Kohlhammer, 1889) 5, "An die Spitze stellen wir billig das Tier, welches, wie kein zweites, von den Alten in Sage und Dichtung verherrlicht worden ist: den Delphin." See also the similar comment of Otto Keller, *Die antike Tierwelt* (Leipzig: Cramer, 1909–13) I, 408, "Kein zweites Meertier speilt in der Sage und Poesie des Altertums eine so hervorragende Rolle wie der Delphin. Man schätzte ihn geradezu als Freund des Menschen."

3 Masson and McCarthy 166.

4 This concept is developed in Richard Dawkins, *The Selfish Gene* (Oxford: Oxford University Press, 1976). Dawkins ends his work, 215, with the sobering hope that man may one day cultivate "pure, disinterested altruism – something that has no place in nature, something that has never existed before in the whole history of the world."

5 For instances of such adoptions, see, for example, Rodd 213–214; deWaal 124; and Masson and McCarthy 75–76. On elephants who aid their own kind and other species when injured, see Masson and McCarthy 154–155 and deWaal 53–54.

6 Rodd 214.

7 deWaal 83.

8 Steve F. Sapontzis, "Are Animals Moral Beings?," *American Philosophical Quarterly* 17, 1 (1980) 45.

9 Ibid. 47.

10 Ibid. 50.

11 Ibid. 51.

12 Marx 5, "Der Delphin hat von einem Menschen einmal in irgend welcher Form eine bedeutende Wohlthat empfangen; später, in einem Augenblicke grosser Not, vergilt er dies demselben durch eine Wohlthat seinerseits."

13 deWaal 135; on reciprocal altruism, see also Hauser 235–239. Hauser records a particularly fascinating example of reciprocal altruism among vampire bats, which he characterizes, 238, as animals that "tend to miss out on the trophies for cleverness." Vampire bats, which live in large social groups, recognize each other by voice and develop social relationships, will regurgitate blood to feed their fellows if those bats have previously done that for them, but they will not feed bats that have not regurgitated in the past. This behavior is not limited to kin. On this, Hauser makes the intriguing comment, 239, "A selfish gene perspective cannot explain this pattern."

14 deWaal 136.

15 Although it is dated, there is much of value in W. C. Allee, *Cooperation among Animals, with Human Implications* (New York: Henry Schuman, 1951). Allee maintains that observation of cooperative behavior in animals can aid human beings in their own social relations and can even help human societies to choose international cooperation over war that arises from flawed notions of national superiority and from selfish sorts of cooperative alliances.

16 Hauser 238.

17 Griffin, *Animal Minds* 214.

18 Ibid. 214.

19 Ibid. 214.

20 Barrow 116.

21 See Chapter 3, p. 63.

22 Pliny's nephew relates a somewhat similar tale (*Epistulae* IX. 33) which, though innocent in itself, has a rather grotesque ending. A dolphin befriended a boy and in time came up on shore to dry off. Eventually the spectacle drew such a crowd of locals that the officials of the town, troubled that their home was becoming noisy and crowded with tourists, slew the creature! Pliny draws no moral conclusions on the animal's behavior, and merely suggests to the poet Caninius Rufus, addressee of the letter, that the incident would make an interesting poem.

23 On Aristotle's denial of a sense of justice to animals, see above, Chapter 3, p. 56.

6 ANIMAL APPETITES

1 Harold Cherniss and William C. Helmbold, *Plutarch's Moralia* XII 537. The idea that *De esu carnium* dates from early in Plutarch's career is found as well in Babut 66; Urs Dierauer, *Tier und Mensch im Denken der Antike: Studien zur Tierpsychologie, Anthropologie und Ethik* (Amsterdam: Grüner, 1977) 287; and D. A. Russell, "On Reading Plutarch's *Moralia*," *Greece and Rome* 15 (1968) 131, where the work is called "a youthful extravagance." It is interesting to note, however, that Seneca (*Epistulae* 108) recounts that, under the influence of the Neopythagorean philosopher Sotion, he followed a vegetarian lifestyle for a year, a style of life that he found not only easy but pleasant (*non tantum facilis erat mihi consuetudo, sed dulcis, Epistulae* 108. 22). He eventually abandoned vegetarianism on the urging of his father, however, not, Seneca assures us, because his father feared his son might be charged with dangerous superstitious practices, but because he hated philosophy (*Epistulae* 108. 22). Seneca notes that his father had no trouble persuading his son to "eat better" once again (*nec difficiliter mihi ut inceperem melius cenare persuasit, Epistulae* 108. 22)!

2 Frederick E. Brenk, *In Mist Apparelled: Religious Themes in Plutarch's Moralia and Lives* (Leiden: Brill, 1977) 70.

3 Brenk 70.

4 Aldo Tirelli, "Etica e Dietetica nei *De Tuenda Sanitate Praecepta*," in Gallo, *Plutarco e le Scienze* 391, "In uno scritto giovenile sull'argomento, *De esu carnium*, egli aveva sostenuto, ligio al vegetarismo pitagorico, una posizione di pressoché assoluta intransigenza."

5 Tirelli 392, "ecco il *bon sens* del Plutarco maturo."

6 Nick Fiddes, *Meat: A Natural Symbol* (London: Routledge, 1991) 23–27.

7 Fiddes 159–161.

8 Fiddes 200.

9 Regan 222–223. Regan is here countering Singer's utilitarian argument for vegetarianism and for animal rights in general.

10 Dombrowski, *Philosophy of Vegetarianism* 6.

11 Ibid. 6–7. It is worth noting that John Passmore, "The Treatment of Animals," *Journal of the History of Ideas* 36 (1975) 200, points out that St. Francis' highly touted love of animals is a fairly recent notion that appears first in print in the 1890s.

12 Ryder 160.

13 See the epigraph to Chapter 4.

14 Barigazzi 302.

15 Cherniss and Helmbold, *Plutarch's Moralia* XII 537.

16 Barrow, xiv, observes that while the chronology of Plutarch's works is notoriously difficult to determine, it seems likely that many of the treatises contained in the *Moralia* date from the later years of their author's life, specifically from around the reign of Trajan (98–117 CE).

17 Tirelli 392.

18 It is difficult to judge how much weight should be given to Plutarch's remark (*De fortuna* 98E) that fish is the tastiest food and pork the fattest, but both are nourishing and tempting for humans (ἥδύτατον ἰχθὺς καὶ πολύσαρκον ὕς, ἀνθρώπῳ δὲ τροφὴ καὶ ὄψον ἐστί). The comment appears to endorse meat eating. The context of the passage is a discussion of ways in which humans excel animals and they excel humans, and humans are declared to be superior because of their reason. The excellences of animals, including their high spirits and speed, are put into service by man, who thereby appears to be superior. Plutarch seems to include the option of eating animal flesh as one example of man's use of animals, but the passage does not seem to contradict the strongly negative attitude toward

meat eating that he expresses elsewhere. Plutarch is speaking here of the relative superiorities of the species rather than of dietary choices, and he makes no further comment here, positive or negative, on human diet.

19 See above, Chapter 2, pp. 19–20, on the difficulties involved in assessing the motivations for Pythagoras' vegetarianism.

20 Haussleiter 228, "Fragen wir endlich, wer vor allem Plutarch die Anregung zu seiner Überzeugung gab, so ist in erster Linie natürlich Pythagoras und seine Schule zu nennen."

21 Babut 65.

22 Brenk 86.

23 On ancient pronouncements concerning the extent of Pythagoras' ban on animal flesh, see above, Chapter 2, p. 20.

24 In the dialogue *Septem sapientium convivium* (*Banquet of the Seven Sages*), Plutarch portrays Solon as dismissing the abstention of the Orphics, a sect whose allegiance to vegetarianism is usually thought to have derived, like that of the Pythagoreans, from a belief in metempsychosis, as a mere quibble rather than as a concern with avoiding injustice in eating (τὸ δ' ἀπείχεσθαι σαρκῶν ἐδωδῆς, ὥσπερ Ὀρφέα τὸν παλαιὸν ἱστοροῦσι, σόφισμα μᾶλλον ἢ φυγὴ τῶν περὶ τροφὴν ἀδικημάτων ἐστί, 159C). Solon's point here is that all human nourishment involves acts of injustice toward what is eaten, be that plant or animal, so that total abstention from meat is largely a pointless gesture that does not save man from this injustice. Although Solon does not specifically mention metempsychosis here, the passage does not suggest that Plutarch holds it in very high regard in any case. On Orphism and vegetarianism, see Haussleiter 83–96 and 151–157.

25 Montserrat Jufresa, "La Abstinencia de Carne y el Origen de la Civilización en Plutarco," in J. A. Fernández Delgado and F. Pordomingo Pardo, eds *Estudios sobre Plutarco: Aspectos Formales* (Salamanca: Ediciones Clásicas, 1996) 220–222.

26 Barigazzi 303–304.

27 Tsekourakis 379. In contrast to Tsekourakis, however, Dombrowski, *Philosophy of Vegetarianism* 45, suggests that one consideration figuring in Pythagoras' case for abstention was his conviction that animals are sentient and capable of suffering. Extant sources do not seem to bear out Dombrowski's view, at least insofar as it pertains to animal suffering. The consideration that humans must show to animals, in Pythagoras' system, appears to arise from the fact that animals may be humans and not from any intrinsic qualities or capacities that they may possess *as animals*.

28 Tsekourakis 383.

29 Tsekourakis 391. He implies, 390, that Socrates' dedication to moderation in living included a commitment to vegetarianism, which might have influenced Plutarch. There is little evidence to support the view that Socrates was a vegetarian. Indeed, Porphyry, *De abstinentia* I. 15, suggests that he was not.

30 Santese, Introduction to Inglese and Santese, *Il Cibarsi de Carne* 43.

31 See above, Chapter 3, pp. 62–63 and note 57. We should recall that Sorabji, 176, had detected an anticipation of what Regan would term the Harm as Deprivation Argument in Porphyry's discussion, *De abstinentia* II. 12, of Theophrastus' belief that depriving an animal of life constitutes a harm to it. Sorabji does not connect the doctrine with Regan or employ Regan's designation for the argument, nor does he mention the occurrence of the argument in Plutarch.

32 Singer 8.

33 Singer 9.

34 Regan 100.

35 Regan 330–338.

36 Regan 335.

37 Pliny, *Naturalis historia* XI. 210–211, reports, with remarkable detachment and no trace of moral reserve, that the udders of sows that have just miscarried are tastier than those of sows that have delivered without complications, while next tastiest are the udders of sows slaughtered the day after giving birth if the animal has not been given the opportunity to suckle its young. Although Plutarch may have taken a hint from the subject matter of Pliny for his own discussion of the horrors perpetrated upon sows, he would hardly have admired the clinical approach of Pliny.

38 Michael W. Fox, *Inhumane Society: The American Way of Exploiting Animals* (New York: St. Martin's Press, 1990) 30. On factory farming, see in general Jim Mason and Peter Singer, *Animal Factories* (New York: Harmony Books, 1990); Singer 92–158; and Masson, *The Pig Who Sang to the Moon* 38–44, 67–68, and 185–187.

39 Scully 120.

40 Scully 282.

41 Scully 283. For specifics on the treatment of animals in modern slaughterhouses, see especially Gail A. Eisnitz, *Slaughterhouse: The Shocking Story of Greed, Neglect, and Inhumane Treatment Inside the U. S. Meat Industry* (Amherst: Prometheus, 1997).

42 Diogenes Laertius, VII. 4, reports that Zeno had written a treatise on living "in accord with nature" (γέγραφε . . . Περὶ τοῦ κατὰ φύσιν βίου). F. H. Sandbach, *The Stoics* (New York: Norton, 1975) 53–59 offers a helpful overview of interpretations of what living "in accord with nature" may entail for the Stoics. He concludes that it may well have meant living a life that is self-consistent and contains no element of conflict that can hinder human happiness. It necessarily entailed living in accord with reason, which, of course, the Stoics had denied to animals.

43 See above, pp. 91–92.

44 In his thoroughgoing defense of a vegetarian regimen for humans, John Robbins, *Diet for a New America* (Walpole, NH: Stillpoint, 1987) 283–284 emphasizes the anatomical differences between true carnivores and humans, arguing, "Their digestive secretions are far more highly acidic than ours. . . . Their teeth are long and pointed, suited for seizing prey and ripping off chunks of flesh. Our teeth, in contrast, are designed for the grinding of grains, vegetables and fruits." Similarly, in her popularly intended treatise on vegetarian philosophy, Vistara Parham, *What's Wrong with Eating Meat?* (Corona, NY: PCAP, 1981) 7, observes, "The human digestive system, tooth and jaw structure, and bodily functions are completely different from carnivorous animals. . . . Human beings clearly are not carnivores by physiology."

45 In like manner, Robbins 284, "Without the aid of steak knives and cooking, we'd be hard-pressed indeed to handle flesh." The issue of cooking animal flesh before consuming it reappears in Porphyry in an intriguing transformation. In his early survey of ancient arguments *against* abstention, Porphyry (*De abstinentia* I. 13) notes that some carnivorous humans have maintained that no people on earth abstains from animal flesh, and that since no race of humans regularly eats animal flesh raw, perhaps humans should correctly be designated not as creatures vegetarian by nature but rather as creatures who by nature cook flesh before eating it!

46 On the Epicurean denial of the possibility of a covenant of justice between humans and animals, see above, Chapter 3, p. 55.

47 Tsekourakis 373.

48 See pp. 90–91.

49 See Plato, *Phaedo* 64a–67b. In this passage, Socrates maintains that the philosopher desires death because it offers that separation of soul from body that frees the soul from those impediments weighing it down in mortal life, including all those things that constitute the pleasures of the body and the senses. The soul cannot attain to truth when the body deceives it. The body causes constant disturbances by its need for nourishment (μυρίας μὲν γὰρ ἡμῖν ἀσχολίας παρέχει τὸ σῶμα διὰ τὴν ἀναγκαίαν τροφήν , 66b).
50 On indirect duty views, see above, Chapter 2, p. 16 and note 38.
51 Dombrowski 121.
52 See above, Chapter 3, pp. 49–50 and chapter 6, pp. 92–94.
53 Dombrowski 123.
54 Dombrowski 123.

7 CONCLUSION

1 Ryder 6–7.
2 Clark, *The Moral Status of Animals* 21–22.

BIBLIOGRAPHY

d'Agostino, Vittorio, "Sulla Zoopsicologia di Plutarco," *Archive Italiano di Psicologia* 11 (1933) 21–42.

Allee, W. C., *Cooperation among Animals, with Human Implications* (New York: Henry Schuman, 1951; revised edition).

Babut, Daniel, *Plutarque et le Stoïcisme* (Paris: Presses Universitaires de France, 1969).

Barigazzi, Adelmo, "Implicanze Morali nella Polemica Plutarchea sulla Psicologia degli Animali," in Italo Gallo, ed. *Plutarco e le Scienze* (Genoa: Sagep Editrice, 1992) 297–315.

Barrow, R. H., *Plutarch* (London: Chatto and Windus, 1967).

Becchi, F., "Biopsicologia e Giustizia verso gli Animali in Teofrasto e Plutarco," *Prometheus* 27 (2001) 119–135.

—— "Irrazionalità e Razionalità degli Animali," *Prometheus* 26 (2000) 205–225.

—— "Istinto e Intelligenza negli Scritti Zoopsicologici di Plutarco," in Michele Bandini and Federico G. Pericoli, eds *Scritti in Memoria di Dino Pieraccioni* (Florence: Istituto Papirologico G. Vitelli, 1993) 59–83.

Bentham, Jeremy, *An Introduction to the Principles of Morals and Legislation*, ed. J. H. Burns and H. L. A. Hurt (Oxford: Clarendon Press, 1996).

Bergua Cavero, Jorge, "Cinismo, Ironía y Retorica en el *Bruta ratione uti* de Plutarco," in *Estudios sobre Plutarco: Paisaje y Naturaleza* (Madrid: Ediciones Clásicas, 1991) 13–19.

Bodson, Liliane, "Attitudes towards Animals in Greco-Roman Antiquity," *International Journal for the Study of Animal Problems* 4 (1983) 312–320.

Brenk, Frederick E., *In Mist Apparelled: Religious Themes in Plutarch's Moralia and Lives* (Leiden: Brill, 1977).

Brink, C. O., "Οἰκείωσις and Οἰκειότης: Theophrastus and Zeno on Nature in Moral Theory," *Phronesis* 1 (1955–56) 123–145.

Brophy, Brigid, "The Rights of Animals," *Sunday Times*, October 10, 1965; reprinted in Brigid Brophy, *Don't Never Forget: Collected Views and Reviews* (New York: Holt, Rinehart and Winston, 1966) 15–21.

Caballero, Raúl, "ΟΙΚΕΙΩΣΙΣ en Plutarco," in A. Pérez Jiménez, J. García Lopez and R. Ma. Aguilar, eds *Plutarco, Platón y Aristóteles: Actas del V. Congreso Internacional de la I. P. S. (Madrid-Cuenca, 4–7 de mayo de 1999)* (Madrid: Ediciones Clásicas, 1999) 549–566.

Carruthers, Peter, *The Animals Issue: Moral Theory in Practice* (Cambridge: Cambridge University Press, 1992).

Cartmill, Matt, *A View to a Death in the Morning: Hunting and Nature through History* (Cambridge, Mass.: Harvard University Press, 1993).

Cherniss, Harold, and William Helmbold, eds *Plutarch's Moralia XII* (Cambridge, Mass.: Harvard University Press, 1984; reprint of the edition of 1957).

Clark, Gillian, trans. *Porphyry: On Abstinence from Killing Animals* (Ithaca: Cornell University Press, 2000).

Clark, Stephen R. L., *The Moral Status of Animals* (Oxford: Oxford University Press, 1984).

Dawkins, Marian Stamp, *Through Our Eyes Only? The Search for Animal Consciousness* (Oxford: Freeman, 1993).

Dawkins, Richard, *The Selfish Gene* (Oxford: Oxford University Press, 1976).

DeGrazia, David, *Taking Animals Seriously: Mental Life and Moral Status*, (Cambridge: Cambridge University Press, 1996).

Dickerman, Sherwood Owen, "Some Stock Illustrations of Animal Intelligence in Greek Psychology," *Transactions and Proceedings of the American Philological Association* 42 (1911) 123–130.

Dierauer, Urs, *Tier und Mensch im Denken der Antike: Studien zur Tierpsychologie, Anthropologie und Ethik* (Amsterdam: Grüner, 1977).

—— "Das Verhältnis von Mensch und Tier im griechisch-römischen Denken," in Paul Münch and Rainer Walz, eds *Tiere und Menschen: Geschichte und Aktualität eines prekären Verhältnisses* (Paderborn: Schöningh, 1998) 37–85.

Dirlmeier, Franz, 'Die Oikeiosis-Lehre Theophrasts," *Philologus Supplementband* 30 (1937) 1–100.

Dombrowski, Daniel A., *The Philosophy of Vegetarianism* (Amherst: University of Massachusetts Press, 1984).

—— "Porphyry and Vegetarianism: A Contemporary Philosophical Approach," *Aufstieg und Niedergang der römischen Welt* II, 36, 2 (1987) 774–791.

Duff, Tim, *Plutarch's Lives: Exploring Virtue and Vice* (Oxford: Clarendon Press, 1999).

Dyroff, Adolf, *Die Tierpsychologie des Plutarchos von Chaironeia* (Würzburg: Bonitas-Bauer, 1897).

Edelstein, L. and I. G. Kidd, eds *Posidonius, I: The Fragments* (Cambridge: Cambridge University Press, 1972).

Eisnitz, Gail A., *Slaughterhouse: The Shocking Story of Greed, Neglect, and Inhumane Treatment inside the U. S. Meat Industry* (Amherst: Prometheus, 1997).

Fiddes, Nick, *Meat: A Natural Symbol* (London: Routledge, 1991).

Fouts, Roger and Stephen Tukel Mills, *Next of Kin: What Chimpanzees Have Taught Me about Who We Are* (New York: William Morrow and Company, 1997).

Fox, Michael, *Inhumane Society: The American Way of Exploiting Animals* (New York: St. Martin's Press, 1990).

Francione, Gary L., *Rain without Thunder: The Ideology of the Animal Rights Movement* (Philadelphia: Temple University Press, 1996).

Freece, Rod and Lorna Cunningham, *Animal Welfare and Human Values* (Waterloo: Wilfred Laurier University Press, 1993).

French, Roger, *Ancient Natural Histories: Histories of Nature* (London: Routledge, 1994).

Frey, R. G., *Interests and Rights: The Case against Animals* (Oxford: Clarendon Press, 1980).

Gallo, Italo, ed. *Plutarco e le Scienze* (Genoa: Sagep Editrice, 1992).

Gauthier, David, *Morals by Agreement* (Oxford: Clarendon Press, 1986).

Giankaris, C. J., *Plutarch* (New York: Twayne, 1970).

Griffin, Donald R., *Animal Minds* (Chicago: University of Chicago Press, 1992).

—— *The Question of Animal Awareness: Evolutionary Continuity of Mental Experience* (Los Altos: William Kaufmann, 1981).

Hauser, Marc D., *Wild Minds: What Animals Really Think* (New York: Henry Holt and Company, 2000).

Haussleiter, Johannes, *Der Vegetarismus in der Antike* (Berlin: Töpelmann, 1935).

Hershbell, Jackson P., "Plutarch and Stoicism," *Aufstieg und Niedergang der römischen Welt* II, 36, 5 (1992) 3336–3352.

Hughes, Donald R., *Pan's Travail: Environmental Problems of the Ancient Greeks and Romans* (Baltimore: Johns Hopkins University Press, 1994).

Indelli, Giovanni, ed. and trans. *Plutarco: Le Bestie Sono Esseri Razionali* (Naples: D'Auria, 1995).

—— "Plutarco, *Bruta Animalia Ratione Uti*: Qualche Riflessione," in Gallo, *Plutarco e le Scienze* 317–352.

Inglese, Lionello and Giuseppina Santese, eds *Plutarco: Il Cibarsi di Carne, Introduzione, Testo Critico, Traduzione e Commento* (Naples: D'Auria, 1999).

Jufresa, Montserrat, "La Abstinencia de Carne y el Origen de la Civilización," in J. A. Fernández Delgado and F. Pordomingo Pardo, eds *Estudios sobre Plutarco: Aspectos Formales* (Salamanca: Ediciones Clásicas, 1996) 219–226.

Keller, Otto, *Die Antike Tierwelt* (Leipzig: Cramer, 1909–1913; reprint 1963).

Lamberton, Robert, *Plutarch* (New Haven: Yale University Press, 2001).

Lecky, William Edward Hartpole, *History of European Morals from Augustus to Charlemagne* (New York: George Braziller, 1955; reprint of edition of 1867).

Linzey, Andrew, *Animal Theology* (Urbana: University of Illinois Press, 1995).

Lovejoy, Arthur O., *The Great Chain of Being* (Cambridge, Mass.: Harvard University Press, 1936).

Magel, Charles R., *Keyguide to Information Sources in Animal Rights* (Jefferson, NC: McFarland, 1989).

Manes, Christopher, *Other Creations: Rediscovering the Spirituality of Animals* (New York: Doubleday, 1997).

Martin, Hubert, "Plutarch's *De Sollertia Animalium* 959B–C: The Discussion of the Encomium on Hunting," *American Journal of Philology* 100 (1979) 99–106.

Martos Montiel, Juan Francisco, "*Sophrosyne o Akrasía*: Los Animales como Modelo de Comportamiento en los *Moralia* de Plutarco," in J. A. Fernández Delgado and F. Pordomingo Pardo, eds *Estudios sobre Plutarco: Aspectos Formales* (Salamanca: Ediciones Clásicas, 1996) 205–210.

Marx, August, *Griechische Märchen von dankbaren Tieren und Verwandtes* (Stuttgart: Kohlhammer, 1889).

Masson, Jeffrey Moussaieff, *The Pig Who Sang to the Moon: The Emotional Lives of Farm Animals* (New York: Ballantine, 2003).

Masson, Jeffrey and Susan McCarthy, *When Elephants Weep: The Emotional Lives of Animals* (New York: Delacorte Press, 1995).

Mason, Jim and Peter Singer, *Animal Factories* (New York: Harmony Books, 1990).

Midgley, Mary, *Animals and Why They Matter* (Athens: University of Georgia Press, 1984).

Mitchell, Robert, Nicholas S. Thompson and H. Lyn Miles, eds *Anthropomorphism, Anecdotes and Animals* (Albany: State University of New York Press, 1997).

Mortenson, Joseph, *Whale Songs and Wasp Maps: The Mystery of Animal Thinking* (New York: Dutton, 1987).

Mühl, Max, "Der λόγος ἐνδιάθετος und πφοφοριχός von der älteren Stoa bis zur Synode von Sirmium 351," *Archiv für Begriffsgeschichte* 7 (1962) 7–56.

Newmyer, Stephen T., "Just Beasts? Plutarch and Modern Science on the Sense of Fair Play in Animals," *Classical Outlook* 74, 3 (1997) 85–88.

—— "Of Pigs and People: Plutarch and the French Beast Fable," *Ploutarchos* 13, 1 (1996) 15–22.

—— "Ovid on the Moral Grounds for Vegetarianism," in Werner Schubert ed. *Ovid: Werk und Wirkung*, (Frankfurt: Peter Lang, 1999) I, 477–486.

—— "Paws to Reflect: Ancients and Moderns on the Religious Sensibilities of Animals," *Quaderni Urbinati di Cultura Classica* NS 75, 3 (2003) 111–129.

—— "Philo on Animal Psychology: Sources and Moral Implications," in Samuel Kottek and Manfred Horstmanshoff, eds *From Athens to Jerusalem: Medicine in Ancient Jewish and Early Christian Literature* (Rotterdam: Erasmus Publishing, 2000) 143–155.

—— "Plutarch on the Moral Grounds for Vegetarianism," *Classical Outlook* 72, 2 (1995) 41–43.

—— "Plutarch on the Treatment of Animals: The Argument from Marginal Cases," *Between the Species* 12, 1–2 (1996) 40–46.

—— "Speaking of Beasts: The Stoics and Plutarch on Animal Reason and the Modern Case against Animals," *Quaderni Urbinati di Cultura Classica* NS 63, 3 (1999) 99–110.

Obbink, Dirk, "The Origins of Greek Sacrifice: Theophrastus on Religion and Cultural History," in William W. Fortenbaugh and Robert W. Sharples, eds *Theophrastean Studies on Natural Science, Physics and Metaphysics, Ethics, Religion, and Rhetoric* (New Brunswick: Transaction Books, 1988) 272–295.

Parham, Vistara, *What's Wrong with Eating Meat?* (Corona, NY: PCAP, 1981).

Passmore, John, "The Treatment of Animals," *Journal of the History of Ideas* 36 (1975) 195–218.

Pembroke, S. J., "Oikeiôsis," in A. A. Long, ed. *Problems in Stoicism* (London: Athlone, 1971) 114–149.

Preus, Anthony, "Biological Theory in Porphyry's *De Abstinentia*," *Ancient Philosophy* 3 (1983) 149–159.

Regan, Tom, *The Case for Animal Rights* (Berkeley: University of California Press, 1983).

Renehan, Robert, "The Greek Anthropocentric View of Man," *Harvard Studies in Classical Philology* 85 (1981) 239–259.

Robbins, John, *Diet for a New America* (Walpole, NH: Stillpoint, 1987).

Rodd, Rosemary, *Biology, Ethics and Animals* (Oxford: Clarendon Press, 1992).

Rogers, Lesley J., *Minds of Their Own: Thinking and Awareness in Animals* (Boulder: Westview Press, 1997).

Rollin, Bernard, *Animal Rights and Human Morality* (Buffalo: Prometheus Books, 1992).

deRomilly, Jacqueline, *La Douceur dans la Pensée Grecque* (Paris: Les Belles Lettres, 1979).

Russell, D. A., "On Reading Plutarch's *Moralia*," *Greece and Rome* 15 (1968) 130–146.

—— *Plutarch* (London: Duckworth, 1972).

Ryder, Richard D., *Animal Revolution: Changing Attitudes towards Speciesism* (Oxford: Blackwell, 1989).

Salt, Henry S., *Animals' Rights Considered in Relation to Social Progress* (Clarks Summit, Pa.: Society for Animal Rights, 1980; reprint of edition of 1892).

Santese, Giuseppina, "Animali e Razionalità in Plutarco," in S. Castignone and G. Lanata, eds *Filosofi e Animali nel Mondo Antico* (Pisa: Edizioni ETS, 1994) 141–170.

Sapontzis, S. F., "Are Animals Moral Beings?," *American Philosophical Quarterly* 17, 1 (1980) 45–52.

—— *Morals, Reason, and Animals* (Philadelphia: Temple University Press, 1987).

Schuster, Max, *Untersuchungen zu Plutarchs Dialog De sollertia animalium, mit Besonderer Berücksichtigung der Lehrtätigkeit Plutarchs* (Augsburg: Himmer, 1917).

Scully, Matthew, *Dominion: The Power of Man, the Suffering of Animals, and the Call to Mercy* (New York: St. Martin's Press, 2002).

Shelton, Jo-Ann, "Contracts with Animals: Lucretius, *De Rerum Natura*," *Between the Species* 11 (1995) 115–121.

Singer, Peter, *Animal Liberation: A New Ethics for Our Treatment of Animals* (New York: Avon Books, 1977).

Skutch, Alexander F., *The Minds of Birds* (College Station: Texas A&M University Press, 1996).

Sorabji, Richard, *Animal Minds and Human Morals: The Origins of the Western Debate* (Ithaca: Cornell University Press, 1993).

Striker, Gisela, "The Role of *Oikeiosis* in Stoic Ethics," *Oxford Studies in Ancient Philosophy* 1 (1983) 145–167.

Teodorsson, Sven-Tage, "Plutarco Naturalista attraverso le Questioni Conviviali," in Gallo, *Plutarco e le Scienze* 199–210.

Terian, Abraham, *Philonis Alexandrini de Animalibus: The Armenian Text with an Introduction, Translation and Commentary* (Chico, Calif.: Scholars Press, 1981).

Terrace, Herbert, *Nim* (New York: Knopf, 1979).

Tirelli, Aldo, "Etica e Dietetica nei *De Tuenda Sanitate Praecepta*," in Gallo, *Plutarco e le Scienze* 385–403.

Tovar Paz, Francisco Javier, "Aproximación al Contenido de *De Sollertia Animalium* de Plutarco," *Anuario de Estudios Filológicas XIV* (Cáceres: Universidad de Estremadura, 1991) 491–501.

Toynbee, J. M. C., *Animals in Roman Life and Art* (Ithaca: Cornell University Press, 1973).

Tsekourakis, Damianos, "Pythagoreanism or Platonism and Ancient Medicine? The Reasons for Vegetarianism in Plutarch's Moralia," *Aufstieg und Niedergang der römischen Welt* II, 36, 1 (1987) 366–393.

deWaal, Frans, *Good Natured: The Origins of Right and Wrong in Humans and Other Animals* (Cambridge, Mass.: Harvard University Press, 1996).

West, Robert Francis, "Animal Suffering in Roman Literature" (Thesis: University of Calgary, 1997).

Wise, Steven M., *Drawing the Line: Science and the Case for Animal Rights* (Cambridge: Perseus Books, 2002).

INDEX LOCORUM

DK = Hermann Diels and Walher Kranz, eds, *Die Fragmente der Vorsokratiker*, 6th ed. (Berlin: Weidmann, 1951)

EK = L. Edelstein and I. G. Kidd, eds, *Posidonius* (Cambridge: Cambridge University Press, 1972–99)

SVF = Johannes von Arnim, ed., *Stoicorum Veterum Fragmenta* (Stuttgart: Teubner, 1964; reprint of the edition of 1905)

INDEX

Related titles from Routledge

Animal Ethics Reader

Edited by Susan Armstrong and Richard Botzler

The *Animal Ethics Reader* is the first comprehensive, state-of-the-art anthology of readings on this substantial area of study and interest. A subject that regularly captures the headlines, the book is designed to appeal to anyone interested in tracing the history of the subject, as well as providing a powerful insight into the debate as it has developed. The recent wealth of material published in this area has not, until now, been collected in one volume. Readings are arranged thematically, carefully presenting a balanced representation of the subject as it stands. It will be essential reading for students taking a course in the subject as well as being of considerable interest to the general reader. Articles are arranged under the following headings:

- Theories of Animal Ethics
- Animal Capacities
- Animals for Food
- Animal Experimentation
- Genetic Engineering of Animals
- Ethics and Wildlife
- Zoos, Aquaria, and Animals in Entertainment
- Companion Animals
- Legal Rights for Animals

Readings from leading experts in the field including Peter Singer, Mary Midgely and Bernard Rollin are featured as well as selections from Donald Griffin, Mark Bekoff, Jane Goodall, Raymond Frey, Barbara Orlans, Tom Regan, and Baird Callicott. There is an emphasis on balancing classic and contemporary readings with a view to presenting debates as they stand at this point in time.

Each chapter is introduced by the editors and study questions feature at the end. The foreword has been written by Bernard Rollin.

This will be appropriate reading for students taking courses in philosophy, ethics, zoology, animal science, psychology, veterinary medicine, law, environmental science and religion.

Hb: 0–415–27588–1
Pb: 0–415–27589–X

Available at all good bookshops

For ordering and further information please visit:
www.routledge.com

Related titles from Routledge

Animals, Gods and Humans
Changing attitudes to animals in Greek, Roman and early Christian thought

Ingvild Sælid Gilhus

Ingvild Sælid Gilhus explores the transition from traditional Greek and Roman religion to Christianity in the Roman Empire and the effect of this change on the concept of animals, illustrating the main factors in the creation of a Christian conception of animals. One of the underlying assumptions of the book is that changes in the way animal motifs are used and the way human–animal relations are conceptualized serve as indicators of more general cultural shifts. Gilhus attests that in late antiquity, animals were used as symbols in a general redefinition of cultural values and assumptions.

A wide range of key texts are consulted and range from philosophical treaties to novels and poems on metamorphoses; from biographies of holy persons such as Apollonius of Tyana and Antony, the Christian desert ascetic, to natural history; from the New Testament via Gnostic texts to the church fathers; from pagan and Christian criticism of animal sacrifice to the acts of the martyrs. Both the pagan and the Christian conception of animals remained rich and multilayered through the centuries and this book presents the dominant themes and developments in the conception of animals without losing that complexity.

Hb: 0–415–38649–7
Pb: 0–415–38650–0

Available at all good bookshops

For ordering and further information please visit:
www.routledge.com

Related titles from Routledge

Classical Philosophy
A Contemporary Introduction

Christopher Shields

Classical Philosophy is a comprehensive examination of early philosophy from the Presocratics through to Aristotle. The aim of the book is to provide an explanation and analysis of the ideas that flourished at this time and considers their relevance both to the historical development of philosophy and to contemporary philosophy today. From these ideas we can see the roots of arguments in metaphysics, epistemology, ethics and political philosophy.

Christopher Shields's style is inviting, refreshing and ideal for anyone coming to the subject for the first time. He provides a balanced account of the central topics and ideas that emerged from the period and includes helpful further reading and chapter overviews.

Hb: 0–415–23397–6
Pb: 0–415–23398–4

Available at all good bookshops

For ordering and further information please visit:
www.routledge.com

Related titles from Routledge

The Roman Philosophers

Mark Morford

The philosophers of the Roman world were asking questions whose answers had practical effects on people's lives in antiquity, and which still influence our thinking to this day. In spite of being neglected in the modern era, this important age of philosophical thought is now undergoing a revival of interest.

Mark Morford's lively survey makes these recent scholarly developments accessible to a wide audience, examining the writings and ideas of both famous and lesser known figures – from Cato the Censor in 155 BC to Marcus Aurelius in 180 AD. Based around extensive and fully translated quotations from the philosophical texts of the era, full consideration is given throughout to historical, political and cultural context.

Hb: 0–415–18851–2
Pb: 0–415–18852–0

Available at all good bookshops

For ordering and further information please visit:
www.routledge.com